OMNI
Visions
Two

Edited by Ellen Datlow

OMNI Books
Greensboro, North Carolina

Introduction © 1994 by Ellen Datlow
"Against Babylon," © 1986 by Robert Silverberg
"The Gods Of Mars," © 1985 by Jack Dann, Gardner Dozois, & Michael Swanwick
"Pictures Made of Stones," © 1987 by Lucius Shepard
"E-Ticket to Namland," © 1988 by Dan Simmons
"The Domino Master," © 1988 by Michael Blumlein
"The Circular Library of Stones," © 1987 by Carol Emshwiller
"Reason Seven," © 1985 by Barry N. Malzberg
"Fire Catcher," © 1986 by Richard Kadrey
"Dead Run," © 1985 by Greg Bear
"Adeste Fideles," © 1987 by Frederik Pohl
"The Lions Are Asleep This Night," © 1986 by Howard Waldrop
"The Dragon Seed," © 1985 by Kate Wilhelm
"Permafrost," © 1986 by Roger Zelazny

Cover art © Gervasio Gallardo/Jeff Lavaty & Associates

Printed in the United States of America

10 9 8 7 6 5 4 3 2 1

ISBN 0-87455-308-3

Omni is a registered trademark of Omni Publications International Ltd. Omni Books, 324 West Wendover Avenue, Suite 200, Greensboro, North Carolina 27408, is a General Media International Company.

Contents

Introduction

Ellen Datlow

Omni Visions One began a new *Omni* anthology series. The title of this new series of reprint anthologies reflects the attitude of *Omni*'s fiction. In 1981, *Omni* published William Gibson's first Sprawl story, "Johnny Mnemonic," heralding the advent of the cyberpunk movement. His novelette "Burning Chrome," published by *Omni* in 1982, first used the expression "cyberspace." The same year, *Omni* published Dan Simmons's story, "Eyes I Dare Not Meet in Dreams," which subsequently became incorporated into the novel *The Hollow Man* and one year later, in 1983, *Omni* published the novelette that eventually became his horror novel *Carrion Comfort.* Clive Barker made his American magazine debut in *Omni* in 1986; in 1988 we published K.W. Jeter's first short story; and, in 1990, we published Terry Bisson's first short story.

In addition, *Omni* has assiduously brought those writers who cross genres to the attention of our readers, blurring the artificial boundaries in order to publish the most interesting and diverse fiction available. Thus *Omni* has published stories by Patricia Highsmith, William Kotzwinkle, Stephen King, Ursula K. Le Guin, Gahan Wilson, Jonathan Carroll, Joyce Carol Oates, Jack Cady, Pat Cadigan, Gardner Dozois, Whitley Strieber, Karen Joy Fowler, Bruce Sterling, and William Burroughs.

Perhaps most important, *Omni* has encouraged science fiction's growth into a sophisticated literature for adult men and women. The stories in this volume were all originally published by *Omni* between 1985 and 1988. The stories range from the weird, almost-mainstream stories of Carol Emshwiller and Kate Wilhelm through the fantasies of Greg Bear and Howard Waldrop to the science fiction of Robert Silverberg, Richard Kadrey, and Roger Zelazny.

Several of the stories included here were nominated for the Nebula and/or Hugo Award. "Permafrost" by Roger Zelazny won the Hugo for best novelette of 1986. *Omni Visions Two* is a good representation of the diversity of theme, tone, and style of *Omni* magazine's fiction.

Against Babylon

Robert Silverberg

Robert Silverberg has written science fiction, horror, fantasy, historical, and erotic literature as well as nonfiction books on science, history, and archaeology. He has won five Nebula Awards and four Hugo Awards. His many novels include *Dying Inside, The Book of Skulls, Born With the Dead, Tom O'Bedlam, Lord Valentine's Castle, The Face on the Waters, Kingdoms of the Wall,* and *Hot Sky at Midnight.* His collections of short fiction include *The Conglomeroid Cocktail Party, Majipoor Chronicles,* and *The Collected Stories of Robert Silverberg, Volume 1: Secret Sharers.*

In addition, he has edited several anthologies including *New Dimensions* and, currently (with Karen Haber), the *Universe* series.

Alien encounters is a common theme in Silverberg's short fiction. "Against Babylon" is about such an encounter and its effect on human relationships. Silverberg incidentally does a brilliant job of depicting one of the great (and justified) fears of Nothern California, where he lives—fire.

Against Babylon

Robert Silverberg

Carmichael flew in from New Mexico that morning, and the first thing they told him when he put his little plane down at Burbank was that fires were burning out of control all around the Los Angeles basin. He was needed badly, they told him. It was late October, the height of the brushfire season in Southern California, and a hot, hard, dry wind was blowing out of the desert, and the last time it had rained was the fifth of April. He phoned the district supervisor right away, and the district supervisor told him, "Get your ass out here on the line double fast, Mike."

"Where do you want me?"

"The worst one's just above Chatsworth. We've got planes loaded and ready to go out of Van Nuys Airport."

"I need time to pee and to phone my wife. I'll be in Van Nuys in fifteen, okay?"

He was so tired that he could feel it in his teeth. It was nine in the morning, and he'd been flying since half past four, and it had been rough all the way, getting pushed around by that same fierce wind out of the heart of the continent that was now threatening to fan the flames in L.A. At this moment all he wanted was home and shower and Cindy and bed. But Carmichael didn't regard fire-fighting work as optional. This time of year, the whole crazy city could go in one big fire storm. There were times he almost wished that it would. He hated this smoggy, tawdry Babylon of a city, its endless tangle of freeways, the strange-looking houses, the filthy air, the thick, choking, glossy foliage everywhere, the drugs, the booze, the divorces, the laziness, the sleaziness, the porno shops and the naked encounter parlors and the massage joints, the weird people

3

wearing their weird clothes and driving their weird cars and cutting their hair in weird ways. There was a cheapness, a trashiness, about everything here, he thought. Even the mansions and the fancy restaurants were that way: hollow, like slick movie sets. He sometimes felt that the trashiness bothered him more than the out-and-out evil. If you kept sight of your own values you could do battle with evil, but trashiness slipped up around you and infiltrated your soul without your even knowing it. He hoped that his sojourn in Los Angeles was not doing that to him. He came from the Valley, and what he meant by the Valley was the great San Joaquin, out behind Bakersfield, and not the little, cluttered San Fernando Valley they had here. But L.A. was Cindy's city, and Cindy loved L.A. and he loved Cindy, and for Cindy's sake he had lived here seven years, up in Laurel Canyon amidst the lush, green shrubbery, and for seven Octobers in a row he had gone out to dump chemical retardants on the annual brushfires, to save the Angelenos from their own idiotic carelessness. You had to accept your responsibilities, Carmichael believed.

The phone rang seven times at the home number before he hung up. Then he tried the little studio where Cindy made her jewelry, but she didn't answer there either, and it was too early to call her at the gallery. That bothered him, not being able to say hello to her right away after his three-day absence and no likely chance for it now for another eight or ten hours. But there was nothing he could do about that.

As soon as he was aloft again he could see the fire not far to the northwest, a greasy black column against the pale sky. And when he stepped from his plane a few minutes later at Van Nuys he felt the blast of sudden heat. The temperature had been in the mid-eighties at Burbank, damned well hot enough for nine in the morning, but here it was over a hundred. He heard the distant roar of flames, the popping and crackling of burning underbrush, the peculiar whistling sound of dry grass catching fire.

The airport looked like a combat center. Planes were coming and going with lunatic frenzy, and they were lunatic planes, too, antiques of every sort, forty and fifty years old and even older, converted B-17 Flying Fortresses and DC-3s and a Douglas Invader and, to Carmichael's astonishment, a Ford Trimotor from the 1930's that had been hauled, maybe, out of some movie studio's collection. Some were equipped with tanks that held fire-retardant chemicals, some were water pumpers, some were mappers with infrared and electronic scanning equipment glistening on their snouts. Harried-looking men and women ran back and forth, shouting into CB handsets, supervising the loading process. Carmichael found his way to Operations HQ, which was full of haggard people staring into computer screens. He knew most of them from

4

other years.

One of the dispatchers said, "We've got a DC-3 waiting for you. You'll dump retardants along this arc, from Ybarra Canyon eastward to Horse Flats. The fire's in the Santa Susana foothills, and so far the wind's from the east, but if it shifts to northerly it's going to take out everything from Chatsworth to Granada Hills and right on down to Ventura Boulevard. And that's only *this* fire."

"How many are there?"

The dispatcher tapped his keyboard. The map of the San Fernando Valley that had been showing disappeared and was replaced by one of the entire Los Angeles basin. Carmichael stared. Three great scarlet streaks indicated fire zones: this one along the Santa Susanas, another nearly as big way off to the east in the grasslands north of the 210 Freeway around Glendora or San Dimas, and a third down in eastern Orange County, back of Anaheim Hills. "Ours is the big one so far," the dispatcher said. "But these other two are only about forty miles apart, and if they should join up somehow—"

"Yeah," Carmichael said. A single wall of fire running along the whole eastern rim of the basin, maybe—with Santa Ana winds blowing, carrying sparks westward across downtown L.A., across Hollywood, Beverly Hills, all the way to the coast, to Venice, Santa Monica, Malibu. He shivered. Laurel Canyon would go. Everything would go. Worse than Sodom and Gomorrah, worse than the fall of Nineveh. Nothing but ashes for hundreds of miles. "Everybody scared silly of Russian nukes, and a carload of dumb kids tossing cigarettes can do the job just as easily," he said.

"But this wasn't cigarettes, Mike," the dispatcher said.

"No? What then, arson?"

"You haven't heard."

"I've been in New Mexico for the last three days."

"You're the only one in the world who hasn't heard, then."

"For Christ's sake, heard what?"

"About the E.T.'s," said the dispatcher wearily. "They started the fires. Three spaceships landing at six this morning in three different corners of the L.A. basin. The heat of their engines ignited the dry grass."

Carmichael did not smile. "You've got one weird sense of humor, man."

The dispatcher said, "I'm not joking."

"Spaceships? From another world?"

"With critters fifteen feet high on board," the dispatcher at the next computer said. "They're walking around on the freeways right this minute. Fifteen feet high, Mike."

5

"Men from Mars?"

"Nobody knows where the hell they came from."

"Jesus Christ, God," Carmichael said.

Wild updrafts from the blaze buffeted the plane as he took it aloft and gave him a few bad moments. But he moved easily and automatically to gain control, pulling the moves out of the underground territories of his nervous system. It was essential, he believed, to have the moves in your fingers, your shoulders, your thighs, rather than in the conscious realms of your brain. Consciousness could get you a long way, but ultimately you had to work out of the underground territories or you were dead.

He felt the plane responding and managed a grin. DC-3s were tough old birds. He loved flying them, though the youngest of them had been manufactured before he was born. He loved flying anything. Flying wasn't what Carmichael did for a living—he didn't actually do anything for a living, not anymore—but flying was what he did. There were months when he spent more time in the air than on the ground, or so it seemed to him, because the hours he spent on the ground often slid by unnoticed, while time in the air was intensified, magnified.

He swung south over Encino and Tarzana before heading up across Canoga Park and Chatsworth into the fire zone. A fine haze of ash masked the sun. Looking down, he could see the tiny houses, the tiny swimming pools, the tiny people scurrying about, desperately trying to hose down their roofs before the flames arrived. So many houses, so many people, filling every inch of space between the sea and the desert, and now it was all in jeopardy. The southbound lanes of Topanga Canyon Boulevard were as jammed with cars, here in midmorning, as the Hollywood Freeway at rush hour. Where were they all going? Away from the fire, yes. Toward the coast, it seemed. Maybe some television preacher had told them there was an ark sitting out there in the Pacific, waiting to carry them to safety while God rained brimstone down on Los Angeles. Maybe there really was. In Los Angeles anything was possible. Invaders from space walking around on the freeways even. Jesus. Jesus. Carmichael hardly knew how to begin thinking about that.

He wondered where Cindy was, what *she* was thinking about it. Most likely she found it very funny. Cindy had a wonderful ability to be amused by things. There was a line of poetry she liked to quote, from that Roman, Virgil: A storm is rising, the ship has sprung a leak, there's a whirlpool to one side and sea monsters on the other, and the captain turns to his men and says, "One day perhaps we'll look back and laugh even at all this." That was Cindy's way, Carmichael thought. The Santa Anas are blowing and three big brushfires are burning and invaders from space have arrived at the same time, and one day perhaps we'll look back and laugh even at all this. His heart overflowed with love for her, and longing. He had never known anything about poetry before he had met her. He closed his eyes a moment and brought her onto the screen of his mind. Thick cascades of jet-black hair; quick, dazzling smile; long, slender, tanned body all aglitter with those amazing rings and necklaces and pendants she designed and fashioned. And her eyes. No one else he knew had eyes like hers, bright with strange mischief, with that altogether original way of seeing that was the thing he most loved about her. *Damn* this fire, just when he'd been away three days! *Damn* the stupid men from Mars!

Where the neat rows and circles of suburban streets ended there was a great open stretch of grassy land, parched by the long summer to the color of a lion's hide, and beyond that were the mountains, and between the grassland and the mountains lay the fire, an enormous, lateral red crest topped by a plume of foul, black smoke. It seemed to already cover hundreds of acres, maybe thousands. A hundred acres of burning brush, Carmichael had heard once, creates as much heat energy as the atomic bomb they dropped on Hiroshima.

Through the crackle of radio static came the voice of the line boss, directing operations from a helicopter hovering at about four o'clock. "DC-3, who are you?"

"Carmichael."

"We're trying to contain it on three sides, Carmichael. You work on the east, Limekiln Canyon, down the flank of Porter Ranch Park. Got it?"

"Got it," Carmichael said.

He flew low, less than a thousand feet. That gave him a good view of the action: sawyers in hard hats and orange shirts chopping burning trees to make them fall toward the fire, bulldozer crews clearing brush ahead of the blaze, shovelers carving firebreaks, helicopters pumping water into isolated tongues of flame. He climbed five hundred feet to avoid a single-engine observer plane, then went up to five hundred more to avoid the smoke and air turbulence of the fire itself. From that altitude he had a clear picture of it, running like a bloody gash from west to east, wider at its western end. Just east of the fire's far tip he saw a circular zone of grassland perhaps a hundred acres in diameter that had already burned out, and precisely at the center of that zone stood something that looked like an aluminum silo, the size of a ten-story building, surrounded at a considerable distance by a cordon of military vehicles. He felt a wave of dizziness rock through his mind. That thing, he realized, had to be the E.T. spaceship.

It had come out of the west in the night, Carmichael thought, floating like

7

a tremendous meteor over Oxnard and Camarillo, sliding toward the western end of the San Fernando Valley, kissing the grass with its exhaust, and leaving a trail of flame behind it. And then it had gently set itself down over there and extinguished its own brushfire in a neat little circle about itself, not caring at all about the blaze it had kindled farther back, and God knows what kind of creatures had come forth from it to inspect Los Angeles. It figured that when the UFOs finally did make a landing out in the open, it would be in L.A. Probably they had chosen it because they had seen it so often on television—didn't all the stories say that UFO people always monitored our TV transmissions? So they saw L.A. on every other show, and they probably figured it was the capital of the world, the perfect place for the first landing. But why, Carmichael wondered, had the bastards needed to pick the height of the fire season to put their ships down here?

He thought of Cindy again, how fascinated she was by all this UFO and E.T. stuff, those books she read, the ideas she had, the way she had looked toward the stars one night when they were camping in Kings Canyon and talked of beings that must live up there. "I'd love to see them," she said. "I'd love to get to know them and find out what their heads are like." Los Angeles was full of nut cases who wanted to ride in flying saucers, or claimed they already had, but it didn't sound nutty to Carmichael when Cindy talked that way. She had the Angeleno love of the exotic and the bizarre, yes, but he knew that her soul had never been touched by the crazy corruption here, that she was untainted by the prevailing craving for the weird and irrational that made him loathe the place so much. If she turned her imagination toward the stars, it was out of wonder, not out of madness: It was simply part of her nature, that curiosity, that hunger for what lay outside her experience, to embrace the unknowable. He had had no more belief in E.T.s than he did in the tooth fairy, but for her sake he had told her that he hoped she'd get her wish. And now the UFO people were really here. He could imagine her, eyes shining, standing at the edge of that cordon staring at the spaceship. Pity he couldn't be with her now, feeling all that excitement surging through her, the joy, the wonder, the magic. But he had work to do. Swinging the DC-3 back around toward the west, he swooped down as close as he dared to the edge of the fire and hit the release button on his dump lines. Behind him a great crimson cloud spread out: a slurry of ammonium sulfate and water, thick as paint, with a red dye mixed into it so they could tell which areas had been sprayed. The retardant clung in globs to anything and would keep it damp for hours.

Emptying his four five-hundred-gallon tanks quickly, he headed back to Van Nuys to reload. His eyes were throbbing with fatigue, and the stink of the wet charred earth below was filtering through every plate of the old plane. It was not quite noon. He had been up all night. At the airport they had coffee ready, sandwiches, tacos, burritos. While he was waiting for the ground crew to fill his tanks he went inside to call Cindy again, and again there was no answer at home, none at the studio. He phoned the gallery, and the kid who worked there said she hadn't been in touch all morning.

"If you hear from her," Carmichael said, "tell her I'm flying fire control out of Van Nuys on the Chatsworth fire, and I'll be home as soon as things calm down a little. Tell her I miss her, too. And tell her that if I run into an E.T. I'll give it a big hug for her. You got that? Tell her just that."

Across the way in the main hall he saw a crowd gathered around someone carrying a portable television set. Carmichael shouldered his way in just as the announcer was saying, "There has been no sign yet of the occupants of the San Gabriel or Orange County spaceships. But this was the horrifying sight that astounded residents of the Porter Ranch area beheld this morning between nine and ten o'clock." The screen showed two upright tubular figures that looked like squid walking on the tips of their tentacles, moving cautiously through the parking lot of a shopping center, peering this way and that out of enormous yellow, platter-shaped eyes. At least a thousand onlookers were watching them at a wary distance, appearing both repelled and at the same time irresistibly drawn. Now and then the creatures paused to touch their foreheads together in some sort of communion. They moved very daintily, but Carmichael saw that they were taller than the lampposts—twelve feet high, maybe fifteen. Their skins were purplish and leathery looking, with rows of luminescent orange spots glowing along the sides. The camera zoomed in for a close-up, then jiggled and swerved wildly just as an enormously long elastic tongue sprang from the chest of one of the alien beings and whipped out into the crowd. For an instant the only thing visible on the screen was a view of the sky; then Carmichael saw a shot of a stunned-looking girl of about fourteen, caught around the waist by that long tongue, being hoisted into the air and popped like a collected specimen into a narrow green sack. "Teams of the giant creatures roamed the town for nearly an hour," the announcer intoned. "It has definitely been confirmed that between twenty and thirty human hostages were captured before they returned to their spacecraft. Meanwhile, fire-fighting activities desperately continue under Santa Ana conditions in the vicinity of all three landing sites, and—"

Carmichael shook his head. Los Angeles, he thought. The kind of people that live here, they walk right up and let the E.T.s gobble them like flies.

Maybe they think it's just a movie and everything will be okay by the last reel. And then he remembered that Cindy was the kind of people who would

9

walk right up to one of these E.T.s. Cindy was the kind of people who lived in Los Angeles, he told himself, except that Cindy was *different*. Somehow.

He went outside. The DC-3 was loaded and ready.

In the forty-five minutes since he had left the fire line, the blaze seemed to have spread noticeably toward the south. This time the line boss had him lay down the retardant from the De Soto Avenue freeway interchange to the northeast corner of the Porter Ranch. When he returned to the airport, intending to call Cindy again, a man in military uniform stopped him as he crossed the field and said, "You Mike Carmichael, Laurel Canyon?"

"That's right."

"I've got some troublesome news for you. Let's go inside."

"Suppose you tell me here, okay?"

The officer looked at him strangely. "It's about your wife," he said. "Cynthia Carmichael? That's your wife's name?"

"Come *on*," Carmichael said.

"She's one of the hostages, sir."

His breath went from him as though he had been kicked.

"Where did it happen?" he demanded. "How did they get her?"

The officer gave him a strange, strained smile. "It was the shopping-center lot, Porter Ranch. Maybe you saw some of it on TV."

Carmichael nodded. That girl jerked off her feet by that immense elastic tongue, swept through the air, popped into that green pouch. And Cindy—?

"You saw the part where the creatures were moving around? And then suddenly they were grabbing people, and everyone was running from them? That was when they got her. She was up front when they began grabbing, and maybe she had a chance to get away, but she waited just a little too long. She started to run, I understand, but then she stopped—she looked back at them—she may have called something out to them—and then—well, and then—"

"Then they scooped her up?"

"I have to tell you that they did."

"I see," Carmichael said stonily.

"One thing all the witnesses agreed, she didn't panic, she didn't scream. She was very brave when those monsters grabbed her. How in God's name you can be brave when something that size is holding you in midair is something I don't understand, but I have to assure you that those who saw it—"

"It makes sense to me," Carmichael said.

He turned away. He shut his eyes for a moment and took deep, heavy pulls of the hot, smoky air.

Of course she had gone right out to the landing site. Of course. If there was anyone in Los Angeles who would have wanted to get to them and see them with her own eyes and perhaps try to talk to them and establish some sort of rapport with them, it was Cindy. She wouldn't have been afraid of them. She had never seemed to be afraid of anything. It wasn't hard for Carmichael to imagine her in that panicky mob in the parking lot, cool and radiant, staring at the giant aliens, smiling at them right up to the moment they seized her. In a way he felt very proud of her. But it terrified him to think that she was in their grasp.

"She's on the ship?" he asked. "The one that we have right up back here?"

"Yes."

"Have there been any messages from the hostages? Or from the aliens?"

"I can't divulge that information."

"*Is* there any information?"

"I'm sorry, I'm not at liberty to—"

"I refuse to believe," Carmichael said, "that that ship is just sitting there, that nothing at all is being done to make contact with—"

"A command center has been established, Mr. Carmichael, and certain efforts are under way. That much I can tell you. I can tell you that Washington is involved. But beyond that, at the present point in time—"

A kid who looked like a Eagle Scout came running up. "Your plane's all loaded and ready to go, Mike!"

"Yeah," Carmichael said. The fire, the fucking fire! He had almost managed to forget about it. *Almost.* He hesitated a moment, torn between conflicting responsibilities. Then he said to the officer, "Look, I've got to get back out on the fire line. Can you stay here a little while?"

"Well—"

"Maybe half an hour. I have to do a retardant dump. Then I want you to take me over to that spaceship and get me through the cordon, so I can talk to those critters myself. If she's on that ship, I mean to get her off it."

"I don't see how it would be possible—"

"Well, try to see," Carmichael said. "I'll meet you right here in half an hour."

When he was aloft he noticed right away that the fire was spreading. The wind was even rougher and wilder than before, and now it was blowing hard from the northeast, pushing the flames down toward the edge of Chatsworth. Already some glowing cinders had blown across the city limits, and Carmichael saw houses afire to his left, maybe half a dozen of them. There would be more, he knew. In fire fighting you come to develop an odd sense of which way the struggle is going, whether you're gaining on the blaze or it's gaining on you, and that sense told him now that the vast effort that was under way was failing, that

11

the fire was still on the upcurve, that whole neighborhoods were going to be ashes by nightfall.

He held on tight as the DC-3 entered the fire zone. The fire was sucking air like crazy now, and the turbulence was astounding: It felt as if a giant's hand had grabbed the ship by the nose. The line boss's helicopter was tossing around like a balloon on a string.

Carmichael called in for orders and was sent over to the southwest side, close by the outermost street of houses. Fire fighters with shovels were beating on wisps of flame rising out of people's gardens down there. The skirts of dead leaves that dangled down the trunks of a row of towering palm trees were blazing. The neighborhood dogs had formed a crazed pack, running desperately back and forth.

Swooping down to treetop level, Carmichael let go with a red gush of chemicals, swathing everything that looked combustible with the stuff. The shovelers looked up and waved at him, and he dipped his wings to them and headed off to the north, around the western edge of the blaze—it was edging farther to the west too, he saw, leaping up into the high canyons out by the Ventura County line—and then he flew eastward along the Santa Susana foothills until he could see the spaceship once more, standing isolated in its circle of blackened earth. The cordon of vehicles seemed to be even larger, what looked like a whole armored division deployed in concentric rings beginning half a mile or so from the ship.

He stared intently at the alien vessel as though he might be able to see through its shining walls to Cindy within.

He imagined her sitting at a table, or whatever the aliens used instead of tables, sitting at a table with seven or eight of the huge beings, calmly explaining Earth to them and then asking them to explain their world to her. He was altogether certain that she was safe, that no harm would come to her, that they were not torturing her or dissecting her or sending electric currents through her simply to see how she reacted. Things like that would never happen to Cindy, he knew.

The only thing he feared was that they would depart for their home star without releasing her. The terror that that thought generated in him was as powerful as any kind of fear he had ever felt.

As Carmichael approached the aliens' landing site he saw the guns of some of the tanks below swiveling around to point at him, and he picked up a radio voice telling him brusquely, "You're off limits, DC-3. Get back to the fire zone. This is prohibited air space."

"Sorry," he said. "No entry intended."

But as he started to make his turn he dropped down even lower so that he could have a good look at the spaceship. If it had portholes and Cindy was looking out one of those portholes, he wanted her to know that he was nearby. That he was watching, that he was waiting for her to come back. But the ship's hull was blind-faced, entirely blank.

Cindy? Cindy?

She was always looking for the strange, the mysterious, the unfamiliar, he thought. The people she brought to the house: a Navajo once, a bewildered Turkish tourist, a kid from New York. The music she played, the way she chanted along with it. The incense, the lights, the meditation. "I'm searching," she liked to say. Trying always to find a route that would take her into something that was wholly outside herself. Trying to become something more than she was. That was how they had fallen in love in the first place, an unlikely couple, she with her beads and sandals, he with his steady no-nonsense view of the world: She had come up to him that day long ago when he was in the record shop in Studio City, and God only knew what he was doing in that part of the world in the first place, and she had asked him something and they had started to talk, and they had talked and talked, talked all night, she wanting to know everything there was to know about him, and when dawn came up they were still together, and they had rarely been parted since. He never had really been able to understand what it was that she had wanted him for—the Valley redneck, the aging flyboy—although he felt certain that she wanted him for something real, that he filled some need for her, as she did for him, which could for lack of a more specific term be called love. She had always been searching for that too. Who wasn't? And he knew that she loved him truly and well, though he couldn't quite see why. "Love is understanding," she liked to say. "Understanding is loving." Was she trying to tell the spaceship people about love right this minute? *Cindy, Cindy, Cindy.*

Back in Van Nuys a few minutes later, he found that everyone at the airport seemed to know by this time that his wife was one of the hostages. The officer whom Carmichael had asked to wait for him was gone. He was not very surprised by that. He thought for a moment of trying to go over to the ship by himself, to get through the cordon and do something about getting Cindy free, but he realized that that was a dumb idea: The military was in charge and they wouldn't let him or anybody else get within a mile of that ship, and he'd only get snarled up in stuff with the television interviewers looking for poignant crap about the families of those who had been captured.

Then the head dispatcher came down to meet him on the field, looking almost about ready to burst with compassion, and in funereal tones told

Carmichael that it would be all right if he called it quits for the day and went home to await whatever might happen. But Carmichael shook him off. "I won't get her back by sitting in the living room," he said. "And this fire isn't going to go out by itself, either."

It took twenty minutes for the ground crew to pump the retardant slurry into the DC-3s tanks. Carmichael stood to one side, drinking Cokes and watching the planes come and go. People stared at him, and those who knew him waved from a distance, and three or four pilots came over and silently squeezed his arm or rested a hand consolingly on his shoulder. The northern sky was black with soot, shading to gray to east and west. The air was sauna-hot and frighteningly dry: You could set fire to it, Carmichael thought, with a snap of your fingers. Somebody running by said that a new fire had broken out in Pasadena, near the Jet Propulsion Lab, and there was another in Griffith Park. The wind was starting to carry firebrands, then. Dodger Stadium was burning, someone said. So is Santa Anita Racetrack, said someone else. The whole damned place is going to go, Carmichael thought. And my wife is sitting inside a spaceship from another planet.

When his plane was ready he took it up and laid down a new line of retardant practically in the faces of the fire fighters working on the outskirts of Chatsworth. They were too busy to wave. In order to get back to the airport he had to make a big loop behind the fire, over the Santa Susanas and down the flank of the Golden State Freeway, and this time he saw the fires burning to the east, two huge conflagrations marking the places where the exhaust streams of the other two spaceships had grazed the dry grass and a bunch of smaller blazes strung out on a line from Burbank or Glendale deep into Orange County. His hands were shaking as he touched down at Van Nuys. He had gone without sleep now for thirty-two hours, and he could feel himself starting to pass into that blank, white fatigue that lies somewhere beyond ordinary fatigue.

The head dispatcher was waiting for him again as he left his plane. "All right," Carmichael said at once. "I give in. I'll knock off for five or six hours and grab some sleep, and then you can call me back to—"

"No. That isn't it."

"That isn't what?"

"What I came out here to tell you, Mike. They've released some of the hostages."

"Cindy?"

"I think so. There's an Air Force car here to take you to Sylmar. That's where they've got the command center set up. They said to find you as soon as you came off your last dump mission and send you over there so you can talk with your wife."

"So she's free," Carmichael said. "Oh, Jesus, she's free!"

"You go on along, Mike. We'll look after the fire without you for a while, okay?"

The Air Force car looked like a general's limo, long and low and sleek, with a square-jawed driver in front and a couple of very tough-looking young officers to sit with him in back. They said hardly anything, and they looked as weary as Carmichael felt. "How's my wife?" he asked, and one of them said, "We understand that she hasn't been harmed." The way he said was stiff and strange. Carmichael shrugged. The kid has seen too many old movies, he told himself.

The whole city seemed to be on fire now. Within the air-conditioned limo there was only the faintest whiff of smoke, but the sky to the east was terrifying, with streaks of red bursting like meteors through the blackness. Carmichael asked the Air Force men about that, but all he got was a clipped, "It looks pretty bad, we understand." Somewhere along the San Diego Freeway between Mission Hills and Sylmar, Carmichael fell asleep, and the next thing he knew they were waking him gently and leading him into a vast, bleak, hangarlike building near the reservoir. The place was a maze of cables and screens, with military personnel operating what looked like a thousand computers and ten thousand telephones. He let himself be shuffled along, moving mechanically and barely able to focus his eyes, to an inner office where a gray-haired colonel greeted him in his best this-is-the-tense-part-of-the-movie style and said, "This may be the most difficult job you've ever had to handle, Mr. Carmichael."

Carmichael scowled. Everybody was Hollywood in this damned town, he thought.

"They told me the hostages were being freed," he said. "Where's my wife?"

The colonel pointed to a television screen. "We're going to let you talk to her right now."

"Are you saying I don't get to see her?"

"Not immediately."

"Why not? Is she all right?"

"As far as we know, yes."

"You mean she hasn't been released? They told me the hostages were being freed."

"All but three have been let go," said the colonel. "Two people, according to the aliens, were injured as they were captured and are undergoing medical treatment aboard the ship. They'll be released shortly. The third is your wife, Mr. Carmichael. She is unwilling to leave the ship."

It was like hitting an air pocket.

15

"Unwilling—?"

"She claims to have volunteered to make the journey to the home world of the aliens. She says she's going to serve as our ambassador, our special emissary. Mr. Carmichael, does your wife have any history of mental imbalance?"

Glaring, Carmichael said, "She's very sane. Believe me."

"You are aware that she showed no display of fear when the aliens seized her in the shopping-center incident this morning?"

"I know, yes. That doesn't mean she's crazy. She's unusual. She has unusual ideas. But she's not crazy. Neither am I, incidentally." He put his hands to his face for a moment and pressed his fingertips lightly against his eyes.

"All right," he said. "Let me talk to her."

"Do you think you can persuade her to leave the ship?"

"I'm sure as hell going to try."

"You are not yourself sympathetic to what she's doing, are you?" the colonel asked.

Carmichael looked up. "Yes, I am sympathetic. She's an intelligent woman doing something that she thinks is important and doing it of her own free will. Why the hell shouldn't I be sympathetic? But I'm going to try to talk her out of it, you bet. I love her. I want her. Somebody else can be the goddamned ambassador to Betelgeuse. Let me talk to her, will you?"

The colonel gestured, and the big television screen came to life. For a moment mysterious colored patterns flashed across it in a disturbing, random way; then Carmichael caught glimpses of shadowy catwalks, intricate metal strutworks crossing and recrossing at peculiar angles; and then for an instant one of the aliens appeared on the screen. Yellow platter-eyes looked complacently back at him. Carmichael felt altogether wide awake now.

The alien's face vanished and Cindy came into view. The moment he saw her, Carmichael knew he had lost her.

Her face was glowing. There was a calm joy in her eyes verging on ecstasy. He had seen her look something like that on many occasions, but this was different: This was beyond anything she had attained before. She had seen the beatific vision, this time.

"Cindy?"

"Hello, Mike."

"Can you tell me what's been happening in there, Cindy?"

"It's incredible. The contact, the communication."

Sure, he thought. If anyone could make contact with the space people it would be Cindy. She had a certain kind of magic about her: the gift of being able to open any door.

She said, "They speak mind to mind, you know, no barriers at all. They've come in peace, to get to know us, to join in harmony with us, to welcome us into the confederation of worlds."

He moistened his lips. "What have they done to you, Cindy? Have they brainwashed you or something?"

"No! No, nothing like that! They haven't done a thing to me, Mike! We've just talked."

"*Talked!*"

"They've showed me how to touch my mind to theirs. That isn't brainwashing. I'm still me. I, me, Cindy. I'm okay. Do I look as though I'm being harmed? They aren't dangerous. Believe me."

"They've set fire to half the city with their exhaust trails, you know."

"That grieves them. It was an accident. They didn't understand how dry the hills were. If they had some way of extinguishing the flames, they would, but the fires are too big even for them. They ask us to forgive them. They want everyone to know how sorry they are." She paused a moment. Then she said, very gently, "Mike, will you come on board? I want you to experience them as I'm experiencing them."

"I can't do that, Cindy."

"Of course you can! Anyone can! You just open your mind, they touch you, and—"

"I know. I don't want to. Come out of there and come home, Cindy. Please. Please. It's been three days—four, now—I want to hug you, I want to hold you—"

"You can hold me as tight as you like. They'll let you on board. We can go to their world together. You know that I'm going to go with them to their world, don't you?"

"You aren't. Not really."

She nodded gravely. She seemed terribly serious. "They'll be leaving in a few weeks, as soon as they've had a chance to exchange gifts with Earth. I've seen images of their planet—like movies, only they do it with their minds— Mike, you can't imagine how beautiful it is! How eager they are to have me come!"

Sweat rolled out of his hair into his eyes, making him blink, but he did not dare wipe it away for fear she would think he was crying.

"I don't want to go to their planet, Cindy. And I don't want you to go either."

She was silent for a time.

Then she smiled delicately and said, "I know, Mike."

17

He clenched his fists and let go and clenched them again. "I *can't* go there."

"No. You can't. I understand that. Los Angeles is alien enough for you, I think. You need to be in your Valley, in your own real world, not running off to some far star. I won't try to coax you."

"But you're going to go anyway?" he asked, and it was not really a question.

"You already know what I'm going to do."

"Yes."

"I'm sorry. But not really."

"Do you love me?" he said, and regretted saying it at once.

She smiled sadly. "You know I do. And you know I don't want to leave you. But once they touched my mind with theirs, once I saw what kind of beings they are—do you know what I mean? I don't have to explain, do I? You always know what I mean."

"Cindy—"

"Oh, Mike, I do love you so much."

"And I love you, babe. And I wish you'd come out of that goddamned ship."

"You won't ask that. Because you love me, right? Just as I won't ask you again to come on board with me, because I really love you. Do you understand that, Mike?"

He wanted to reach into the screen and grab her.

"I understand, yes," he made himself say.

"I love you, Mike."

"I love you, Cindy."

"They tell me the round-trip takes forty-eight of our years, but it will only seem like a few weeks to me. Oh, Mike! Good-bye, Mike! God bless, Mike!" She blew kisses to him. He saw his favorite rings on her fingers, the three little strange star sapphire ones that she had made when she first began to design jewelry. He searched his mind for some new way to reason with her, some line of argument that would work, and could find none. He felt a vast emptiness beginning to expand within him, as though he were being made hollow by some whirling blade. Her face was shining. She seemed like a stranger to him suddenly. She seemed like a Los Angeles person, one of *those*, lost in fantasies and dreams, and it was as though he had never known her, or as through he had pretended she was something other than she was. No. No, that isn't right. She's not one of those, she's Cindy. Following her own star, as always. Suddenly he was unable to look at the screen any longer, and he turned away, biting his lip, making a shoving gesture with his left hand. The Air Force men in the room

18

wore the awkward expressions of people who had inadvertently eavesdropped on someone's most intimate moments and were trying to pretend they had heard nothing.

"She isn't crazy, Colonel," Carmichael said vehemently. "I don't want anyone believing she's some kind of nut."

"Of course not, Mr. Carmichael."

"But she's not going to leave that spaceship. You heard her. She's staying aboard, going back with them to wherever the hell they came from. I can't do anything about that. You see that, don't you? Nothing I could do, short of going aboard that ship and dragging her off physically, would get her out of there. And I wouldn't ever do that."

"Naturally not. In any case, you understand that it would be impossible for us to permit you to go on board, even for the sake of attempting to remove her."

"That's all right," Carmichael said. "I wouldn't dream of it. To remove her or even just to join her for the trip. I don't want to go to that place. Let her go: That's what she was meant to do in this world. Not me. Not me, Colonel. That's simply not my thing." He took a deep breath. He thought he might be trembling. "Colonel, do you mind if I get the hell out of here? Maybe I would feel better if I went back out there and dumped some more gunk on that fire. I think that might help. That's what I think, Colonel. All right? Would you send me back to Van Nuys, Colonel?"

He went up one last time in the DC-3. They wanted him to dump the retardants along the western face of the fire, but instead he went to the east, where the spaceship was, and flew in a wide circle around it. A radio voice warned him to move out of the area, and he said that he would.

As he circled a hatch opened in the spaceship's side and one of the aliens appeared, looking gigantic even from Carmichael's altitude. The huge, purplish thing stepped from the ship, extended its tentacles, seemed to be sniffing the smoky air.

Carmichael thought vaguely of flying down low and dropping his whole load of retardants on the creature, drowning it in gunk, getting even with the aliens for having taken Cindy from him. He shook his head. That's crazy, he told himself. Cindy would feel sick if she knew he had ever considered any such thing. But that's what I'm like, he thought. Just an ordinary, ugly, vengeful Earthman. And that's why I'm not going to go that other planet, and that's why she is.

He swung around past the spaceship and headed straight across Granada Hills and Northridge into Van Nuys Airport. When he was on the ground he sat at the controls of his plane a long while, not moving at all. Finally one of the dispatchers came out and called up to him, "Mike, are you okay?"

"Yeah. I'm fine."

"How come you came back without dropping your load?"

Carmichael peered at his gauges. "Did I do that? I guess I did that, didn't I?"

"You're not okay, are you?"

"I forgot to dump, I guess. No, I didn't forget. I just didn't feel like doing it."

"Mike, come on out of that plane."

"I didn't feel like doing it," Carmichael said again. "Why the hell bother? This crazy city—there's nothing left in it that I would want to save anyway." His control deserted him at last, and rage swept through him like fire racing up the slopes of a dry canyon. He understood what she was doing, and he respected it, but he didn't have to like it. He didn't like it at all. He had lost Cindy, and he felt somehow that he had lost his war with Los Angeles as well. "Fuck it," he said. "Let it burn. This crazy city. I always hated it. It deserves what it gets. The only reason I stayed here was for her. She was all that mattered. But she's going away now. Let the fucking place burn."

The dispatcher gaped at him in amazement. "Mike—"

Carmichael moved his head slowly from side to side as though trying to shake a monstrous headache from it. Then he frowned. "No, that's wrong," he said. "You've got to do the job anyway, right? No matter how you feel. You have to put the fires out. You have to save what you can. Listen, Tim, I'm going to fly one last load today, you hear? And then I'll go home and get some sleep. Okay? Okay?" He had the plane in motion, going down the short runway. Dimly he realized that he had not requested clearance. A little Cessna spotter plane moved desperately out of his way, and then he was aloft. The sky was black and red. The fire was completely uncontained now, and maybe uncontainable. But you had to keep trying, he thought. You had to save what you could. He gunned and went forward, flying calmly into the inferno in the foothills, until the wild thermals caught his wings from below and lifted him and tossed him like a toy skimming over the top and sent him hurtling toward the waiting hills to the north.

Thus saith the Lord; Behold, I will raise up against Babylon, and against them that dwell in the midst of them that rise up against me, a destroying wind;

And will send unto Babylon fanners, that shall fan her, and shall empty her land: For in the day of trouble they shall be against her round about.

Jeremiah 51: 1-2

The Gods of Mars

Gardner Dozois, Jack Dann, and Michael Swanwick

Individually nominees and/or winners of numerous Nebula and Hugo Awards, the collaborators on "The Gods of Mars" wrote the story during a particularly prolific period as collaborators. Gardner Dozois has won two Nebulas for his short fiction and is currently the award-winning editor of *Asimov's Science Fiction Magazine*. Jack Dann has just finished a novel about Leonardo da Vinci titled *The Path of Remembrance*, and Michael Swanwick, winner of the Nebula Award for Best Novel of 1992 for *Stations of the Tide*, is the author of the recent fantasy novel *The Iron Dragon's Daughter*.

"The Gods of Mars," an homage to Edgar Rice Burroughs, was nominated for the Hugo and Nebula Awards. It was first published March 1985.

The Gods of Mars

Gardner Dozois, Jack Dann, and Michael Swanwick

They were outside, unlashing the Mars lander, when the storm blew up.

With Johnboy and Woody crowded against his shoulders, Thomas snipped the last lashing. In careful cadence, the others straightened, lifting the ends free of the lander. At Thomas's command, they let go. The metal lashing soared away, flashing in the harsh sunlight, twisting like a wounded snake, dwindling as it fell below and behind their orbit. The lander floated free, tied to the *Plowshare* by a single, slim umbilicus. Johnboy wrapped a spanner around a hex-bolt over the top strut of a landing leg and gave it a spin. Like a slow, graceful spider leg, it unfolded away from the lander's body. He slapped his spanner down on the next bolt and yanked. But he hadn't braced himself properly, and his feet went out from under him in a slow somersault. He spun away, laughing, to the end of his umbilicus. The spanner went skimming back toward the *Plowshare*, struck its metal skin, and sailed off into space.

"You meatballs!" Thomas shouted over the open intercom. The radio was sharp and peppery with sun static, but he could hear Woody and Johnboy laughing. "Cut it out! No skylarking! Let's get this done."

"Everything okay out there?" asked Commander Redenbaugh, from inside the *Plowshare*. The commander's voice had a slight edge to it, and Thomas grimaced. The last time the three of them had gone out on EVA, practicing this very maneuver, Johnboy had started to horse around and had accidentally sent a dropped lug nut smashing through the source-crystal housing, destroying the laser link to Earth. And hadn't the commander gotten on their asses about *that*; NASA had been really pissed, too—with the laser link

23

gone, they would have to depend solely on the radio, which was vulnerable to static in an active sun year like this.

It was hard to blame the others too much for cutting up a little on EVA, after long, claustrophobic months of being jammed together in the *Plowshare*, but the responsibility for things going smoothly was his. Out here, *he* was supposed to be in command. That made him feel lonely and isolated, but after all, it was what he had sweated and strived for since the earliest days of flight training. The landing party was his command, his chance for glory, and he wasn't going to let anybody or anything ruin it.

"Everything's okay, Commander," Thomas said. "We've got the lander unshipped, and we're almost ready to go. I estimate about twenty minutes to separation." He spoke in the calm, matter-of-fact voice that tradition demanded, but inside he felt the excitement building again and hoped his pulse rate wasn't climbing too noticeably on the readouts. In only a few minutes, they were going to be making the first manned landing on Mars! Within the hour, he'd be down there, where he'd dreamed of being ever since he was a boy. On *Mars*.

And *he* would be in command. *How about that, Pop*, Thomas thought, with a flash of irony. *That good enough for you? Finally?*

Johnboy had pulled himself back to the *Plowshare*.

"Okay, then," Thomas said dryly. "If you're ready, let's get back to work. You and Woody get that junk out of the lander. I'll stay out here and mind the store."

"Yes, *sir*, sir," Johnboy said with amiable irony, and Thomas sighed. Johnboy was okay but a bit of a flake—you had to sit on him a little from time to time. Woody and Johnboy began pulling boxes out of the lander; it had been used as storage space for supplies they'd need on the return voyage, to save room in *Plowshare*. There were jokes cracked about how they ought to let some of the crates of flash-frozen glop that NASA straight-facedly called food escape into space, but at last, burdened with boxes, the two space-suited figures lumbered to the air lock and disappeared inside.

Thomas was alone, floating in space.

You really *were* alone out here, too, with nothing but the gaping immensity of the universe surrounding you on all sides. It was a scary, but at the same time something to savor after long months of being packed into the *Plowshare* with three other men. There was precious little privacy aboard ship—out here, alone, there was nothing *but* privacy. Just you, the stars, the void...and, of course, Mars.

Thomas relaxed at the end of his tether, floating comfortably, and watched as Mars, immense and ruddy, turned below him like some huge, slow-spinning, rusty-red top. Mars! Lazily, he lets his eyes trace the familiar landmarks. The ancient dead-river valley of Kasei Vallis, impact craters puckering its floor...the reddish brown and gray of haze and frost in Noctis Labyrinthus, the Labyrinth of Night...the immense scar of the Vallis Marineris, greatest of canyons, stretching two thirds of the way around the equator...the great volcanic constructs in Tharsis...and there, the Chryse Basin, where soon they would be walking.

Mars was as familiar to him as the streets of his hometown—more so, since his family spent so much time moving from place to place when he was a kid. Mars had stayed a constant, though. Throughout his boyhood, he had been obsessed with space and with Mars in particular...as if he'd somehow always known that one day he'd be here, hanging disembodied like some ancient god over the slowly spinning red planet below. In high school he had done a paper on Martian plate tectonics. When he was only a gangly grade-school kid, ten or eleven, maybe, he had memorized every available map of Mars, learned every crater and valley and mountain range.

Drowsily, his thoughts drifted even further back, to that day in the attic of the old house in Wrightstown, near McGuire Air Force Base—the sounds of jets taking off mingling with the lazy Saturday afternoon sounds of kids playing baseball and yelling, dogs barking, lawn mowers whirring, the rusty smell of pollen coming in the window on the mild, spring air—when he'd discovered an old, dog-eared copy of Edgar Rice Burroughs's *A Princess of Mars*.

He'd stayed up there for hours reading it, while the day passed unnoticed around him, until the light got so bad that he couldn't see the type anymore. And that night he'd surreptitiously read it in bed, under the covers with a pencil flashlight, until he'd finally fallen asleep, his dreams reeling with giant, four-armed green men, thoats, zitidars, longsword-swinging heroes and beautiful princesses...the Twin Cities of Helium...the dead sea bottoms lit by the opalescent light of the two hurtling moons...the nomad caverns of the Tharks, the barbaric riders draped with glittering jewels and rich riding silks. For an instant, staring down at Mars, he felt a childish disappointment that all of that really wasn't waiting down there for him after all, and then he smiled wryly at himself. Never doubt that those childhood dreams had power—after all, one way or another, they'd *gotten* him here, hadn't they?

Right at that moment the sandstorm began to blow up.

It blew up from the hard-pan deserts and plains and, as Thomas watched in dismay, began to creep slowly across the planet like a tarp being pulled over a work site. Down there, winds moving at hundreds of kilometers per hour were racing across the Martian surface, filling the sky with churning, yellow-white clouds of sand. A curtain storm.

"You see that, Thomas?" the commander's voice asked in Thomas's ears.

"Yeah," Thomas said glumly. "I see it."

"Looks like a bad one."

Even as they watched, the storm slowly and relentlessly blotted out the entire visible surface of the planet. The lesser features went first, the scarps and rills and stone fields, then the greater ones. The polar caps went. Finally even the top of Olympus Mons—the tallest mountain in the solar system—disappeared.

"Well, that's it," the commander said sadly. "Socked in. No landing today."

"Son of a *bitch*!" Thomas exploded, feeling his stomach twist with disappointment and sudden rage. He'd been so *close*....

"Watch your language, Thomas," the commander warned. "This is an open channel." Meaning that we mustn't shock the Vast Listening Audience Back Home. Oh, horrors, certainly *not*.

"If it'd just waited a couple more hours, we would have been able to get *down* there—"

"You ought to be glad it didn't," the commander said mildly. "Then you'd have been sitting on your hands down there with all that sand piling around your ears. The wind can hit one hundred forty miles an hour during one of those storms. *I'd* hate to have to try to sit one out on the ground. Relax, Thomas. We've got plenty of time. As soon as the weather clears, you'll go down. It can't last forever."

Five weeks later, the storm finally died.

Those were hard weeks for Thomas, who was as full of useless energy as a caged tiger. He had become overaware of his surroundings, of the pervasive, sour human smell, of the faintly metallic taste of the air. It was like living in a jungle-gym factory, all twisting pipes and narrow, cluttered passages, enclosed by metal walls that were never out of sight. For the first time during the long months of the mission, he began to feel seriously claustrophobic.

But the real enemy was time. Thomas was acutely aware that the inexorable clock of celestial mechanics was ticking relentlessly away...that soon the optimal launch window for the return journey to Earth would open and that they *must* shape for Earth then or never get home at all. Whether the storm had lifted yet or not, whether they had landed on Mars or not, whether Thomas had finally gotten a chance to show off his own particular righteous stuff or not, when the launch window opened, they had to go.

They had less than a week left in Mars orbit now, and still the sandstorm raged.

The waiting got on everyone's nerves. Thomas found Johnboy's manic energy particularly hard to take. Increasingly, he found himself snapping at Johnboy during meals and "happy hour," until eventually the commander had to take him aside and tell him to loosen up. Thomas muttered something apologetic, and the commander studied him shrewdly and said, "Plenty of time left, old buddy. Don't worry. We'll get you down there yet!" The two men found themselves grinning at each other. Commander Redenbaugh was a good officer, a quiet, pragmatic New Englander who seemed to become ever more phlegmatic and unflappable as the tension mounted and everyone else's nerves frayed. Johnboy habitually called him Captain Ahab. The commander seemed rather to enjoy the nickname, which was one of the few things that suggested that there might actually be a sense of humor lurking somewhere behind his deadpan facade.

The commander gave Thomas's arm an encouraging squeeze, then launched himself towards the communications console. Thomas watched him go, biting back a sudden bitter surge of words that he knew he'd never say...not up here, anyway, where the walls literally had ears. Ever since *Skylab,* astronauts had flown with the tacit knowledge that everything they said in the ship was being eavesdropped on and evaluated by NASA. Probably before the day was out somebody back in Houston would be making a black mark next to his name in a psychological-fitness dossier, just because he'd let the waiting get on his nerves to the point where the commander had had to speak to him about it. But damn it, it was *easier* for the rest—they didn't have the responsibility of being NASA's token Nigger in the Sky, with all the white folks back home waiting and watching to see how you were going to fuck up. He'd felt like a third wheel on the way out here—Woody and the commander could easily fly the ship themselves and even take care of most of the routine schedule of experiments— but the landing party was supposed to be *his* command, his chance to finally do something other than be the obligatory black face in the NASA photos of Our Brave Astronauts. He remembered his demanding, domineering, hard-driving father saying to him, hundreds of times in his adolescent years, "It's a white man's world out there. If you're going to make it, you got to show that you're *better* than any of them. You got to force yourself down their throats, *make* them need you. You got to be twice as good as any of them...." *Yeah, Pop,* Thomas thought, *you bet, Pop*...thinking, as he always did, of the one and only time he'd ever seen his father stinking, slobbering, falling-down drunk, the night the old man had been passed over for promotion to brigadier general for the third time, forcing him into mandatory retirement. *First they got to give you the chance, Pop,* he thought, remembering, again as he always did, a cartoon by Ron Cobb that he had seen when he was a kid and that had haunted him ever since: a cartoon showing black men in space suits on the moon—sweeping up around the Apollo 58 campsite.

"We're losing Houston again," Woody said. "I jes cain't keep the signal." He turned a dial, and the voice of Mission Control came into the cabin, chopped up and nearly obliterated by a hissing static that sounded like dozens of eggs frying in a huge iron skillet. "...read?...not read you...*Plowshare*...losing..." Sunspot activity had been unusually high for weeks, and just a few hours before, NASA had warned them about an enormous solar flare that was about to flood half the solar system with radio noise. Even as they listened, the voice was completely drowned out by static; the hissing noise kept getting louder and louder. "Weh-ayl," Woody said glumly, "that does it. That solar flare's screwing *every*thing up. If we still had the laser link"—here he flashed a sour look at Johnboy, who had the grace to look embarrassed—"we'd be okay, I guess, but with*out* it...weh-ayl, shit, it could be days before reception clears up. *Weeks,* maybe."

Irritably, Woody flipped a switch, and the hissing static noise stopped. All four men were silent for a moment, feeling their suddenly increased isolation. For months, their only remaining contact with Earth had been a faint voice on the radio, and now, abruptly, even that link was severed. It made them feel lonelier than ever and somehow farther away from home.

Thomas turned away from the communications console and automatically glanced out the big observation window at Mars. It took him a while to notice that there was something different about the view. Then he realized that the uniform, dirty yellow-white cloud cover was breaking up and becoming streaky, turning the planet into a giant, mottled Easter egg, allowing tantalizing glimpses of the surface. "Hey!" Thomas said, and at the same time Johnboy crowed, "Well, *well,* lookie there! Guess who's back, boys!"

They all crowded around the observation window, eagerly jostling one another.

As they watched, the storm died all at once, with the suddenness of a conjuring trick, and the surface was visible again. Johnboy let out an ear-splitting rebel yell. Everyone cheered. They were all laughing and joking and slapping one another's shoulders, and then, one by one, they fell silent.

Something was *wrong.* Thomas could feel the short hairs prickling erect along his back and arms, feel the muscles of his gut tightening. Something was *wrong.* What was it? What...? He heard the commander gasp, and at the same time realization broke through into his conscious mind, and he felt the blood draining from his face.

Woody was the first to speak.

"But..." Woody said, in a puzzled, almost petulant voice, like a bewildered child. "But...*that's not Mars.*"

The air is thin on Mars. So thin it won't hold up dust in suspension unless the wind is traveling at enormous speeds. When the wind dies, the dust falls like pebbles, fast and all at once.

After five weeks of storm, the wind died. The dust fell.

Revealing entirely the wrong planet.

The surface was still predominantly a muddy reddish orange, but now there were large mottled patches of green and grayish ocher. The surface seemed softer now, smoother, with much less rugged relief. It took a moment to realize why: The craters—so very like those on the moon both in shape and distribution—were gone, and so were most of the mountains, the scarps and rills, the giant volcanic constructs. In their place were dozens of fine, perfectly straight blue lines. They were bordered by bands of green and extended across the entire planet in an elaborate crisscrossing pattern, from polar icecap to polar icecap.

"I cain't *find* anything," Woody was saying exasperatedly. "What *happened* to everything? I cain't even see Olympus Mons, for Christsake! The biggest fucking volcano in the solar system! Where is it? And what the fuck are those lines?"

Again Thomas felt an incredible burst of realization well up inside him. He gaped at the planet below, unable to speak, unable to answer, but Johnboy did it for him.

Johnboy had been leaning close to the window, his jaw slack with amazement, but now an odd, dreamy look was stealing over his face, and when he spoke, it was a matter-of-fact, almost languid voice. "They're canals," he said.

"Canals my ass!" the commander barked, losing control of his temper for the first time on the mission. "There aren't any canals on Mars! That idea went out with Schiaparelli and Lowell."

Johnboy shrugged. "Then what are *those?*" he asked mildly, jerking his thumb toward the planet, and Thomas felt a chill feather up along his spine.

A quick visual search turned up no recognizable surface features, none of the landmarks familiar to them all from the *Mariner 9* and Viking orbiter photomaps—although Johnboy annoyed the commander by pointing out that the major named canals that Percival Lowell had described and mapped in the nineteenth century—Strymon, Charontis, Erebus, Orcus, Dis—*were* there, just as Lowell had said that they were.

"It's *got* to be the sandstorm that did it," Thomas said, grasping desperately for some kind of rational explanation. "The wind moving the sand around from one place to another, maybe, covering up one set of surface features while at the same time exposing *another* set...."

He faltered to a stop, seeing the holes in that argument even as Johnboy snorted and said, "Real good, sport, *real* good. But Olympus Mons just isn't *there,* a mountain three times higher than Mount Everest! Even if you could cover it up with sand, then what you'd have would be a fucking *sand dune* three times higher than Everest...but there don't seem to be any big mountains down there at all anymore."

"I know what happened," Woody said before Thomas could reply.

His voice sounded so strange that they all turned to look at him. He had been scanning the surface with the small optical telescope for the Mars-Sat experiments, but now he was leaning on the telescope mounting and staring at them instead. His eyes were feverish and unfocused and bright and seemed to have sunken into his head. He was trembling slightly, and his face had become waxen and pale.

He's scared, Thomas realized, *he's just plain scared right out of his skull....*

"This has all happened before," Woody said hoarsely.

"What in the world are you talking about?" Thomas asked.

"Haven't you read your history?" Woody asked. He was a reticent man, slow voiced and deliberate, like most computer hackers, but now the words rushed from his mouth in a steadily accelerating stream, almost tumbling over one another in their anxiety to get out. His voice was higher than usual, and it held the ragged overtones of hysteria in it. "The *Mariner 9* mission, the robot probe. Back in 1971. Remember? Jes as the probe reached Mars orbit, before it could start sending back any photos, a great big curtain storm came up, jes like this one. Great *big* bastard. Covered *everything.* Socked the whole planet in for weeks. No surface visiblity at all. Had the scientists back home pulling their hair out. But when the storm finally did lift, and the photos did start coming in, everybody was jes flat-out *amazed.* None of the Lowellian features, no canals, *nothing*—jes craters and rills and volcanoes, all the stuff we expected to see *this* time around." He gave a shaky laugh.

"So everybody jes shrugged and said Lowell had been wrong—poor visibility, selector bias, he jes *thought* he'd seen canals. Connected up existing surface features with imaginary lines, maybe. He'd seen what he wanted to see." Woody paused, licking at his lips, and then began talking faster and shriller than ever. "But that wasn't *true,* was it? We *know* better, don't we boys? We can see the proof right out that window! My crazy ol' uncle Barry, *he* had the right of it from the start, and everybody else was *wrong.* He tole me what happened, but I was jes too dumb to believe him! It was the *space* people, the UFO people! The Martians! *They* saw the probe coming, and they whomped that storm up, to keep us from seeing the surface, and then they changed everything. Under the cover of the sandstorm, they changed the whole damn planet to fool us, to keep us from finding out *they* were there! This *proves* it! They changed it *back!* They're out there right *now,* the flying saucer people! They're *out* there—"

"Bullshit!" the commander said. His voice was harsh and loud and cracked like a whip, but it was the unprecedented use of obscenity that startled them more than anything else. They turned to look at him, where he floated near the command console. Even Woody, who had just seemed on the verge of a breakdown, gasped and fell silent.

When he was sure he had everyone's attention, the commander smiled coldly and said, "While you were all going through your little psychodrama, I've been doing a little elementary checking. Here's the telemetry data, and you know what? *Every*thing shows up the same as it did before the sandstorm. Exactly...the...same. Deep radar, infrared, everything." He tapped the command console. "It's just the same as it ever was: no breathable air, low atmospheric pressure, subzero temperatures, nothing but sand and a bunch of goddamn rusty-red rocks. No vegetation, no surface water, *no canals.*" He switched the view from the ship's exterior cameras onto the cabin monitor, and there for everyone to see was the familiar Mars of the Mariner and Viking probes: rocky, rugged, cratered, lifeless. No green oases. No canals.

Everyone was silent, mesmerized by the two contradictory images.

"I don't know what's causing this strange visual hallucination we're all seeing," the commander said, gesturing at the window and speaking slowly and deliberately. "But I do know it is a hallucination. It doesn't show up on the cameras, it doesn't show up in the telemetry. It's just not real."

They adjourned the argument to the bar. Doofus the Moose—an orange inflatable toy out of Johnboy's personal kit—smiled benignly down on them as they sipped from bags of reconstituted citrus juice (NASA did not believe that they could be trusted with a ration of alcohol, and the hip flask Woody had smuggled aboard had been polished off long before) and went around and around the issue without reaching any kind of consensus. The "explanations" became more and more farfetched, until at last the commander uttered the classic phrase *mass hypnosis,* causing Johnboy to start whooping in derision.

There was a long, humming silence. Then Johnboy, his mood altering, said very quietly, "It doesn't matter anyway. We're never going to find out anything more about what's happening from up here." He looked soberly around at the others. "There's really only one decision we've got to make: Do we go on down, or not? Do we land?"

Even the commander was startled. "After all this—you still want to land?"

Johnboy shrugged. "Why not? It's what we came all the way out here for, isn't it?"

"It's too dangerous. We don't even know what's happening here."

"I thought it was only mass hypnosis," Johnboy said slyly.

"I think it is," the commander said stoutly, unperturbed by Johnboy's sarcasm. "But even if it is, we still don't know *why* we're having these hallucinations, do we? It could be a sign of organic deterioration or dysfunction of some sort, caused by who *knows* what. Maybe there's some kind intense electromagnetic field out there that we haven't detected that's disrupting the electrical pathways of our nervous systems; maybe there's an unforeseen flaw in the recycling system that causing some kind of toxic buildup that affects brain chemistry....The point is, we're not *functioning* right; we're seeing things that aren't there!"

"None of that stuff matters," Johnboy said. He leaned forward, speaking now with great urgency and passion. No one had ever seen him so serious or so ferociously intent. "We have to land. Whatever the risk. It was hard enough funding *this* mission. If we fuck up out here, there may never be another one. NASA itself might not survive." He stared around at his crewmates. "How do *you* think it's going to look, Woody? We run into the greatest mystery the human race has ever encountered, and we immediately go scurrying home with our tails tucked between our legs without even investigating it? That sound good to you?"

Woody grunted and shook his head. "Sure doesn't, ol' buddy," he said. He glanced around the table and then coolly said, "Let's get on *down* there." Now that he was apparently no longer envisioning the imminent arrival of UFO-riding astronaut mutilators, Woody seemed to be as cool and unflappable and ultramacho as possible, as if to prove that he hadn't really been frightened after all.

There was another silence, and slowly Thomas became aware that everyone else was staring at him.

It all came down to him now. The deciding vote would be *his*. Thomas locked eyes with Johnboy, and Johnboy stared back at him with unwavering intensity. The question didn't even need to be voiced; it hung in the air between them and charged the lingering silence with tension. Thomas moved uneasily under the weight of all those watching eyes. How *did* he feel? He didn't really know—strange, that was about the closest he could come to it...hung up between fear and some other slowly stirring emotion he couldn't identify and didn't really want to think about. But there was one thing he suddenly was certain about: They weren't going to abandon *his* part of the mission, not after he'd come this far! Certainly he was never going to get another chance to get into the history books. Probably that was Johnboy's real motive, too, above and beyond the jazz about the survival of NASA. Johnboy was a cool enough head to realize that if they came home without landing, they'd be laughingstocks, wimps instead of heroes, and somebody *else* on some future mission would get all the glory. Johnboy's ego was much too big to allow him to take a chance on *that*. And he was right! Thomas had even more reason to be afraid of being passed over, passed by: When you were black, opportunities like this certainly didn't knock more than once.

"We've still got almost three days until the launch window opens," Thomas said, speaking slowly and deliberately. "I think we should make maximum use of that time by going down there and finding out as much as we can." He raised his eyes and stared directly at the commander. "I say we *land*."

Commander Redenbaugh insisted on referring the issue to Houston for a final decision, but after several hours of trying, it became clear that he was not going to be able to get through to Earth. For once, the buck was refusing to be passed.

The commander sighed and ran his fingers through his hair. He felt old and tired and ineffectual. He knew what Houston would probably have said, anyway. With the exception of the commander himself (who had been too well-known *not* to be chosen), *de facto* policy for this mission had been to select unmarried men with no close personal or family ties back home. That alone spoke volumes. They were *supposed* to be taking risks out here. That was what they were here for. It was part of their job.

At dawn over Chryse, they went down.

As commander of the landing party, Thomas was first out of the lander. Awkward in his suit, he climbed backward out of the hatch and down the exterior ladder. He caught reeling flashes of the Martian sky, and it was orange, as it should be. His first, instinctive reaction was relief, followed by an intense stab of perverse disappointment, which surprised him. As he hung from the ladder, one foot almost touching the ground, he paused to reel off the words that some P.R. man at NASA had composed for the occasion: "In the name of all humanity, we dedicate the planet of war to peace. May God grant us this." He put his foot down from the ladder, twisting around to get a good look at the spot he was standing on.

"Jesus *Christ,*" he muttered reverently. Orange sky or not, there were *plants* of some kind growing here. He was standing almost knee-deep in them, a close-knit, springy mat of grayish-ocher vegetation. He knelt down and gingerly touched it.

"It looks like some kind of moss," he reported. "It's pliant and giving to the touch, springs slowly back up again. I can break it off in my hand."

The transmission from the *Plowshare* crackled and buzzed with static. "Thomas," said the commander's voice in his ear, "what are you *talking* about? Are you okay?"

Thomas straightened up and took his first long, slow look around. The ocher-colored moss stretched out to the orange horizon in all directions, covering both the flat plains immediately around them and a range of gently rolling hills in the middle distance to the north. Here and there the moss was punctuated by tight clusters of spiny, misshapen shrubs, usually brown or glossy black or muddy purple, and even occasionally by a lone tree. The trees were crimson, about ten feet high; the trunks glistened with the color of fresh, wet blood, and their flat, glassy leaves glittered like sheets of amethyst. Thomas dubbed them flametrees.

The lander was resting only several hundred yards away from a canal.

It was wide, the canal; and its still, perfectly clear waters reflected the sky as dark as wine, as red as blood. Small yellow flowers trailed delicate tentacles into the water from the edging walls, which were old and crumbling and carved with strange geometrical patterns of swirls and curlicues that might, just possibly, be runes.

It can't possibly be real, Thomas thought dazedly.

Johnboy and Woody were clambering down the ladder, clumsy and troll-like in their hulking suits, and Thomas moved over to make room for them.

"Mother dog!" Woody breathed, looking around him, the wonder clear in his voice. "*This* is really something, ain't it?" He laid a gloved hand on Thomas's shoulder. "*This* is what we saw from up there."

"But it's impossible," Thomas said.

Woody shrugged. "If it's a hallucination, then it's sure as hell a *beautiful* one."

Johnboy had walked on ahead without a word, until he was several yards away from the ship; now he came to a stop and stood staring out across the moss-covered plain to the distant hills. "It's like being born again," he whispered.

The commander cut in again, his voice popping and crackling with static. "Report in! What's going *on* down there?"

Thomas shook his head. "Commander, I wish I knew."

He unlashed the exterior camera from the lander, set it up on its tripod, removed the lens cover. "Tell me what you see"

"I see sand, dust, rocks...what else do you *expect* me to see?"

"No canals?" Thomas asked sadly. "No trees? No moss?"

"Christ, you're hallucinating again, aren't you?" the commander said. "This is what I was afraid of. All of you, listen to me! Listen good! There aren't any goddamn*canals*down there. Maybe there's water down a few dozen meters as permafrost. But the surface is as dry as the moon."

"But there's some sort of moss growing all over the place," Thomas said. "Kind of grayish-ocher color, about a foot and a half high. There's clumps of bushes. There's even *trees* of some kind. Can't you see any of that?"

"You're hallucinating," the commander said. "Believe me, the camera shows nothing but sand and rock down there. You're standing in a goddamn lunar desert and babbling to me about trees, for Christ's sake! That's enough for me. I want everybody back up here, right *now*. I shouldn't have let you talk me into this in the first place. We'll let Houston unravel all this. It's no longer our problem. Woody, come back here! Stick together, dammit!"

Johnboy was still standing where he had stopped, as if entranced, but Woody was wandering toward the canal, poking around, exploring.

"Listen up!" the commander said. "I want everybody back in the lander, right now. I'm going to get you out of there before somebody gets hurt. Everybody back *now*. That's an order! That's a direct order!"

Woody turned reluctantly and began bounding slowly toward the lander, pausing every few yards to look back over his shoulder at the canal.

Thomas sighed, not sure whether he was relieved to be getting out of here or heartbroken to be going so soon.

"Okay, Commander," Thomas said. "We read you. We're coming up. Right away." He took a few light, buoyant steps forward—fighting a tendency to bounce kangaroolike off the ground—and tapped Johnboy gently on the arm. "Come on. We've got to go back up."

Johnboy turned slowly around. "Do we?" he said. "Do we *really?*"

"Orders," Thomas said uneasily, feeling something began to stir and turn over ponderously in the deep backwaters of his own soul. "I don't want to go yet, either, but the commander's right. If we're hallucinating..."

"Don't give me that shit!" Johnboy said passionately. "Hallucinating, my ass! You *touched* the moss, didn't you? You *felt* it. This isn't a hallucination, or mass hypnosis, or any of that other crap. This is a *world,* a new world, and it's ours!"

"Johnboy, get in the lander right now!" the commander broke in. "That's an order!"

"Fuck you, Ahab!" Johnboy said. "And fuck your orders, too!"

Thomas was shocked—and at the same time felt a stab of glee at the insubordination, an emotion that surprised him and that he hurried uneasily to deny, saying, "You're out of line, Johnboy. I want you to listen to me, now—"

"No, you listen to *me,*" Johnboy said fiercely. "Look around you! I know you've read Burroughs. You *know* where you are! A dead sea bottom, covered with ocher-colored moss. Rolling hills. A *canal.*"

"Those are the very reasons why it can't be real," Thomas said uneasily.

"It's real if we *want* it to be real," Johnboy said. "It's here *because* of us. It's made for us. It's made *out* of us."

"Stop gabbing and get in the lander!" the commander shouted. "Move! Get your asses in gear!"

Woody had come up to join them. "Maybe we'd better—" he started to say, but Johnboy cut in with:

"Listen to me! I knew what was happening the moment I looked out and saw the Mars of Schiaparelli and Lowell, the *old* Mars. Woody, you said that Lowell saw what he wanted to see. That's *right,* but in a different way than you meant it. You know, other contemporary astronomers looked at Mars at the same time as Lowell, with the same kind of instruments, and saw no canals at all. You ever hear of consensual reality? Because Lowell wanted to see it, it existed for him! Just as it exists for us—because we want it to exist! We don't have to accept the gray reality of Ahab here and all the other gray little men back at NASA. They *want* it to be rocks and dust and dead, drab desert; they *like* it that way—"

"For God's sake!" the commander said. "Somebody get that nut in the lander!"

"—but *we* don't like it! Deep down inside of us—Thomas, Woody—we don't *believe* in that Mars. We believe in this one—the *real* one. That's why it's here for us! That's why it's the way it is—it's made of our dreams. Who knows what's over those hills: bone white faerie cities? four-armed green men? beautiful princesses? the Twin Cities of Helium? There could be *anything* out there!"

"Thomas!" the commander snapped. "Get Johnboy in the lander *now*. Use force if necessary, but *get him in there*. Johnboy! You're emotionally unstable. I want you to consider yourself under house arrest!"

"I've been under house arrest all my life," Johnboy said. "Now I'm *free*." Moving deliberately, he reached up and unsnapped his helmet.

Thomas started forward with an inarticulate cry of horror, trying to stop him, but it was too late. Johnboy had his helmet completely off now and was shaking his head to free his shaggy, blond hair, which rippled slightly in the breeze. He took a deep breath, another, and then grinned at Thomas. "The air smells *great*," he said. "And, my God, is it clean!"

"Johnboy?" Thomas said hesitantly. "Are you *okay?*"

"Christ!" the commander was muttering. "Christ! Oh my God! Oh my sweet God!"

"I'm fine," Johnboy said. "In fact, I'm *terrific*." He smiled brilliantly at them, then sniffed at the inside of his helmet and made a face. "Phew! Smells like an armpit in there!" He started to strip off his suit.

"Thomas, Woody," the commander said leadenly. "Put Johnboy's body into the lander, and then get in there yourselves, fast, before we lose somebody else."

"But..." Thomas said, "there's nothing wrong with Johnboy. We're *talking* to him."

"God damn it, *look at your med readouts*."

Thomas glanced at the chinstrap readout board, which was reflected into a tiny square on the right side of his faceplate. There was a tiny red light flashing on Johnboy's readout. "Christ!" Thomas whispered.

"He's *dead*, Thomas, he's *dead*. I can see his body. He fell over like he'd been pole-axed right after he opened his helmet and hemorrhaged his lungs out into the sand. Listen to me! Johnboy's *dead*—anything else is an hallucination!"

Johnboy grinned at them, kicking free of his suit. "I may be dead, kids," he told them quizzically, "but let me tell *you*, dead or not, I feel one-hundred-percent better now that I'm out of that crummy suit, believe it. The air's a little bit cool, but it feels *wonderful*." He raised his arms and stretched lazily, like a cat.

"Johnboy—?" Woody said, tentatively.

"*Listen*," the commander raged. "You're hallucinating! You're talking to yourselves! Get in the lander! That's an *order*."

"Yes, *sir*, sir," Johnboy said mockingly, sketching a salute to the sky. "Are you actually going to *listen* to that asshole?" He stepped forward and took each of them by the arm and shook them angrily. "Do I *feel* dead to you, schmucks?"

Thomas *felt* the fingers close over his arm, and an odd, deep thrill shot through him—part incredulity, part supernatural dread, part a sudden, strange exhilaration. "I can*feel*him," Woody was saying wonderingly, patting Johnboy with his gloved hands. "He's solid. He's *there*. I'll be a son of a *bitch*—"

"Be one?" Johnboy said, grinning. "Ol' buddy, you already *are* one."

Woody laughed. "No hallucination's *that* corny," Woody said to Thomas. "He's real, all right."

"But the readout—" Thomas began.

"Obviously wrong, There's got to be some kind of mistake—"

Woody started to unfasten his helmet.

"No!" the commander screamed, and at the same time Thomas darted forward shouting, "Woody! Stop!" and tried to grab him, but Woody twisted aside and bounded limberly away, out of reach.

Cautiously, Woody took his helmet off. He sniffed suspiciously, his lean, leathery face stiff with tension, then he relaxed, and then he began to smile. "Hoo*ie*," he said in awe.

"Get his helmet back on, quick!" the commander was shouting. But Woody's medical readout was already flashing orange, and even as the commander spoke, it turned red.

"Too late!" the commander moaned. "Oh God, too *late*...."

Woody looked into his helmet at his own flashing readout. His face registered surprise for an instant, and then he began to laugh. "Weh-ayl," Woody drawled, "now that I'm officially a corpse, I guess I don't need *this* anymore." He threw his helmet aside; it bounced and rolled over the spongy moss. "Thomas," Woody said, "*you* do what you want, but I've been locked up in a smelly ol' tin can for months, and what *I'm* going to do is *wash my face* in some honest-to-God, unrecycled water!" He grinned at Thomas and began walking away toward the canal. "I might even take me a *swim*."

"Thomas..." the commander said brokenly, "don't worry about the bodies. Don't worry about *anything* else. Just get in the lander. As soon as you're inside I'm going to trigger the launch sequence."

Johnboy was staring at him quizzically, compassionately—waiting.

"Johnboy..." Thomas said. "Johnboy, how can I tell which is real?"

"You *choose* what's real," Johnboy said quietly. "We all do."

"*Listen* to me, Thomas," the commander pleaded; there was an edge of panic in his voice. "You're talking to yourself again. Whatever you think you're seeing, or hearing, or even *touching*, it's just *isn't real*. There can be tactile hallucinations, too, you know. It's not *real*."

"Old Ahab up there has made his choice, too," Johnboy said. "For him,

38

in his own conceptual universe, Woody and I *are* dead. And that's real, too—for *him*. But you don't have to choose that reality. You can choose *this* one."

"I don't know," Thomas mumbled, "I just don't *know*...."

Woody hit the water in an explosion of foam. He swam a few strokes, whooping, then turned to float on his back. "C'mon in, you guys!" he shouted.

Johnboy smiled, then turned to bring his face close to Thomas's helmet, peering in through the faceplate. Johnboy was still wearing that strange, dreamy look, so unlike his usual animated expression, and his eyes were clear and compassionate and calm. "It calls for an act of faith, Thomas. Maybe that's how every world begins." He grinned at Thomas. "Meanwhile, I think I'm going to take a swim, too." He strolled off toward the canal, bouncing a little at each step.

Thomas stood unmoving, the two red lights flashing on his chinstrap readout.

"They're both going swimming now," Thomas said dully.

"Thomas! Can you hear me, Thomas?"

"I hear you," Thomas mumbled.

They were having *fun* in their new world—he could see that. The kind of fun that kids had...that every child took for granted. The joy of discovery, of everything being *new*...the joy that seemed to get lost in the gray shuffle to adulthood, given up bit by incremental bit....

"You're just going to have to trust me, Thomas. *Trust me.* Take my word for it that I know what I'm talking about. You're going to have to take that on faith. Now *listen* to me: No matter what you think is going on down there, *don't take your helmet off.*"

His father used to lecture him in that same tone of voice, demanding, domineering...and at the same time condescending. Scornful. Daddy knows best. Listen to me, boy, I *know* what I'm talking about! Do what I *tell* you to do!

"Do you hear me? Do *not* take your helmet off! Under any circumstances at all. That's an *order.*"

Thomas nodded, before he could stop himself. Here he was, good boy little Tommy, standing on the fringes again, taking orders, doing what he was told. Getting passed over *again*. And for what?

Something flew by in the distance, headed toward the hills.

It looked to be about the size of a large bird, but like a dragonfly, it had six long, filmy gossamer wings, which it swirled around in a complexly interweaving pattern, as if it were rowing itself through the air.

"Get to the lander, Thomas, and close the hatch."

Never did have any fun. Have to be twice as good as *any* of them, have to bust your goddamn ass—

"That's a direct order, Thomas!"

You've got to make the bastards respect you, you've got to *earn* their respect. His father had said that a million times. And how little time it had taken him to waste away and die, once he'd stopped trying, once he realized that you can't earn what people aren't willing to sell.

A red and yellow lizard ran over his boot, as quick and silent as a tickle. It had six legs.

One by one, he began to undo the latches of his helmet.

"No! Listen to me! If you take off your helmet, you'll *die.* Don't do it! For God's sake, don't do it!"

The last latch. It was sticky, but he tugged at it purposefully.

"You're killing yourself! Stop it! *Please. Stop! You goddamn stupid nigger! Stop—*"

Thomas smiled, oddly enough feeling closer to the commander in that moment than he ever had before. "Too late," he said cheerfully.

Thomas twisted his helmet a quarter turn and lifted it off his head.

When the third red light winked on, Commander Redenbaugh slumped against the board and started to cry. He wept openly and loudly, for they had been good men, and he had failed all of them, even Thomas, the best and steadiest of the lot. He hadn't been able to save a goddamned one of them!

At last he was able to pull himself together. He forced himself to look again at the monitor, which showed three space-suited bodies sprawled out lifelessly on the rusty-red sand.

He folded his hands, bent his head, and prayed for the souls of his dead companions. Then he switched the monitor off.

It was time to make plans. Since the *Plowshare* will be carrying a much lighter-than-anticipated cargo, he had enough excess fuel to allow him to leave a bit early, if he wanted to, and he *did* want to. He began to punch figures into the computer, smiling bitterly at the irony. Yesterday he had been regretting that they had so little time left in Mars orbit. Now, suddenly, he was in a hurry to get home...but no matter how many corners he shaved, he'd still be several long, grueling months in transit—with quite probably a court-martial waiting for him when he got back.

For an instant, even the commander's spirit quailed at the thought of that dreadful return journey. But he soon got himself under control again. It would be a difficult and unpleasant trip, right enough, but a determined man could always manage to do what needed to be done.

Even if he had to do it alone.

* * *

When the *Plowshare's* plasma drive was switched on, it created a daytime star in the Martian sky. It was like a shooting star in reverse, starting out at its brightest and dimming rapidly as it moved up and away.

Thomas saw it leave. He was leaning against his makeshift spear—flametree wood, with a fire-hardened tip—and watching Johnboy preparing to skin the dead hyena-leopard, when he chanced to glance up. "Look," he said.

Johnboy followed Thomas's eyes and saw it, too. He smiled sardonically and lifted the animal's limp paw, making it wave bye-bye. "So long Ahab," Johnboy said. "Good luck." He went back to skinning the beast. The hyena-leopard—a little bit larger than a wildcat, six-legged, saber-tusked, its fur a muddy purple with rusty-orange spots—had attacked without warning and fought savagely; it had taken all three of them to kill it.

Woody looked up from where he was lashing a makeshift flametree-wood raft together with lengths of wiring from the lander. "I'm sure he'll make it okay," Woody said quietly.

Thomas sighed. "Yeah," he said, and then, more briskly, "Let me give you a hand with that raft. If we snap it up, we ought to be ready to leave by morning."

Last night, climbing the highest of the rolling hills to the north, they had seen the lights of a distant city, glinting silver and yellow and orange on the far horizon, gleaming far away across the black midnight expanse of the dead sea bottom like an ornate and intricate piece of jewelry set against ink-black velvet.

Thomas was still not sure if he hoped there would be aristocratic red men there, and giant four-armed green Tharks, and beautiful Martian princesses....

41

Pictures Made of Stones

Lucius Shepard

Lucius Shepard became a major voice in contemporary science fiction and fantasy during the 1980s. His first novel, *Green Eyes,* about sf zombies, was published in Terry Carr's second Ace Special novel series. Shepard's second novel, *Life During Wartime,* is about a futuristic war in Central America. His third, *The Golden,* a lushly written addition to the vampire *oeuvre*, has brought him to the attention of horror readers. Shepard's short fiction is collected in *The Jaguar Hunter* and *The Ends of the Earth.*

"Pictures Made of Stones" showcases Shepard's brilliant use of language and describes a universe he has made his own—the jungle. *Omni* rarely publishes poetry, but this piece was commissioned for the magazine. It appeared in September 1987.

Pictures Made Of Stones

Lucius Shepard

This bunch of neckties drop into the bar for a boost before dinner
and start bullshitting about the war like it was the NFL or something,
tossing off casualty figures, arguing tactics, and I'm amused, right,
so I pull up a chair and say I'd be glad to fill them in about the war, because
    I can't stand to let ignorance flourish...which sets them to muttering.
But before they can work up real hostility, I order a round of drinks
and get to talking about the time the patrol was on recon in Nicaragua,
following the course of the Patuca through thick mountain jungle,
just after a flight of Russian choppers had laid down a cloud of gas.
I found myself alone, feeling relaxed, grinning like a saved Christian.
I'd never been at home in the jungle, but there I was, spacing on the scenery,
    wondering why orchids had faces and monkeys were screaming my
    name,
and not a bit worried by the fact that the rest of the patrol had vanished.
All that mean green was looking beautiful, green like a perfect vice, great
    sweeps and declensions of green, an entire vocabulary of green scripted
    by the curves of leaves and vines...green tenses, green lives.
Even the air seemed to hold a wash of pale emerald throughout.
I'd heard about this gas the beaners had that turned you sideways to reality,
but as good as I was feeling, I didn't care what the hell was behind it.

It was as if I'd become more soldierly, more aligned with warring purpose,

and I understood that war was not an event bounded by time, defined by politics,

but was a principle underlying every life,

the ground upon which our actions were deployed.

Maybe it was foolish to put so much stock in a delusion (I never thought it otherwise),

but I concluded that delusions were standard issue, and if you lucked onto a compelling one,

you didn't discard it just because it didn't accord with Army regs.

I walked higher and higher into the mountains, looking like death,

thin and feverish, my eyes gone black from seeing, fatigues rotting away.

But I was a miracle inside, ribbed with the silver of principle,

armored with the iron of a new intent, one I sensed but could not name.

The waitress, a brunette with trophy-sized balloons, she's been listening,

and now she asks, "What happened to the rest?" I just smile and shrug.

One of the neckties, a real Blow Dry in an Italian suit, onyx cuff links,

he says, "I've never heard of anything like that...that gas or whatever."

I laugh and tell him I could make a whole damn world out of the things he's never heard of,

and that half of everything sounds like fantasy, anyway...take the stock market, for example,

which gets a laugh from the others. But Mr. Blow Dry remains unconvinced.

"I knew lots of guys like you in Nicaragua," I say. "They couldn't believe in what was killing them.

Thought because something wasn't real, it couldn't do them any harm."

The neckties struggle with this concept as I go on talking about war.

I came to a white village ringed by green mountains, with cane and corn

planted on the slopes, and mango trees shading the red tile roofs.

The inhabitants were women, children, and old men with wet black eyes as vacant as turtles' eyes,

who told me that their sons had been executed and buried in a mass grave.

Their voices were soft, unremorseful, their manner calm and resolute,

and I realized this was not evidence of resignation but that they were at peace.

The longer I stayed, the more I understood that this peace

was a by-product of war, filling the valley the way rainwater fills a shell crater,

creating of this violent form a placid surface and a tranquil depth,

and this inadvertent transformation was its only real incidence,

for all those modes of existence we label peace are nothing more than organisms that when irritated produce the pearls we officially sanction as conflicts.

I lived with a young widow, Serafina, in a house with dirt floors,

a charcoal stove, and a faded Madonna on the wall above a crude candlelit altar.

Days, I would put on the cotton shirt and trousers of a campesino and help her in the fields.

Nights, I would tell her stories of America and other dreams.

With us lived Ramon, her son, and her senile mother, Expectacion,

the only person in the village aside from me who was not at peace.

She loathed me and would haunt the doorway while her daughter and I made love,

cursing at me, muttering incoherencies such as "Your shadow is a demon, your hours broken glass,"

and we would be forced to go into the hills to find some privacy.

Serafina was thick-waisted, heavy in the legs, her face written with cares,

but from her I learned that beauty was no measure, rather a kind of lucidity

that communicated perfectly its moods to whomever it permitted to see.

I wanted to be in love with her...more than wanted, I needed that solace

and I believed that love might someday override my other compulsions.

But though I knew passion with her, knew all the trappings of emotion,

I could not fall in love, though I suppose I might have, had I survived.

* * *

Mr. Blow Dry interrupts me, asking if I'm claiming to be a ghost

or if my statement has some symbolic relevance. "Neither," I tell him.

"Life and death are elusive in their meanings." He nods sagely, pretends to
understand,

but the waitress leans close, touching my arm, and asks me to explain.

Her face, though beautiful by any standard, seems now to open,

to expose the revelatory beauty that I once perceived in Serafina's face,

and I see her failed years, her petty aspirations and self-absorption,

all this distilling into a consolation, a desire to provide me with remedies.

Though there may be no explanations, for the sake of her lucid mood,

I tell her of Ramon, eight years old, a slow-witted child with thin arms and
dull eyes,

who would sit all day outside the house, making pictures of the stones

he gathered from the bed of a stream that carved a groove along the base of
the eastern hill.

The stones were black and white, iron-colored and mossy green,

and the pictures had the simplicity of graphics, yet had a certain power.

It was said that Ramon had been blessed with gifts of prophecy and magic,

that he was the spiritual chargeman of the village and of peace itself.

It made sense that peace—like war with its soldiers—should operate

through an agency whose character is of a kind with its essential idea.

But I can only testify that the picture he made on my last night there

showed a shadowy man with a rifle, standing with a hand outstretched,

and just beyond him, as if flung from his hand into the air, a black bird was
flying in a white sky.

And, too, there was that sense I had of his presence, of being always in his
scrutiny.

"Whether or not Ramon was as the villagers claimed," I tell the waitress,

"his truth is undeniable. Our lives are no more than pictures made of stones,
and moment to moment we and the world are transformed utterly.

Only war and the false dream of continuity are immune to these little deaths.

Even peace can last for just so long as it's able to effect a magical denial.

This is not philosophy, but signals a process too subtle to wear a suit of
words."

That last night Serafina and I went into a banana grove to be alone,

and after making love, lying there, watching the ragged shadows of the
fronds

shifting across the thickets of stars and darkness overhead,

she made a disconsolate noise, and when I asked what was wrong ,

she told me she was concerned about Expectacion, her increasing irascibility
and incoherence.

Then as if on cue, Expectacion appeared at the base of the hill, staring at us,

looking like a huge black bird in her peaked shawl, her voice a static of
curses.

We ignored her, and eventually she moved off into the night toward home.

But when we returned to the house, a neighbor told us that Expectacion had
run off into the hills,

heading west toward the great cliff that overlooked the Patuca.

Leaving Serafina to watch over Ramon, I went to bring back Expectacion.

As I climbed the western hill, I could feel my superficial peace dissolving,

my principle resurfacing, claiming me, and everything I saw took on an
eerie valence,

and my thoughts became as black and deviant as the limbs of the trees,

which seemed like weird candelabras tipped with a thousand green flames,

illuminated by a golden full moon like an evil vowel howling silence.

Now and then I saw Expectacion moving above me, a shadow among
shadows,

and I cursed her in my thoughts....Old hag, mad ghost, gloom of a bitch.

A dozen times I nearly had her, but always she eluded me, and at last

I found her waiting at the cliff top. I almost caught her as she leaped,

appearing to vanish up and out into the dark, rather than falling.

I stood a moment, wondering how to tell Serafina what had happened,

and a voice called from the trail leading down to the left of the cliff, commanding me to come toward it, to hold my hands high and not to run.

I did as ordered and soon confronted a patrol of men anonymous in their combat gear,

bulky olive-drab suits and helmets with smoked faceplates through which were visible

reflections of green numerals and diagrams from their computer readouts.

Rockets bristled from their backpacks, gas grenades for igniting the air in tunnels

hung in clusters from their belts, and their computer-linked rifles hummed.

I was confused as to who they were, for their speech was an electric babble

that I translated into frequencies of pure meaning, but I believe now they were Cuban,

though had they been American, it would have made little difference.

They asked about the village, if there were women, if there were soldiers....

I told them how it was, and they were delighted, they talked about the pleasures awaiting them.

They gave me food and drink, and asked me from which village I hailed,

for in my cotton trousers and embroidered shirt, they mistook me for a local.

I pretended to be grateful, but I hated them, I saw the inconstancy

with which they embodied the principle of war, and I knew what must be done.

That night I walked among them as they slept, perfect in my stealth,

a pure warrior, shadowless, free of the drugs of conscience and morality.

I slipped a rifle from a sleeping hand and swung it in a scything burst

that finished all but one, whose legs and arms were pierced by the rounds.

He tried to talk with me, and I think he understood why he was to die

but perhaps this was simply a conceit on my part, reflecting a need for understanding.

The moon was a drop of golden venom in his faceplate, his pleading hurt my head,

and his thoughts scurried like spiders for cover into the crevices of his brain.

I killed them all before they could hide and leave clues to my identity.

Then I stood, feeling more unified in purpose and place than ever.

Though Ramon may have enlisted me in the service of the village,

though in his picture I might be a protector, I saw that my act had been one of initiation,

a reentry into the war, an expression of its art and governance.

I felt a shifting within me, I seemed to hear a click as of stones being set in place.

The border between peace and war divided me, slicing me in half,

but there was no doubt which of them was my ruler, and I went down from the cliff,

away from the valley, dead to one world, already reborn to the next.

The rush of traffic is braiding together with the ashen twilight into dusk,

and the neckties are sitting with their heads down, studying their hands

with the solemnity of men at a Rotary breakfast who are contemplating

some preacherly truth that they hope will sustain them through their business day.

"What happened then?" asks Mr. Blow Dry, and I laugh long and hard

at the absolute ignorance of time and process that his question reveals.

"You want to hear more?" I say. "Sure, I'll tell you stories all night long.

I'll tell about The Volcano That Sang, The Fire That Spoke My Name,

about the four-armed child I once saw during the Battle of Bluefields.

Then you can go from here armed with sad expertise, with a new pose of wisdom,

with a vital and seductive color to add to your cocktail party opinions.

Sure, man! Buy another round! We'll talk, we'll fucking communicate.

I'll make believe you're really here, and you can pretend the world has never ended."

The neckties are alarmed, not wanting their shallowness to be mistaken for what it is,

and they assure me that all I've said has made a difference in their lives,

impressed by the hard-hitting glamour of pain with—wow!—philosophy, too, and ignoring the possibility that I may be deluded or a liar or both.

But the waitress only looks at me, and as peace begins to spill from the bar into the warring street,

instead of her face, her beautiful lucid face that stuns me with its clarity of mood,

its intimations of something more than sympathy, of deeper interest,

I have a vision of a child's enormous grimy fingers reaching toward me....

Listen, Ramon. What good is there in my continued service?

Is it that I am a counterweight, a potent pawn whose movements

help to maintain the delicate border between peace and war?

Even if so, sooner or later the border will erode and a harsh toll will be taken,

harsher for every moment that denies war's dominion.

I have died many times, always for the sake of principle, and I am not afraid.

I have lost the capacity for fear and for much else that makes a man.

But this woman is becoming real to me,

and though she is only an argument against an unendurable truth,

I need a death to consume me in light, to show me those things I might have learned in that valley where peace was the law and magic the rule.

Choose your stones with care, Ramon.

Give me back my world of random choices, of ordinary defeats.

Leave in place the green stone in my skull that is proof against the lie of time.

Stay your hand from the white stone in my groin that admits to heat and angels.

Pluck only the black stone from my heart, and tonight let me die for love.

E-Ticket to Namland

Dan Simmons

Another of several writers in this volume who burst onto the science fiction and fantasy scene during the 1980s, Simmons's "Eyes I Dare Not Meet in Dreams" was one of the first stories I bought as *Omni*'s fiction editor. Subsequently, we published his novelette, "Carrion Comfort," which was later expanded into the acclaimed novel. Simmons's short fiction has been collected in the award-winning *Prayers to Broken Stones*. His most recent book is *LoveDeath,* a collection of five novellas.

"E-Ticket to Namland" is a bitter, cynical look at the undeclared (by the U.S. government) war that divided the nation. The story was published November 1988.

E-Ticket To Namland

Dan Simmons

The twenty-eight Huey gunships moved out in single file, each hovering a precise three meters above the tarmac, the sound of their rotors filling the world with a roar that could be felt in teeth and bones and testicles. Once above the tree line and gaining altitude, the helicopters separated into four staggered V formations, and the noise diminished to the point where shouts could be heard.

"First time out?" cried the guide.

"What?" Justin Jeffries turned away from the open door where he had been watching the shadow of their helicopter slide across the surface of the mirrored rice paddies below. He leaned toward the guide until their combat helmets were almost touching.

"First time out?" repeated the guide. The man was small even for a Vietnamese. He wore a wide grin and the uniform and shoulder patch of the old First Air Cav Division. Jeffries was big even for an American. He was dressed in green shorts, a flowered Hawaiian shirt, Nike running sandals, an expensive Rolex comlog, and a U.S. Army helmet that had become obsolete the year he was born. Jeffries was draped with cameras: a compact Yashica SLR, a Polaroid Holistic-360, and a new Nikon imager. Jeffries returned the guide's grin. "First time for us. We're here with my wife's father."

Heather leaned over to join the conversation. "Daddy was here during...you know...the war. They thought it might be good for him to take the Vet Tour." She nodded in the direction of a short, solid, gray-haired man leaning against the M-60 machine-gun mount near the door's safety webbing. He was the only person in the cabin not wearing a helmet. The back of his blue shirt was soaked with sweat.

55

"Yes, yes," smiled the guide and stepped back to plug his microphone jack into a bulkhead socket. His voice echoed tinnily in every helmet and from hidden speakers. "Ladies and gentlemen, please notice the tree line to your right."

There was a lurch as the passengers shifted their positions and craned for a view. Ten-year-old Sammee Jeffries and his eight-year-old sister, Elizabeth, shoved their way through the crowded space to stand next to where their grandfather sat by the open door. The barrel of Elizabeth's plastic M-16 accidentally struck the older man on his sunburned neck, but he did not turn or speak. Suddenly a series of flashes erupted from the tree line along one rice paddy. The passengers gasped audibly as a line of magnesium-bright tracer bullets rose up and lashed toward their ship, missing the rotors by only a few meters. Immediately one of the gunships at the rear of the V formation dove, curved back the way they had come in a centrifugally perfect arc, and raked the tree line with rocket and minigun fire. Meanwhile, at the guide's urging, Sammee stood on a low box, grasped the two-handed grip of the heavy M-60, swung it awkwardly to bear in the general direction of the now-distant tree line, and depressed the firing studs. The passengers instinctively clutched at their helmets to block their ears. Heavy cartridges, warm but not hot enough to burn anyone, clattered onto the metal deck.

An explosion split the tree line, sending phosphorous streamers fifty meters into the air and setting several tall palms ablaze. Bits of flaming debris splashed into the quiet rice paddy. The passengers laughed and applauded. Sammee grinned back at them and flexed his muscles. Elizabeth leaned against her grandfather and spoke loudly into his ear. "Isn't this *fun*, Grandpa?"

He turned to say something, but at that second the guide announced that their destination would be coming up on the left side of the ship, and Elizabeth was away, shoving her brother aside to get a better view, eager to see the village appear below out of the heat, haze and smoke.

Later that evening five men sat around a table on the fifth-floor terrace of the Saigon Oberoi Sheraton. The air was warm and humid. Occasional gusts of laughter and splashing sounds came up from the pool on the fourth-floor terrace. It was well past nine, but the tropical twilight lingered.

"You were on the village mission-tour this morning, weren't you?" asked Justin Jeffries of the young Oriental next to him.

"Yes, I was. Most interesting." The man sat in a relaxed manner, but something about his bearing, the precisely creased safari suit, the intensity of his gaze, suggested a military background.

"You're Nipponese, aren't you?" asked Justin. At the man's smile and nod, Justin went on, "Thought so. Here with the military mission?"

"No, merely on leave. R and R, I believe your people used to call it."

"Christ," said the overweight American who sat next to Justin's father-in-law. "You've been up north in the PRC fighting Chen's warlords, haven't you?"

"Just so," said the Nipponese and extended his hand to Justin. "Lieutenant Keigo Naguchi."

"Justin Jeffries, Kansas City." Justin's huge hand enclosed the lieutenant's and pumped twice. "This here is my father-in-law, Ralph Disantis."

"A pleasure," said the lieutenant.

"Pleased to meet you," said Disantis.

"I believe I saw you with your grandchildren at the village today," said Naguchi. "A boy and a girl?"

Disantis nodded and sipped his beer. Justin gestured to the heavyset man next to his father-in-law. "And this is Mr...ah...Sears, right?"

"Sayers," said the man. "Roger Sayers. Nice to make your acquaintance, Lieutenant. So how's it going up there? Your guys finally getting those little bastards out of the hill caves?"

"Most satisfactory," said Lieutenant Naguchi. "The situation should be stabilized before the next rainy season."

"Japanese brains and Vietnamese blood, huh?" laughed Sayers. He turned to the fifth man at the table, a silent Vietnamese in a white shirt and dark glasses, and added quickly, "No offense meant. Everybody knows that your basic Viet peasant makes the best foot soldier in the world. Showed us that forty years ago, eh, Mr...ah...?"

"Minh," said the little man and shook hands around the table. "Nguyen van Minh." Minh's hair was black, his face unlined, but his eyes and hands revealed that he was at least in his sixties, closer to Disantis's age than that of the others.

"I saw you on the plane from Denver," said Justin. "Visiting family here?"

"No," said Minh, "I have been an American citizen since 1976. This is my first trip back to Vietnam. I have no family here now." He turned toward Naguchi. "Lieutenant, I am surprised that you choose to spend your leave on an American Veterans' Tour."

Naguchi shrugged and sipped at his gin and tonic. "I find it a sharp contrast to modern methods. Up north I am more technician than warrior. Also, of course, learning more about the first of the helicopter wars is valuable to anyone who is interested in military history. You were a veteran of that war, Mr. Disantis?"

Justin's father-in-law nodded and took a long swallow of beer.

"I just missed it," said Sayers with real regret in his voice. "Too young for Vietnam. Too goddamn old for the Banana Wars."

Justin grunted. "You didn't miss much."

"Ah, you were involved in that period?" asked Naguchi.

"Sure," said Justin. "Everybody who came of age in the discount decade got in on the Banana Wars. The tour today could have been Tegucigalpa or Estanzuelas; just substitute coffee plantations for the rice paddies."

"I want to hear about that," said Sayers and waved a waiter over to the table. "Another round for everyone," he said. From somewhere near the pool a steel drum band started up, unsuccessfully trying to mix American pop tunes, a Caribbean beat, and local musicians. The sound seemed sluggish in the wet, thick air. Tropical night had fallen, and even the stars appeared dimmed by the thickness of atmosphere. Naguchi looked at a band of brighter stars moving toward the zenith and then glanced down at his comlog.

"Checking azimuth for your spottersat, right?" asked Justin. "It's a hard habit to break. I still do it."

Disantis rose. "Sorry I can't stay for the next round, gentlemen. Going to sleep off some of this jet lag." He moved into the air-conditioned brightness of the hotel.

Before going to his room, Disantis looked in on Heather and the children. His daughter was in bed already, but Sammee and Elizabeth were busy feeding data from their father's Nikon through the terminal and onto the wall screen. Disantis leaned against the door molding and watched.

"This is the LZ," Sammee said excitedly.

"What's an LZ?" asked Elizabeth.

"*Landing zone,*" snapped Sammee. "Don't you remember *anything?*"

The wall showed image after image of dust, rotors, the predatory shadows of Hueys coming in above Justin's camera position, the thin line of passengers in combat garb, men and women instinctively bent low despite obvious clearance from the rotors, tourists clutching at their helmets with one hand and hugging cameras, purses, and plastic M-16's to their chests with the other, groups moving away from the raised landing platform along rice paddy dikes.

"There's Grandpa!" cried Elizabeth. Disantis saw himself, aging, over-weight, puffing heavily as he heaved himself down from the helicopter, disdaining the guide's outstretched hand. Sammee tapped at the terminal keys. The picture zoomed and enlarged until only Disantis's grainy face filled the screen. Sammee shifted through colors and widened his grandfather's face until it became a purple balloon ready to pop. *"Stop it,"* whined Elizabeth.

"Crybaby," said Sammee, but some sixth sense made him glance over his shoulder to where Disantis stood. Sammee made no acknowledgment of his grandfather's presence but advanced the picture through a montage of new images.

Disantis blinked and watched the jerky newsreel proceed. The abandoned village of rough huts. The lines of tourist-troops along each side of the narrow road. Close-ups of huts being searched. Heather emerged from a low doorway, blinking in the sunlight, awkwardly lifting her toy M-16, and waving at the camera.

"This is the good part," breathed Sammee.

They had been returning to the LZ when figures along a distant dike had opened fire. At first the tourist milled around in confusion, but at the guide's urging they finally, laughingly had taken cover on the grassy side of the dike. Justin remained standing to take pictures.

Disantis watched as those images built themselves on the wall screen at a rate just slower than normal video. Data columns flashed by to the right. He saw himself drop to one knee on the dike and hold Elizabeth's hand. He remembered noting that the grass was artificial.

The tourists returned fire. Their M-16's flashed and recoiled, but no bullets were expended. The din was tremendous. On the screen a two-year-old near Justin had begun to cry. Eventually the guides helped a young tourist couple use a field radio to call in an air strike. The jets were there in less than a minute—three A-4D Skyhawks with antiquated U.S. naval markings bright and clear on the white wings. They screamed in under five hundred feet high. Justin's camera shook as the explosions sent long shadows across the dikes and made the tourists cringe and hug the earth from their vantage point six hundred meters away. Justin had managed to steady the camera even as the napalm continued to blossom upward.

"Watch," said Sammee. He froze the frame and then zoomed in. The image expanded. Tiny human forms, black silhouettes, became visible against the orange explosions. Sammee enlarged the image even further. Disantis could make out the silhouette of an outflung arm, a shirttail gusting, a conical peasant's hat flying off.

"How'd they do that, Grandpa?" asked Sammee without turning around.

Disantis shrugged. "Holos, maybe."

"Naw, not holos," said Sammee. He did not try to hide his condescension. "Too bright out there. Besides, you can see the pieces fly. Betcha they were animates."

Elizabeth rolled over from where she sprawled. Her pajamas carried a picture of Wonder Duck on the front. "What'd Mr. Sayers mean on the way back, Grandpa?"

"When?"

"In the helicopter, when he said, 'Well, I guess we really showed Charlie today.' " Elizabeth took a breath. "Who's Charlie, Grandpa?"

"Stupid," said Sammee, "Charlie was the VC. The bad guys."

"How come you called him Charlie, Grandpa?" persisted Elizabeth. The frozen explosion on the wall screen cast an orange glow on her features.

"I don't remember," said Disantis. He paused with his hand on the door. "You two better get to bed before your father comes. Tomorrow's going to be a busy day."

Later, alone in his room, sitting in silence broken only by the hum of the air conditioner, Disantis realized that he could *not* remember why the Vietcong had been called Charlie. He wondered if he had ever known. He turned out the light and opened the sliding doors to the balcony. The humid air settled on him like a blanket as he stepped out.

Three floors below, Justin, Sayers, and the others still sat drinking. Their laughter floated up to Disantis and mixed with the rumble of thunder from a storm on the distant and darkened horizon.

On their way to a picnic the next day, Mr. Sayer tripped a claymore mine.

The guide had put them on a simulated patrol down a narrow jungle trail. Sayers was in the lead, paying little attention to the trail, talking to Reverend Dewitt, an airwaves minister from Dothan, Alabama. Justin and Heather were talking with the Newtons, a young couple from Hartford. Disantis was farther back in the line, walking between Sammee and Elizabeth to keep them from quarreling.

Sayers stepped into a thin trip wire stretched across the trail, a section of dirt erupted a meter in front of him, and the claymore jumped three meters into the air before exploding into a white puff.

"Shit," said Sayers. "Excuse me, Reverend." The Vietnamese guide came forward with an apologetic smile and put a red KIA armband on Sayers. The Reverend Dewitt and Tom Newton each received a yellow WIA armband.

"Does this mean I don't get to go to the picnic?" asked Sayers.

The guide smiled and directed the others on how to prepare a medevac LZ in a nearby clearing. Lieutenant Naguchi and Minh cleared underbrush with matchetes, while Heather and Sue Newton helped spread marker panels of iridescent orange plastic. Sammee was allowed to pop the tab on a green smoke marker. The red-cross marked Huey came in with a blast of downdraft that flattened the tall grass and blew Disantis's white tennis hat off. Sayers, Dewitt, and Newton sat propped on their elbows and waved as their stretchers were loaded. The patrol resumed when the medevac copter was just a distant throbbing in the sky.

Justin took point. He moved carefully, frequently holding his hand up to halt the line behind him. There were two more trip wires and a stretch of trail salted with anti-personnel mines. The guide showed them all how to probe ahead with bayonets. For the last half kilometer, they stayed in the grass on either side of the trail.

The picnic ground was on a hill overlooking the sea. Under a thatched pavilion sat three tables covered with sandwich makings, salads, assorted fruits, and coolers of beer. Sayers, Newton, and Dewitt were already there, helping two guides cook hamburgers and hot dogs over charcoal fires. "What kept you?" called Sayers with a deep laugh.

After a long lunch, several of the tourists went down to the beach to swim or sunbathe or take a nap. Sammee found a network of tunnels in the jungle near the picnic pavilion, and several of the children gathered around as the guide showed them how to drop in CS gas and fragmentation grenades before actually searching the tunnels. Then the children and few of the younger adults wiggled in on their bellies to explore the complex. Disantis could hear their excited shouts as he sat alone at one of the picnic tables, drinking his beer and looking out to sea. He could also hear the conversation of his daughter and Sue Newton as they sat on beach towels a few meters away. "We wanted to bring my daddy, but he just refused to come," said the Newton woman. "So Tommy says, 'Well, shoot, as long as the government's paying part of it, let's go ourselves'. So we did."

"We thought it would be good for my father," said Heather. "I wasn't even born then, but when he got back from the war, way back in the seventies, he didn't even come home to Mother. He went and lived in the woods of Oregon or Washington or somewhere for a couple of years."

"Really!" said Sue Newton. "My daddy never did anything crazy like that."

"Oh, he got better after a while," said Heather. "He's been fine the last ten years or so. But his therapy program said that it'd be good for him to come on the Vet's Tour, and Justin was able to get time off 'cause the dealership is doing so good."

The talk turned to children. Shortly after that, it began to rain heavily, and three Hueys and a lumbering Sikorsky picked them up to return them to the Sheraton. The dozen or so people in Disantis's group sang "Ninety-nine Bottles of Beer on the Wall" during the short flight back.

There was nothing scheduled for the afternoon; and after the storm passed, several people decided to go shopping at one of the large malls between the hotel complex and the park. Disantis caught an electric bus into downtown Saigon, where he walked the streets until nightfall.

The change of name to Ho Chi Minh City had never really taken, and the metropolis had officially been renamed Saigon in the early nineties. The city bore little resemblance to the excited jumble of pedestrians, motorbikes, strip joints, bars, restaurants, and cheap hotels Disantis remembered from forty years earlier. The foreign money had all gone into the tourist enclaves near the park, and the city itself reflected the gray era of the New Socialist Reality more than it did the feverish pulse of old Saigon. Efficient, faceless structures and steel-and-glass high rises sat on either side of busy boulevards. Occasionally Disantis would see a decaying side street that reminded him of the cluttered stylishness of Tu-Do Street in the late sixties.

Nguyen van Minh joined him as Disantis waited for a light to change on Thong Nhut Boulevard.

"Mr. Disantis."

"Mr. Minh."

The short Vietnamese adjusted his glasses as they strolled past the park where the Independence Palace had once stood. "You are enjoying the sights?" he asked. "Do you see much that is familiar?"

"No," said Disantis. "Do you?"

Minh paused and looked around him as if the idea had not pertained to him. "Not really, Mr. Disantis," he said at last. "Of course, I rarely visited Saigon. My village was in a different province. My unit was based near Da Nang."

"ARVN?" asked Disantis.

"Hac Bao," said Minh. "The Black Panthers of the First Division. You remember them, perhaps?"

Disantis shook his head.

"We were...I say without pride...the most feared fighting unit in all of South Vietnam...including the Americans. The Hac Bao had put fear into the hearts of the Communist insurgents for ten years before the fall."

Disantis stopped to but a lemon ice from a street vendor. The lights were coming on all along the boulevard.

"You see the embassy there?" asked Minh, pointing to an antiquated six-story structure set back behind an ornate fence.

"That's the old U.S. Embassy?" asked Disantis, without much interest in his voice. "I would have thought that the building would've been torn down by now."

"Oh, no," said Minh, "it is a museum. It has been restored very much to its original appearance."

Disantis nodded and glanced at his comlog.

"I stood here," continued Minh, "right here . . . in April of 1975 and watched the helicopters take the last of the Americans off the roof of the embassy. It was only my third time in Saigon. I had just been released from four days in prison."

"Prison?" Disantis turned to look at Minh.

"Yes. I had been arrested by the government after members of my unit had commandeered the last Boeing 727 out of Da Nang to Saigon. We fought civilians—women and children—to get aboard that plane. I was a lieutenant. I was twenty-three years old."

"So you got out of Vietnam during the panic?"

"They released us from jail when the North Vietnamese were in the suburbs," said Minh. "I was not able to leave the country until several months later."

"Boat?" asked Disantis. The lemon ice was melting quickly in the warm air.

Minh nodded. "And you, Mr. Disantis, when did you leave Vietnam?"

Disantis tossed the paper wrapped into a trash can and licked his fingers. "I came here early in '69," he said.

"And when did you leave?" Minh asked again. Disantis lifted his head as if to sniff the night air. The evening was thick with the scent of tropical vegetation, mimosa blossoms, stagnant water, decay. When he looked at Minh there was a dark gleam in his blue eyes. He shook his head. "I never left," he said.

Justin, Sayers, and Tom Newton came up to the guide as he sat alone at a table near the back of the hotel bar. The three Americans hesitated and looked at each other. Finally Justin stepped forward. "Howdy," he said.

"Good afternoon, Mr. Jeffries," said the guide.

"We...uh...we'd all, I mean the three of us and a couple of other guys, we wanted to see you about something."

"Ahhh, there is some problem with the tour?" asked the guide.

"No, no, everything's great," said Justin and glanced back at the other two. He sat down and leaned toward the Vietnamese. His voice was a hoarse whisper. "We...ah...we wanted a little more than the regular tour."

"Oh?" The guide blinked. His mouth was not quite curled in a smile.

"Yeah," said Justin, "you know. Something *extra.*"

"Something extra?" said the guide.

Roger Sayers stepped forward. "We want some special action," he said.

"Ahhh," said the guide and finished up his drink.

Justin leaned forward again. "Nat Pendrake told us it was okay," he whispered loudly. "He said he...uh...arranged it through Mr. Tho."

"Mr. Tho?" the guide said blankly. But the smile was there now.

"Yeah. Nat said that...uh...a special action would be about a thousand."

"Two thousand," the guide said softly. "Each."

"Hey," interjected Sayers, "Nat was here just a few months ago and..."

"Quiet," said Justin. "All right. That's fine. Here." He slid his universal card across the table.

The Vietnamese smiled and pushed Jeffries's card back.

"Cash, please," he said. "You will have it tonight. American dollars."

"I don't know about..." began Sayers.

"Where?" asked Justin.

"The frontage road beyond the hotel maintenance buildings," said the guide. "Twenty-three hundred hours."

"Right," said Justin as the guide stood up. "See you then."

"Have a nice day," said the guide and was gone.

The trucks transported them to a point in the jungle where the road ended and a trail began. The five men jumped down and followed the guide through the darkness. The trail was muddy from the evening rains, and wet fronds brushed at their cork-smudged faces. Justin Jeffries and Tom Newton kept close to the guide. Behind them, stumbling occasionally in the dark, came Sayers and Reverend Dewitt. Lieutenant Naguchi brought up the rear. Each man was in uniform. Each carried an M-16.

"*Shit,*" hissed Sayers as a branch caught him in the face.

"Shut up," whispered Justin. The guide motioned them to a stop, and the Americans pressed close to peer at a clearing through a gap in the foliage. A few kerosene lanterns threw cold light from the doorways of the dozen huts of the village.

"Vietcong sympathizers," whispered the guide. "They can tell you where the cadre headquarters is. Everyone in the village knows the VC."

"Huh," said Sayers. "So our job is to get the information, right?"

"Yes."

"And they're VC sympathizers?" whispered Tom Newton.

"Yes."

"How many?" asked Lieutenant Naguchi. His voice was barely audible above the drip of water from palm leaves.

"Maybe thirty," said the guide. "No more than thirty-five."

"Weapons?" asked Naguchi.

"There may be some hidden in the huts," said the guide. "Be careful of the young men and women. VC. Well trained."

There was a long silence as they stared at the quiet village.

Finally Justin stood and clicked the safety off on his rifle. "Let's do it," he said. Together they moved into the clearing.

Ralph Disantis and Nguyen van Minh sat together in a dark booth in an old bar not far from what had once been Tu-Do Street. It was late. Minh was quite drunk, and Disantis let himself appear to be in the same condition. An ancient jukebox played recent Japanese hits and oldies but goodies dating back to the eighties.

"For many years after the fall of my country, I thought that America had no honor," said Minh. The only sign of the little man's drunkenness was the great care with which he enunciated each word. "Even as I lived in America, worked in America, became a citizen of America, I was convinced that America had no honor. My American friends told me that during the Vietnam War there was news from my country on the televisions and radios every day, every evening. After Saigon fell...there was nothing. Nothing. It was as if my nation had never existed."

"Hmmm," said Disantis. He finished his drink and beckoned for more.

"But you, Mr. Disantis, you are a man of honor," said Minh. "I know this. I sense this. You are a man of honor."

Disantis nodded at the retreating waiter, removed the swizzle stick from his fresh drink, and placed the plastic saber in a row with seven others. Mr. Minh blinked and did the same thing with his.

"As a man of honor you will understand why I have returned to avenge my family," Minh said carefully.

"Avenge?" said Disantis.

"Avenge my brother who died fighting the North Vietnamese," said Minh. "Avenge my father—a teacher—who spent eight years in a reeducation camp only to die soon after his release. Avenge my sister who was deported by this regime for..." Minh paused. "For alleged crimes against morality. She drowned when their overcrowded boat went down somewhere between here and Hong Kong."

65

"Avenge," repeated Disantis. "How? And with what?"

Minh sat up straight and looked over his shoulder. No one was near. "I will avenge my family's honor by striking against the maggots who have corrupted my nation," he said.

"Yeah," said Disantis. "With what? Do you have a weapon?"

Minh hesitated, licked his lips, and looked for a second like he was sobering. Then he leaned over and grasped Disantis's forearm. "I have a weapon," he whispered. "Two of them. I smuggled them in. A rifle and my service automatic from the Hac Bao."

He hesitated again. "I can tell you this, Mr. Disantis. You are a man of honor." This time it was a question.

"Yes," said Disantis. "Tell me."

Two of the huts were on fire. Justin and the other four had come in shouting and firing. There had been no opposition. The thirty-two villagers, mostly children and old people, knelt in the dust at the center of the village. Sayers had knocked over a lantern in one of the huts, and the thatch and bamboo had blazed like an incendiary flare. The fat American beat uselessly at the flames until Justin called, "Forget the fucking hooch and get back here."

Tom Newton swung his rifle to cover the cringing villagers. "Where are the VC?" he shouted.

"VC!" shouted Sayers. "Where are their tunnels? Tell us, God damn it!" A kneeling woman holding a baby bowed her forehead to the dust. Flames cast bizarre shadows on the dirt, and the smell of smoke made the men's nostrils flare.

"They don't understand what we're saying," said Reverend Dewitt.

"The hell they don't," snapped Justin. "They're just not talking."

Lieutenant Naguchi stepped forward. He was relaxed, but he kept his M-16 trained on the cowering villagers. "Mr. Jeffries, I will stand guard here if you wish to conduct an interrogation."

"Interrogation?" said Justin.

"There is an empty hut there, away from the fire," said the lieutenant. "It is best to isolate them during questioning."

"Yeah," said Justin. "I remember. Tom cut a couple of them out of the herd. Hurry!"

Newton lifted a young man and an old woman by the arm and began moving them toward the hut. "Not her," said Justin. "Too old. Get that one." He pointed to a wide-eyed girl of fifteen or sixteen. "She's probably got a brother or boyfriend fighting with the VC."

Newton pushed the old woman back to her knees and roughly lifted the girl to her feet. Justin felt his mouth go dry. Behind him the flames had set a third hut on fire, and sparks drifted up to mix with the stars.

Disantis set the ninth plastic saber carefully in a row with the others. "How about ammunition?" he asked.

Minh blinked slowly and smiled. "Three thousand rounds for the rifle," he said. He lifted his glass in slow motion, drank, swallowed. "Thirty clips for the .45 caliber service automatic. Enough..." He paused, swayed a second, and straightened his back. "Enough to do the job, yes?"

Disantis dropped money on the table to pay the tab. He helped Minh to his feet and guided the smaller man toward the door. Minh stopped, grasped Disantis's arm in both hands, and brought his face close. "Enough, yes?" he asked.

Disantis nodded. "Enough," he said.

"Shit," said Tom Newton, "he's not going to tell us anything." The young man from the village knelt before them. His black shirt had been pulled back to pin his arms. Blood was smeared from the corners of his mouth and nostrils. There were cigarette burn marks dotted across his chest.

"Bring the girl here," said Justin. Sayers pushed her to her knees, took a fistful of hair, and jerked her head back sharply.

"Where are the VC?" asked Justin. Smoke came through the open door of the hooch. "Tunnels? VC?"

The girl said nothing. Her eyes were very dark and dilated with fear. Small, white teeth showed between her slightly parted lips. "Hold her arms," Justin said to Newton and Sayers. He took a long knife out of his sheath on his web belt, slipped the point under her buttoned shirtfront, and slashed upward. Cloth ripped and parted.

The girl gasped and writhed, but the two Americans held her tightly. Her breasts were small, conical, and lightly filmed with moisture.

"Jesus," said Newton and giggled.

Justin tugged her black pants halfway down, slapped her knee aside when she kicked, and used the knife to tear the cloth away from her ankles.

"Hey!" yelled Sayers. The young Vietnamese had lurched to his feet and was struggling to free his arms. Justin turned quickly, dropped the knife, lifted the M-16, and fired three times in rapid succession. Flesh exploded from the boy's chest, throat, and cheeks. He kicked backward, spasmed once, and lay still in a growing red pool.

67

"Oh, Jesus," Newton said again. "Jesus Christ, this is something."

"Shut up," said Justin. He placed the butt of his rifle against the dazed girl's collarbone and pushed her onto her back. "Hold her legs," he said. "You'll get your turns."

After seeing Minh to his hotel room and putting him to bed, Disantis went back to his own room and sat out on the balcony. Sometime after three A.M., his son-in-law and four other men materialized out of the darkness and sat down around one of the round tables on the abandoned terrace below. Disantis could hear the sounds of beer cans being tossed into trash bins, the pop of more tabs, and bits of conversation.

"How the hell did all the firing start out there?" asked Justin in the darkness. Several of the others giggled drunkenly.

A firm voice with a Japanese accent answered, "One of them ran. The reverend opened fire. I joined him in stopping them from escaping."

"...damn brains all over the place." Disantis recognized Sayers's voice. "I'd like to know how they did that."

"Blood bags and charges every six centimeters or so under the synflesh," came the slurred voice of the young man named Newton. "Used to work for Disney. Know all about that animate stuff."

"If they *were* animates," said the Sayers shadow, and someone giggled.

"You damn well know that they were," came Justin's voice. "We never even got out of the goddamned park. Ten thousand goddamn bucks."

"It was so...*real*," said a voice that Disantis recognized as belonging to the airwaves minister. "But surely there were no...bullets."

"Hell, no," said Newton. " 'Scuse me, Reverend. But they couldn't use real slugs. Customers'd kill each other by mistake."

"Then how..."

"Lasered UV pulses." said Justin.

"Triggered the charges under the skin." said Newton. "Easy to reset."

"But the blood," said Reverend Dewitt in the darkness. "The...the brain matter. The bone fragments..."

"All right, already!" shouted Sayers so loudly that the other men shushed him. "Come on, let's just say we got our money's worth, okay? They can buy a lot of spare parts for that much, right?"

"You can but a lot of spare gooks for that much," said Newton, and there was a ripple of laughter. "Jesus," he went on, "did you see that gook girl wiggle when Jeffries slipped it to her the first time...?"

Disantis listened for a few minutes more and then went into his room and carefully closed the sliding door.

The morning was beautiful, with tall, white clouds piled up above the sea to the east when the family had a leisurely breakfast on the restaurant terrace. Sammee and Elizabeth had eggs, toast, and cereal. Heather ordered an omelet. Disantis had coffee. Justin joined them late, cradled his head in his hands, and ordered a Bloody Mary. "You came in late last night, dear," said Heather.

Justin messaged his temples. "Yeah. Tom and some of us went to the gaming rooms and played poker 'til late."

"You missed the excitement this morning, Dad," said Sammee.

"Yeah, what?" Justin sipped at his drink and grimaced.

"They arrested Mr. Minh this mornin'," Sammee said happily.

"Oh?" Justin looked at his wife.

"It's true, dear," said Heather. "He was arrested this morning. Something to do with illegal contraband in his luggage."

"Yeah," said Sammee, "I heard the guy downstairs tellin' somebody that he had a rifle. You know, like ours, only *real.*"

"Well, I'll be damned," said Justin. "Is he going to stand trial or what?"

"No," said Disantis. "They just asked him to leave. They shipped him out on the morning shuttle to Tokyo."

"There're a lot of nuts around," muttered Justin. He opened the menu. "I think I will have breakfast. Do we have time before the morning tour?"

"Oh, yes," said Heather. "The helicopters don't leave until ten-thirty this morning. We're going up the river somewhere. Dad says that it should be very interesting."

"I think all this junk is *boring*," whined Elizabeth.

"That's 'cause you think *every*thing's boring, stupid," said Sammee.

"Be quiet, both of you," said Heather. "We're here for your grandfather's benefit. Eat your cereal."

The twenty-eight Huey gunships moved out in single file, climbed above the line of trees, and sorted themselves into formation as they leveled off at three thousand feet. The panorama of highways and housing developments beneath them changed to rice paddies and jungle as they entered the park. Then they were over the river and heading west. Peasants poling small craft upstream looked up and waved as shadows of the gunships passed over them.

Disantis sat in the open door, hands hooked in the safety webbing, and let his legs dangle. On his back was Sammee's blue backpack. Justin dozed on a cushioned bench. Elizabeth sat on Heather's lap and complained of the heat. Sammee swung the heavy M-60 to the left and right and made machine-gun noises. The guide plugged his microphone into the bulkhead. "Ladies and gentlemen, today we are on a mission up the Mekong River. Our goal is twofold—to intercept illicit river traffic and to inspect any area of jungle near Highway 1 where movement of NVA regulars has been reported. Following completion of the mission, we will tour an eight-hundred-year-old Buddhist temple. Lunch will be served after the temple tour."

The helicopter throbbed north and westward. Elizabeth complained that she was hungry. Reverend Dewitt tried to get everyone to sing camp songs, but few people were interested. Tom Newton pointed out several historical landmarks to his wife. Justin awoke briefly, shot a series of images with his Nikon, and then went back to sleep.

Sometime later the guide broke the silence. "Please watch the river as we turn south. We will be searching for any small boats which look suspicious or attempt to flee at our approach. We should see the river in the next few minutes."

"No, we won't," said Disantis. He reached under his flowered shirt and removed the heavy .45 from his waistband. He aimed it at the guide's face and held it steady. "Please ask the pilot to turn north."

The cabin resounded with babble and then fell silent as the guide smiled. "A joke, Mr. Disantis, but not a funny one, I am afraid. Please let me see the..."

Disantis fired. The slug ripped through the bulkhead padding three centimeters from the guide's face. People screamed, the guide flinched and raised his hands instinctively, and Disantis swung his legs into the cabin. "North, please," he said. "Immediately."

The guide spoke quickly into his microphone, snapped two monosyllabic answers to unheard questions from the pilot, and the Huey swung out of formation and headed north.

"*Daddy,*" said Heather.

"What the fuck do you think you're doing, Ralph?" said Justin. "Now give me that goddamn relic before someone gets..."

"Shut up," said Disantis.

"Mr. Disantis," said Reverend Dewitt, "you know, there are women and children aboard this aircraft. If we could just talk about whatever..."

"Put the damn gun down, Ralph," growled Justin and began to rise from the bench.

"Be quiet." Disantis swung the pistol in Justin's direction, and the big man froze in mid-movement. "The next person to speak will be shot."

Sammee opened his mouth, looked at his grandfather's face, and remained silent. For several minutes the only sound was the throb of the rotors and Heather's soft weeping.

"Take it down here," Disantis said at last. He had been watching the jungle, making sure they were well out of the park. "Here."

The guide paused and then spoke rapid-fire Vietnamese into his mike. The Huey began to descend, circling in toward the clearing Disantis had pointed to. He could see two black Saigon Security Hovercraft coming quickly from the east, the down blast of their fans rippling the leaf canopy of the jungle as they roared ten meters above it.

The Huey's skids touched down, and the high grass rippled and bent from the blast of the rotors.

"Come on, kids," said Disantis. He moved quickly, helping Elizabeth out and then tugging Sammee from his perch before Heather could grab him. Disantis jumped down beside them.

"The *hell* you say," bellowed Justin and vaulted down.

Disantis and the children had moved a few feet and were crouching in the whipping grass. Disantis half-turned and shot Justin in the left leg. The force of the blow swung the big man around. He fell back toward the open doorway as people screamed and reached for him.

"This is real," Disantis said softly. "Goodbye." He fired twice past the cockpit windshield. Then he took Elizabeth by the hand and pulled her toward the jungle as the helicopter lifted off. A multitude of hands pulled Justin in the open door as the Huey swung away over the trees.

Sammee hesitated for a moment, looked at the empty sky, and then stumbled after his sister and grandfather. The boy was sobbing uncontrollably.

"Hush," said Disantis and pulled Sammee inside the wall of vegetation. There was a narrow trail extending into the jungle darknness. Disantis removed the light backpack and took out a new clip for the automatic. He ejected the old magazine and clicked the new one in with a slap of his palm. Then he grabbed both children and moved as quickly as he could in a counterclockwise jog around the perimeter of the clearing, always remaining concealed just within the jungle. When they stopped he pushed the children down behind a fallen tree. Elizabeth began to wail. "Hush," Disantis said softly.

The Huey gunship came in quickly, the guide leaped to the ground, and then the helicopter was spiraling upward again, clawing for altitude. A second later the first of the Saigon Security Hovercraft roared in over the treetops and settled next to the guide. The two who jumped out wore black armor cloth and carried Uzi miniguns. The guide pointed to the spot on the opposite side of the clearing where Disantis had first entered the jungle.

71

They lifted their weapons and took a step in that direction. Disantis walked out behind them, dropped to one knee when he got to within five meters, braced the pistol with both hands, and fired as they turned. He shot the first policeman in the face. The second man had time to raise his gun before he was struck twice in the chest. The bullets did not penetrate the armor cloth, but the impact knocked him onto his back. Disantis stepped forward, straightened his arm, and shot the man in the left eye.

The guide turned and ran into the jungle. Disantis fired once and then crouched next to the dead policeman as a wash of hot air struck him. The Hovercraft was ten meters high and turning toward the trees when Disantis lifted the policeman's Uzi and fired. He did not bother to aim. The minigun kicked and flared, sending two thousand fléchettes a second skyward. Disantis had a brief glimpse of the pilot's face before the entire canopy starred and burst into white powder. The Hovercraft listed heavily to the left and plowed into the forest wall. There was heavy sound of machinery and trees breaking but no explosion.

Disantis ran back to the jungle just as the second Hovercraft appeared. It circled once and then shot straight up until it was lost in the sun. Disantis grabbed the children and urged them on, circling the edge of the clearing again until they reached the spot where the guide had entered the forest. The narrow trail led away from the light into the jungle.

Disantis crouched for a second and then touched the high grass at the side of the trail. Drops of fresh blood were visible in the dappled light. Disantis sniffed at his fingers and looked up at the white faces of Sammee and Elizabeth. They had stopped crying. "It's all right," he said, and his voice was soft and soothing. Behind them and above them there were the sounds of rotors and engines. Gently, ever so gently, he turned the children and began leading them, unresisting, along the path into the jungle. It was darker there, quiet and cool. The way was marked with crimson. The children moved quickly to keep up with their grandfather.

"It's all right," he whispered and touched their shoulders lightly to guide them down the narrowing path. "Everything's all right. I know the way."

The Domino Master

Michael Blumlein

In one life, Michael Blumlein is a practicing physician living in the San Francisco Bay area. In his other, he is author of the novels *The Movement of Mountains* and *X, Y* and the short stories collected in *The Brains of Rats*. His short fiction often makes good use of his medical experience.

"The Domino Master" was originally titled "The Man Who Loved Children" but, although perfectly appropriate to the story, I felt it problematic. First, there exists a classic novel by Christina Stead with the same title. Second, *Omni* had just published "The Girl Who Loved Animals," by Bruce McAllister, a few issues previously, and third, there are unfortunate and unfair connotations implied by the title. So, with Blumlein's begrudging consent, we retitled the story. It appeared in June 1988.

"The Domino Master" is more traditional in style than much of Blumlein's short fiction but as powerful as his best.

The Domino Master

Michael Blumlein

I first met Jake the night my father came home all drunk. My mother was drunk, too, and they yelled at each other, and then she hit him over the head with a bottle. His hair got red, and blood started coming over his face and eyes. She screamed, and I got scared. She ran to help him, and I ran out of the apartment.

When I got to the stairs I stopped. I wasn't supposed to go out by myself, but I couldn't go back. I took a deep breath and stepped on the first step. When nothing happened, I took another. Suddenly the door at the top of the stairs opened. I froze. Then a cat came out. It was a tired-looking cat, black and white, with the longest fur I'd ever seen. It yawned and trotted off down the stairs. The door stayed open, and suddenly a face appeared in the crack. It had old-looking eyes and bushy eyebrows, but it wasn't much higher than a kid.

"Stupid cat," it said. "You'd think he'd know by now." The eyes turned to me. "Wouldn't you think he'd know?"

I stared at him. I didn't know what he was talking about, and besides, I wasn't supposed to talk to strangers. Especially not if this was the man who lived at the end of the hall.

"*You* know," he kept on. "You're the right size. I'm sure you know." He shook his head. "You'd think a cat would. Especially that cat."

"Know what?"

"Maybe he's just too old. I know he knows. Maybe he just can't do anything about it."

"About what, Mister?"

He looked at me and blinked once. He had whiskers and mussed-up gray hair on the sides of his head. The top was completely bald.

75

"Come in and see for yourself. See what you think. Then you tell me."

He disappeared, and the door opened wider. Everything inside looked orange. Some kind of song was playing, but I couldn't hear exactly what. I took a step toward the door, then stopped. I listened.

"The ants go marching one by one, hurrah, hurrah. The ants go marching one by one, hurrah, hurrah. The ants go marching one by one, the little one stops to have some fun...." I knew the song from school and went inside to hear more. As soon as I got in, I saw him again. He was kneeling on the rug inside the door, staring at it and looking glum. If this was the man who lived in the apartment, he didn't seem so scary to me. In fact, he seemed kind of sad.

I went over, but when I got close he put out a hand.

"Hold it," he said. "You don't want to step in it." He shook his head. "Stupid cat. My favorite carpet, too."

I looked down. It was dark but not too dark to see the stain on the rug.

"Is that it, Mister?"

"Jake," he said.

"Is that it, Mister Jake? Is that what your cat did?"

"Not my cat. Not mine. Sometimes I wish it were, but of course, it isn't. Can't be."

"Huh?"

He looked at me. "Don't be simple. You know as well as I do what that cat did. Would you do that on your rug?"

I stared at him, a little scared but not too scared, and shook my head.

"Of course you wouldn't. You've got manners."

"Sometimes I wet my bed."

"Of course you do. Sometimes I do, too. But not the rug. Not that. Stupid cat."

"Maybe it didn't mean to. Maybe it was just a mistake."

He opened his mouth to say something but then shut it. He sighed and sat back on his heels.

"You're very wise, my friend. It *was* a mistake, that's the sad part."

"My name is Johnny."

"When you wet the bed, it's a part of growing up. When we do, it's a sign of growing down."

He ran his fingers through the bunches of hair above his ears. "Poor cat."

"I'll help you clean it up. I know how."

"Do you?" That perked him up. "By all means, then, help."

"I need some salt."

He pushed himself up and left the room. In a minute he came back with an old glass jar with the letters NaCl written across the front. He took off the top and handed the jar to me.

"This is it?"

"From the Dead Sea itself, John. I may call you that, if I may. May I?" I shrugged and poured the salt on the spot. Pretty soon it got caked up, and the yellow began to show through, so I poured out more. By the time I finished, nearly the whole jar was gone.

"You're quite a handy little man, aren't you? I must tell Arsenio your trick. He would want to know."

"Who's he?"

"A little friend. I'm sure you'll meet him, or rather I'm not sure, but you might. But here..." He got up again, I guess because he saw that his rug was going to be okay, and took my hand. Then he started to march. Up and down went his legs, and then he started to sing: "The ants go marching one by one, hurrah, hurrah. The ants go marching one by one, then John he comes to have some fun, and they all go marching round and around to get out of the rain, boom, boom, boom...." I joined in, and in a minute the two of us were in the orange room, marching around and around, singing and clapping every time we came to the "boom, boom, boom." When we got to ten we went through the whole song again, which no grown-up ever did with me before. After the second time we stopped. Jake was breathing hard, too hard, I guess, to keep going.

He went to the side of the room and flopped down on a stack of pillows on the floor. He stuck out his legs and closed his eyes. I waited for something to happen. When nothing did, I decided to look around.

At first it seemed like the room was full of junk. Things were hanging all over the place, from the walls and tables and even over the backs of chairs. There was stuff piled up high on the floor, and boxes everywhere. I thought what my mom would do if my room ever looked like that, but then I stopped thinking about it because I didn't want to. Instead I looked at the boxes.

All of them were long and skinny, all kind of the same but different. Some of them shined bright like the sun, and some were so dark you couldn't even see what was on them. On top of one were drawings of funny-looking animals, almost but not quite like ones at the zoo. One was a horse with a tail and everything, but also it had wings. There was another horse, too, but that one had the face of a woman with long hair, kind of like a girl I knew from school. And there was a dragon on the box, and a bird flying up out of a big fire. I liked looking at it, but also it seemed stupid to have animals that weren't really animals. So I stopped looking and went to another box.

This one was blue and bright. It flashed on and off like the police lights when they run their sirens. I wanted to open it, but I couldn't figure out how. So I picked it up.

Some things rattled inside, which scared me. Real fast I put it down and walked away. I didn't want Jake to know that I even touched it. Luckily, his eyes were still closed. I couldn't tell if he was asleep or awake, and I went over to see. The room was so crowded that by mistake I bumped into a table. It hurt my leg, and I stooped over to rub it. Then I saw the box on top.

It was the blackest black I had ever seen, blacker even than my friend Joey's birthmark on his face. It was so black it seemed like it wasn't even there, like a hole or something. I put out my hand to see if it was real, and then all of a sudden Jake woke up.

"Don't touch that!" he said.

I jerked my hand back and looked at him.

"Good boy." He leaned over and snatched the box away, stuffing it behind one of the pillows

"How about some milk? Little boys like milk."

I shook my head. "I gotta go home."

"Of course you do. How could I be so sleepy? Your parents must be worried." He smiled and reached into one of his pockets. He held out something in his hand.

"Here. It's a present."

I wasn't supposed to, but it didn't seem anything bad. So I took it. It was a pin, and attached to one side were two white squares joined together by a black line in the middle. On each square were some black dots.

"A domino," he said. "Can you put it on yourself?"

I nodded and showed him. Then I turned around and went home.

I didn't see him again for a long time, but I didn't stop thinking about him. Especially that black box which he snatched away from me. I would've gone back sooner, except that after that night my mom moved out of our apartment and took me with her. We moved to her friend Ginny's place, which was even smaller than ours. After a while Ginny said that we had to leave, it was just too crowded. Mom said it was okay because by then she and Dad were seeing each other again. They were back in love, she said. Dad said the same thing when I saw him. He gave me a big hug, which hurt a little. "Welcome back, Johnny boy," he said. He cooked us all a big breakfast, eggs and toast and pancakes, and he gave me a new GI Joe. He gave Mom a real short nightgown, and after breakfast they told me to play by myself for a while. They went into the bedroom, locked the door, and started giggling. I knew what that meant, so I went and turned on the TV. But it was broke, so I played with Joe. He was okay, but after a while I got tired of him because all he wanted to do was hit the other soldiers and make them bleed on their heads. I thought about Jake. And the box.

From the noise they were making I figured Mom and Dad wouldn't miss me. So I told Joe not to tell, and the other guys, and I tiptoed out the door and down the hall. When I got to Jake's, I looked for a button to push, but there wasn't one. There wasn't a doorknob either. I was afraid to knock because of the noise, and I didn't know what to do. Then I heard music.

It was faraway and real soft. I shut my eyes and leaned against the door. I listened hard.

"The ants go marching four by four, hurrah, hurrah. The ants go marching four by four, the little one stops to knock at the door...." And all of a sudden I found myself knocking at Jakes's door. Nothing happened, and I knocked again. And the door, without even the smallest creak, opened.

"Come in, come in," a voice said, and right away I knew it was him. I went in, and the door shut behind me. I walked through the little hall into the orange room.

"Hi," I said when I saw him, and he waved me in. He was lying on the pillows, looking the same as before except for the pipe in his mouth. It was a long one, almost as long as his whole body. It was so long, in fact, that he could hardly light it, which he was trying to do with a long, skinny match. By the time he got his hand steady enough to put the flame over the bowl of the pipe, the match had burned down so much that he had to move his hand again. He kept having to stretch out farther and farther. Finally he got the pipe smoking, but then the match went out. He groaned and looked at me.

"I'd use pyrotechnics, but I might burn down the house. Give me a hand, will you?"

I went over and stood next to him.

"A hand," he said. "You've got ears, haven't you?"

I held one out—a hand, I mean—and he lit a match and gave it to me.

"Now, put it there. Over the bowl."

I did what he told me, and he began to puff. The stuff in the bowl glowed red, and then he took the pipe out of his mouth and blew out the match.

"I could do that," I said.

He looked at me while he had some more puffs. Then he took the match and began rubbing its tip between his finger and thumb. He stopped, and in a second it burst into flame. I stared. It was such a great trick that I forgot about blowing the match out. Just before it burned his fingers, I remembered and blew. He looked at me.

"I apologize if I'm a bit out of sorts," he said, "but that cat went and did it again. It seems as though your visits trigger something in him."

"I didn't do anything, Mister Jake. Honest I didn't."

"Of course you didn't. And it's just Jake."

"I can clean it up. Like before."

"I've already taken care of it. Or rather Arsenio has. Or is. He should be just about finished." Before I could ask who Arsenio was, a kid came walking into the room. He was smaller than me and looked rich, like one of those kids you see sometimes in the store getting their hair done up just like they were grown-up. His was slicked down and shiny and parted right down the middle. It made him look funny. He had on dark pants and a matching jacket and black shoes that were as shiny as his hair. To top it off, he was wearing a bow tie, which I had never seen anyone except old men on the street wear. He looked like a picture of a guy I'd seen once in a museum, except he wasn't a guy but a kid.

"Arsenio, this is John. John, Arsenio."

He came over, folded his arm in front and bowed to me! Then he straightened up and held out his hand.

"Very pleased to meet you."

I didn't know what to do, so I shook it. It seemed stupid. Then he turned to Jake.

"I did as you suggested. The salt is nearly gone, but the spot, I think, is out."

"John here is the one who showed me that trick."

"Then it is you I should thank," he said to me. "I'm always excited to find new ways to clean up."

Not only did he look funny, but he talked funny, too. There was something else. Something that made me think I'd seen him before or could have.

"Arsenio is half of the double two," Jake said. "Judith's the other. Where is she hiding out?"

"I put her in the closet. The one with all the old clothes and paper and crayons."

Jake nodded and puffed on his pipe. "Why don't you introduce John to her?"

Arsenio made a face, the kind that if I'd made I would have got a whipping. He didn't budge.

"Go on," Jake said.

"I don't want to."

"I can see that; but you must. She's undoubtedly already made a big mess."

"Do I have to?"

Jake frowned, as if the question didn't make sense at all. He puffed on his pipe, then lay back on the pillows and stared off into space. Arsenio sighed, then turned around and started off.

"Come on," he said.

I followed him out of the room into a hall with doors. Partway down I saw the pile of salt and made sure I didn't step in it. He stopped at one of the doors and straightened his bow tie. He smoothed down his hair with his hands. He was stalling, and I felt sorry for him.

"I live down the hall." I said.

He nodded. "Me, too."

"Apartment 206. With my mom and dad."

"I live down *that* hall," he said, pointing to the one we had just walked down.

"You mean here? You live with Jake?"

He nodded. "So does Judith. We live here together."

"Is she your sister?"

"She's my double. She lives on the other side."

"Which one is your room?"

He pointed to the orange one, which surprised me. I was about to ask him where his bed was, when all of a sudden there was a scream from the closet. It was loud and scary. Arsenio threw the door back and jumped inside. I took a step in and stopped. The place was a total mess. In back, under a pile of clothes, was a girl. She had long hair that was all tangled, and her face was dirty. It was also red. That was because she was screaming.

"My foot...it's stuck...it hurts. It hurts!"

Arsenio didn't waste a minute. He jumped through the boxes and clothes and crumpled-up papers, found where her foot was stuck, and pulled it out. Then he straightened up and fixed his bow tie.

"Judith," he said, "you're a mess."

"So what?" she answered. She tore up a bunch of paper and threw it in the air. While it floated down, she wiggled around like a worm. Then she started on the clothes.

She was already wearing a dress, and she put pants on top of it and then a shirt and then another shirt and then a vest. She found some socks, all different colors, and put those on, too. A hat and then shoes. There was a mirror on the inside of the door, and she looked at herself and smiled. Then she looked at me.

"Hi," she said.

"Hi."

81

"My name's Judith."

"Mine's Johnny."

"Want a sock?"

She gave me a red one, then a green one. Then she handed me her hat. Before I knew it, she was pulling clothes off as fast as she had put them on. They flew into the hall, and as fast as they landed, Arsenio picked them up and folded them. She got down to her undies and took those off, too. Then she ran down the hall, squealing.

"Oh, no," Arsenio said. "We've got to catch her."

He ran after her, and I ran, too. He caught her, but she slipped away. He started after her again but stopped when he got to the orange room. "Too late," he groaned.

Judith was already across the room. She was jumping up and down on the pillows, laughing and giggling with Jake. He was having fun, too, and I wondered why Arsenio was so glum.

"Fun now," he said, "but he can only take it for a while. Then we have to go back."

I shrugged and wandered over. Pretty soon the three of us were rolling in the pillows, having a great time. But in a little while Jake's breathing got hard. He stopped playing, and then he told me and Judith to stop, too. Neither of us wanted to, and Judith kept bouncing, which made me do it, too. Jake said stop again, not loud but so you knew he meant it. He told Judith it was time for her to go.

"No, no, no," she begged. "Please don't make me."

"We just got here," Arsenio said.

"Please," I joined in, "can't we stay just a little longer?"

He looked at each of us, and then he sighed. It was three against one. When he looked back, his eyes were twinkling.

"All right. A little longer. Time enough for a game of dominoes."

We all cheered, even though I didn't know what that meant. Jake told Arsenio to fetch the dominoes. Arsenio went to the table with the blue box on it, the one that flashed on and off and rattled when you shook it. He picked it up with both hands and brought it over. This time it reminded me of waves of water when the sun hits. I still couldn't see a lid.

From somewhere behind his back Jake brought out a cup of water. At first I thought he was thirsty, but he didn't drink it. Instead he lifted it up in the air, turned it over, and poured it on top of the box. That seemed like a silly thing to do because he'd just have to clean up the mess. But when I looked, there wasn't any mess.

Instead of spilling on the floor, the water fell right into the top of the box. Into the wavy blue light. Suddenly a tower of spray shot out, like steam from a teakettle, only cool. It misted the air, making it hard to see. I had to wipe my eyes, and when I looked again, the box was open.

It was a great trick. I wanted to ask Jake how he did it, but Judith and Arsenio had already started taking the things out. The dominoes. I'd never seen one before. They were all white except for the dots on top, which were black. Some of them had a lot of dots, and some had only a few. Judith and Arsenio took them all out and put them together with the dots facing up. Already it looked like a fun game, and I waited to see what was next.

"We all get to choose a game," said Jake. "One game each, and then everyone goes home."

Judith was the first to shout out: "Trains!" Right away she and Arsenio started picking up the dominoes and lining them up on their edges, one in front of the other. By the time I joined in, they had already used up most of the pieces. In the end Judith had the longest line, and I had the shortest. Mine wasn't so straight, either; it kind of curved, but no one said anything.

"You go first," Judith said.

"Okay," I said, and I sat there, waiting for something to happen.

"Go on," she said, "push it."

"Huh?"

"Like this..." She touched the domino at the end of her line, tilting it forward and making it hit against the one in front of it. That one fell down and hit the next one, and then all of a sudden, faster than I could see, the whole line fell down. Judith let out a whoop, and Arsenio laughed. I just stared. It seemed like magic.

Arsenio did the same thing with his, and it happened just like before. This time we all laughed. Then I pushed mine, and the line went down like theirs, only in a curve. I loved the way it fell, and especially I loved the clacking sound when it did. We all clapped, Jake too, and then Arsenio said, "Now it's my game."

He took the dominoes out of the piles and started putting one on top of the other. Soon he had a tower that was almost as big as he was. He tried one more on the very top, but it was too many. The tower fell over with a crash.

Judith built hers, but before it got too tall she stopped. She built another right next to it. When the second one was as tall as the first, she sat back. The corners of her mouth curled up, and I got ready for something. Quick as a mouse her hand jerked out, knocking the bottom dominoes out. For a second the towers leaned, and then the whole thing came crashing down. I laughed. Then it was my turn.

I built three towers next to each other, and when I was done, I looked for something to balance on top. Something special. The first thing I thought of was the black box. It was back on the table, looking even blacker than before. It seemed to suck at me, and I couldn't keep still. I went to it. I was afraid not to. I reached out. Then Jake began to whistle.

It was a low, cold sound, like the wind in winter. I stopped and listened. He cupped his hands in front of his mouth, and the sound changed. It got higher, prettier, like sometimes you hear in the park. It filled the room, and then he separated his hands. In his palm was a tiny, blue bird. Its beak was open, and it was singing.

Jake held it to his lips and blew on it. The bird flew into the air. It circled the room, singing its pretty song, then landed on my towers. Its tiny beak opened, and it sang its song to me. It turned to Arsenio, then to Judith, singing to each of them. Last of all it turned to Jake. It sang to him, and Jake sang the same song back. Then he opened his mouth. The bird leapt into the air, flew once more around the room, then dived between Jake's lips. That scared me, but nothing happened. Jake closed his mouth, and then we all started clapping.

"No need for that," he said. "It's really not difficult. And now it's time for John's game."

They all looked at me, and I looked down in my lap. I shrugged.

"Make one up," Judith said.

"Yeah," said Arsenio.

I shook my head. "You."

The two of them looked at Jake.

"Fine," he said. "I'll be the last. We'll play the matching game."

"Matches?" I said, thinking of the one he lit with his fingers. He hushed me.

"Listen, and I'll tell you. Each domino has one or more than one dot on it, except for the one that has no dots. That one is called the double blank, and also it's called the soul. Every other one has a name, too. There are twenty-eight in all, and every person in the world has one that is special to him. After the soul comes the sun, the one that has a blank on one side of the black line and one dot on the other. It's called the moon, too, sometimes, and the eye. After that comes the double one, with one dot on each side of the line. Its name is moon eyes and snake eyes, and in some places it's called the scream. The next one has one dot on one side and two on the other—the funny man or the cripple. Then there's the double two."

"That's ours," said Arsenio and Judith.

"The twin," Jake nodded. "The mirror. The dots go all the way up to six;

84

the domino with the most dots has six on one side and six on the other, twelve in all. It's called double six, tracks, the journey, and sometimes it's called grief."

I looked at the dominoes, trying to get what he was talking about. But after a while, all the dots started floating and mixing together. I had to blink to make them stop. I liked hearing the names, but building the tower was more fun. I didn't want to hurt Jake's feelings, but I told him anyway.

"More fun now," he said. "But I have to think of the future. I'm the one who has to think of that."

He lined up the dominoes in a different way, so that the dots were matched up.

"You don't have to remember the names," he said. "All we're going to do is match them. Like this."

He put the soul in the middle of the floor, and on one end he put the one with a blank and one dot, and on the other end he put the one with a blank and two dots.

"Judith's turn now."

She snatched up her own special domino, the twin, and matched it with the one on the floor. Then Arsenio picked up one with two dots on one side and six dots on the other.

"What's this called?"

"The goof," Jake said. "Slippery luck."

"Goof," repeated Arsenio, and matched it to the domino on the floor.

I looked around for a good one and spotted the one with six dots on one side and nothing on the other. I picked it up.

"Tracks through snow," said Jake. "Soul in ice. Home."

I matched it with the other one with six dots. Then Jake put one next to it, then Judith, and pretty soon all the dominoes were laid out in a line. It looked neat, like a long snake with spots. Then Judith messed it up. I gave her a look, and so did Arsenio. Then I looked at Jake.

"Again," I said.

He smiled. "Of course. Another time. Now it's time to put them away."

None of us liked that, but we didn't argue. We helped put the dominoes back in the box. When they were all in, the top turned blue like before. Then it started flashing.

"Now it's time to go home," Jake said.

I know two different ways to be sad: One is when someone hurts you or you're afraid they might. The other is when you're having fun and it has to stop. I was sad the second way, which is better than the first. I knew there'd be fun again.

I said good-bye to everyone and walked to the front door. Just as I got there I remembered something I forgot to say, and I turned back. But when I got to the edge of the room, I stopped. Jake and Arsenio and Judith were in the middle of something that looked important. It looked private, too, and I didn't want to butt in. But I didn't want to leave, either. I couldn't.

Arsenio and Judith were standing in the middle of the room with their backs touching. Their eyes were closed, and Jake was whispering to them. He bent down and kissed them on their heads. Then he went to the table with the black box on it. He did something which I couldn't see, then stepped back. The box was open. In his hand was a domino. The twin.

It was white and bright as a cloud. So bright that I had to squint to see it. He held it above Judith and Arsenio, then took his hand away. By some trick the domino stayed. It hung in the air, shining like a cloud, floating. Slowly it began to turn.

Each time the domino turned, Judith and Arsenio got smaller. I don't know how, but little by little they shrank until they weren't much bigger than mice. And they kept shrinking until they were as tiny as bugs.

Then Jake took the domino and put it on the floor next to them. They walked apart, and each grabbed an edge. Pulling hard, they climbed on top. One of them stood on one side of the line, the other on the other. The domino got brighter. And brighter still. Finally it got so bright I had to look away. There was a flash, and when I looked back, they were gone.

Jake put the domino back in the box, and I decided it wasn't so important after all what I was going to say. I turned around and tiptoed away. When I got to the door, I ran as fast as I could home.

I wasn't so lucky when I got there. Mom and Dad weren't in the bedroom anymore. They yelled at me and asked where I'd been. I said on the stairs, and they told me not to lie. Then Dad took off his belt. I tried not to cry because that just makes it worse. Instead I thought of Jake and his dominoes, of Arsenio and Judith and the box. And thinking of them made the whipping not so bad. The hurt seemed farther away.

Things changed for a while after that. Dad lost his job, and Mom got laid off for a few weeks. Everyone was home a lot, which was actually pretty nice. Dad fixed the TV, and Mom cooked and talked about what a nice family we were. Sometimes she worried about money, but that would make Dad leave. He'd come back with beer, and they'd make up. Then they'd get drunk together. I watched TV and played a lot with GI Joe and the other guys, except that I gave them new names, like Jake and Judith and Snake Eyes and Cripple. It was fun being home. Everyone was happy. Then there was a fight.

It started out small, and Dad left. I thought he was going for beer, but he didn't come back for a long time. Mom got madder and madder. I turned off the TV and put away my toys. I stayed as quiet as I could. Finally he came home, as drunk as I'd ever seen him. The two of them yelled at each other, then Mom took off her shoe and threw it. Dad just laughed, and she threw the other one. That one hit him in the face, and he stopped laughing. He took off his belt. Then Mom was the one who laughed. She said he was too drunk to do anything, but she was wrong. He slapped her across the neck. She tried to grab the belt, but he yanked it back and slapped her again. She screamed, and I got scared. I begged them to stop.

"Go to your room," they said, but I couldn't. I just stood there, while they kept on fighting. It was awful, worse than ever, and I almost started crying. But crying was the last thing I wanted to do, so I did what they said. I went to my room. Only I never made it inside. When I got to my door, something happened. I don't know what, but suddenly everything changed, like when a noise you've been listening to for so long you've forgotten about it suddenly stops. Like that, I stopped hearing my mom and dad. Everything got as quiet as could be, and then real soft I heard the ant song. It was up to four.

"The ants go marching four by four, hurrah, hurrah. The ants go marching four by four, the little one marches out the door, and they all go marching down to the ground to get out of the rain, boom, boom, boom...." And I walked to the front door and marched out. Jake's door was open, and I went in. He was lying on the pillows smoking his pipe, blowing little clouds in the air. He smiled when he saw me and waved me over. In his lap was the cat, the black-and-white one with the long fur. He was petting it, and the cat was purring.

"Sit down," he said, and I did. All of a sudden I started to cry.

The tears busted out like rain, and I tried to stop, but that only made me cry harder. Jake wiped my nose with a hankie. He said that the tear lakes had to get dried up, which wasn't easy. It was spring, and all the snow up above was melting. I guess he knew what he was talking about because it did take a long time. But finally the lakes dried. My throat and chest were sore, but I felt better. The first thing I wanted to know was where were Judith and Arsenio.

"Home," he said.

"Can I go there?"

He puffed on his pipe and looked at me.

"There's always room."

"I want to go."

"Patience, my boy. There are many homes, you know."

"I want to see Judith and Arsenio."

"There are others. Thousands. Lost children, sad children, crippled and sickly children. From any war you choose. Any famine, any plague. From Sumer, Saxony, Bombay, Peru. Any place. Any age."

"Huh?"

"Each person has a stone, John."

"A stone?"

"A domino. One that is his own. I told you that before."

"I want to see."

"You shall. If you're going to live here, you need a place."

He pushed himself slowly to his feet. The cat hung on to him as long as it could, then scrambled to the floor. Jake went across the room and got the black box, brought it back, and sat down. He said some words, which I didn't understand. He said them again, and the black hole that was the box got even blacker. Like it was swallowing itself with more and more blackness. There was a hiss, and suddenly it was open. Inside were the dominoes.

On top was a long row, all of them matchers, starting with the soul and ending with the tracks. They were white as snow when it's falling, before the ground makes it dirty. White as new teeth. The dots were like coal. One by one Jake took the dominoes out and laid them on the floor.

"Now you must choose," he said.

"Huh?"

"Pick one."

Well, that was easy. I knew which one I wanted, and I reached for the twin. But when I picked it up, I saw that it wasn't the twin at all. It was the one with six dots on one side and nothing on the other.

"Big ice," Jake said. "The palace."

"I don't want this one," I told him. "I want the other."

"Indeed." His eyebrows came down, and he gave me a sideways look.

"I want the twin." I pointed. "That one."

He rubbed his chin. "Hmm," he mumbled, playing with his hair. Finally he took the domino out of my hand and put it back on the floor. Then he mixed them all up.

"Pick the one you want," he said. "Last chance."

Before they made me dizzy like before, I found the one I wanted. I said to myself, *Okay, this is it,* and took a deep breath. Then I reached down and picked it up.

It was the same one as before. The six and the blank. That got me scared. I glanced at Jake, who didn't seem to be looking, and tried to put it back. Only it didn't go back. It kept sticking to my hand. I didn't know what was happening, if it was magic or what, but I didn't like it. I felt like crying again.

"Help me," I said.

Jake looked up and smiled. He took the domino out of my hand. With his fingers he touched each dot, then he nodded.

"It's yours, John."

I shook my head. "I don't want it."

"Nevertheless..."

"I want to go home."

"Of course."

I got up and started moving my legs, only instead of going forward, I stayed in the same place. When I looked around, it seemed like the room was getting bigger. The chairs, the tables, the pillows were all growing. The dominoes, too. Instead of being flat on the floor, they had turned into little boxes, then big boxes, then bigger ones. And high above me, something was twirling in the air. It sparkled like a mirror in the sun, sending light down on my body. I wondered what it was; then suddenly something grabbed it from the air and put it on the floor next to me. Then I knew.

It was as big as the other dominoes, and I remembered what had happened to Arsenio and Judith.

I had become tiny like them, but I didn't feel scared. Just the opposite, I felt brave and ready for an adventure.

I grabbed the edge of the domino, pulled hard with my arms, and kicked with my legs. I scrambled on top, then nearly fell in one of the holes. It looked safer on the other side, but to get there I had to jump over the line in the middle. I nearly fell in that, too. Then the domino started to glow.

It got brighter and brighter, so bright that I had to cover my eyes. There was a flash, and then the brightness was gone. I opened my eyes, expecting to see Jake, or the cat, or even my mom and dad. But what I saw was a big field of snow, and far away, a building. There were footprints in the snow and lots of kids, but I'm not supposed to tell even that much. If you lived in the dominoes I could, but then I wouldn't have to, because you'd know. And anyway, everybody has his own domino. That's what Jake says. It means that everybody already knows, or they could. And I like that because then I don't have to tell. No matter what, I don't have to.

The Circular Library of Stones

Carol Emshwiller

Carol Emshwiller is the author of the novel *Carmen Dog* and the story collections *Joy in Our Cause, Verging on the Pertinent,* and *The Start of the End of it All*. I'd been reading and admiring Emshwiller's work for several years in literary journals, but it wasn't until she submitted "The Circular Library of Stones" (February 1987) that her fiction got "weird" enough to justify publishing in *Omni*. Since then, Emshwiller has become a regular contributor to the magazine.

"The Circular Library of Stones" can be seen as mainstream or fantasy, depending on one's point of view.

The Circular Library Of Stones

Carol Emshwiller

They said all this wasn't true. That there had been no city on this site since even before the time of the Indians...that there had been no bridge across the (now dried up) river and no barriers against the mud. "If you have been searching for a library here," they said, "or for old coins, you've been wasting your time."

For lack of space I had put some of the small, white stones in plant baskets and hung them from the ceiling by the window. I don't argue with people about what nonexistent city could have existed at this site. I just collect the stones. (Two have *X*s scratched on them, only one of which I scratched myself.) And I continue digging. The earth, though full of stones of all sizes, is soft and easy to deal with. Often it is damp and fragrant. And I disturb very little in the way of trees or plants of any real size here. Also most of the stones, even the larger ones, are of a size that I can manage fairly well by myself. Besides, mainly it's the stones that I want to reveal. I don't want to move them from place to place, except some of the most important small ones, which I take home with me after a day's digging. Often I have found battered aluminum pots and pans around the site. Once I found an old boot and once, a pair of broken glasses; but these, of course, are of no significance whatsoever, being clearly of the present. Gaining access to their books! If I could find the library and learn to read their writing! If I could find, there, stories beyond my wildest dreams. A love story, for instance, where the love is of a totally different kind...a kind of ardor we have never even thought of, more long lasting than our simple attachments, more world-shaking than our simple sexualities. Or a literature that is two things at once, which we can only do in drawings where a body might be, at one and the same time, a face in which the breasts also equal eyes; or two naked ladies sitting

93

side by side, arms raised, that also form a skull, their black hair the eye sockets.

For quite some time now I have had sore legs, so digging is an exercise I can do better than any other, and though at night my back pains me, the pains usually go away quite soon. By morning I hardly feel them. So the digging, in itself, pleases me. There is the pleasure of work. A day well spent. Go home tired and silent. But mostly, of course, it is the slow revelation of the stones that I care about. Sometimes they cluster in groups so that I think that here must have been where a fireplace was, or perhaps a throne. Sometimes they form a long row that I think might have been a wall or a bench. And I have found a mirror. Two feet underground, and so scratched that one can see oneself only in little fish-shaped flashes—a bit of an eye, a bit of lip, but for even that much of it to have been preserved all this time is a miracle. I feel certain that if they had a library, it's logical they would also have had mirrors. Or if they had mirrors, it certainly follows they could have had a library.

I keep the mirror with me in my breast pocket. (I wear a man's old fishing vest.) When people ask me what I'm doing out here, I show the mirror to them along with a few smooth stones.

At night I write. I shut my eyes and let my left hand move as it wishes. Usually it makes only scratchings, but other times words come out. Once I wrote several pages of nothing but *no, no, no, no, no,* and after that, *on, on, on,* and *on,* but more and more often there are larger words now, and more and more often they are making some kind of sense. Yesterday, for instance, I found myself writing: *Let us do let us us do and do and let us not be but do and you do too.* And then, and for the first time, a whole phrase came out clear and simple: *Cool all that summer and at night returned to the library.*

Certainly I would suppose the library, being built of stone, to be always cool in summer, always warm in winter. The phrase is surely, then, true and of the time. It is interesting that the library itself is referred to in this, the first real phrase I've written so far. That is significant. What I have been hoping to do is to reproduce some of the writings from the library, or reasonable facsimiles. Perhaps this is the beginning of one of their books.

The circle is sacred to all peoples except for us. We are the only ones that don't care if a thing is square or a circle or oblong or triangular. The shape has no meaning to us. A circle could be oval for all we care. I'm thinking about this because I think I have come across a giant circle. About a foot down I found what looked like a path of stones, and I dug along it all day thinking I was going in a straight line; but when I turned around to look back on what I had accomplished, I saw that although I had dug only a few yards, clearly I was curving.

Though I had thought to finish for the day, I turned and vigorously revealed another yard of the stones, yet knowing full well it would be perhaps a month before I could uncover a really significant portion of the circle. I was thinking that probably here, at last, was where the very walls of the library had been and that, if true, this would be a great revelation of stones (even though done by an old woman...a useless old woman, so everyone thinks). I felt happy...happy and tired after that, and though I came home very late and my back hurt even more than usual, I sat down, dirty as I was, at my little table. I shut my eyes and let my left hand write: *Let us oh let us do and do and dance and do the dance of the library in the cool in the sanctuary of the library.*

It rained all that night and all the next day, and I knew it had filled up all my pits and paths with mud. I would have to do much of my digging over again, and yet I wasn't terribly unhappy about it. Such things come in every life. It's to be expected. (And doing is digging. Digging is doing. Do, not be. That's my philosophy and it seems to be theirs, too.) And my latest discovery was momentous, to say the least. Who would have thought it: a great white, stone, circular library to be danced in!

Mostly on rainy days like these I do as the other old women do. I knit or make pot holders. I make soup and muffins. While I was there doing old-woman things and looking out the window, I thought, *How nice if I found even only another stone with, perhaps, an O on it. People who search as I do must be happy with small and seemingly insignificant discoveries. People who search as I do must understand, also, that the lack of something is never insignificant; so even if there was nothing to be found, I was never disappointed, because that, too, was significant—as, for instance, a library and only one stone with an X on it. Besides, the less discovered, the more open the possibilities.* I always console myself with that thought.

That night I let my left hand write. It took a long time to get from scratches to *X*s; to *no, no, no;* but finally it wrote: *Let us then stone on stone on stone a library that befits a library each door face the sun one at dawn and one at dusk. Many queens saw it.* (Perhaps they were all queens in those days. Or perhaps when they reached my age they became queens. I would like to think so.)

This was on my mind when I went to sleep and I dreamed a row of dancing women, all my age and all wearing crowns of smooth white pebbles. They were calling to me to wake up...to wake up, that is, into my dream, and I did, and I was still in my boots and fishing vest and my old gray pants. I didn't, in other words, dream myself to be one of them, as some sort of queen or other. I was my dirt-stained self, holding out my grimy hands. And it seemed that they gave me my mirror—the one I had already found, and even in my dream it wasn't

95

shiny and new but just as scratched as when I found it. They showed me that I must place the mirror exactly where I found it in the first place so that I could find it—as I did find it—near the former riverbed and on a slight rise. This I did in my dream as the old women beat stones together with a loud *clack, clack*. And of course it's true; that's where I *did* find the mirror. It all fits together perfectly!

(All those old women lacked grace, but perhaps it's not required.)

My daughters....I suppose they tell me the truth about myself, though no need to. Why do they do it? Why feel free to say such things? Do I talk too much? Do I go on and on about it or about anything? Why, I've almost stopped talking altogether, wanting, now, other kinds of meanings. My argument is one *X*ed stone or a particularly smooth one or several in a row. I let them speak their ambiguities for themselves.

I showed my daughters my moonstone. I wanted to convince them. I said it came from the library.

"What library?"

"You know. Out by the dried-up stream."

"You've always had that moonstone. Grandma gave it to you."

"Well," I said, "I found it lying in the mud there." (I knew I was just making everything worse.)

"You must have dropped it yourself. What were you doing wearing that out there, anyway? You ought to be more careful."

I suppose I should have been. I know it will be theirs someday.

Later they told me about a place (I've seen it) where there's a doctor's office in the basement and art rooms, pot-holder rooms, television rooms, railings along all the halls. Everybody has a cane. I've seen that. I told my daughters no.

Just as crossroads, fire, seashells, oak trees, and circles have special meanings, stones have meanings, too. Some, upright and lumpy on the hillsides, are named after women. All the best houses are of stone, therefore the library also. Molloy sucked them (I have too, sometimes), found them refreshing. Stone doors into the mountain balance on a single point and open at the slightest caress. The sound stone makes as door is not unlike the rustling of pebbles on beaches. It is fitting that stones should be open to question, as my stones are. I liked letting them speak their ambiguities. When I was not out at my dig, I remembered stones. I dreamed them. I imagined I heard their *clack, clack*.

* * *

I warned my daughters that if I should be found awkwardly banging stones together on some moonlit night, it would be neither out of senility nor sentimentality, but a scientific test.

But then I found a stone of a different kind and color: reddish and lumpy. Essentially nine lumps: two in front, two in back, plus one head, two arms, and two leg posts. I recognized it instantly. Fecund *and* wise. Big breasted *and* a scholar. Fat *and* elegant. I wanted to bring this librarian to her true place in the scheme of things. Restore her to her glory. Clearly, she not only had babies and nursed them, but she read all the books.

After this find, I dug in a frenzy. I knew I should be more careful of myself at my age: follow some rules of rest and recreation, but I believe in *do*, not *be*. Do! Though why should I so desperately want more...more, that is, than the mother of the library? (My daughters will call her a lumpy, pink stone.) Am I never satisfied?

Never! (My left hand has written: *Stone on stone on stone on stone on stone,* almost as though I were building the library out of the words.)

And then as I dug frantically, my eyes were blinded by the setting sun. Everything sparkled, and I thought I actually saw the library: all white with a great, clear river before it and a landing where the books (stone books) were brought in on little ships with big sails. The glistening of the waves hurt my eyes, but I could see, even so, the librarians dancing on the beach in front of the sacred circle of the library. And they were all old. Old as I am or even older—wrinkled, hobbling women—I could see that their backs were hurting them too, but they kept on with the dancing, just as I kept on with my digging. And I heard the soft, sweet, fluty music of the library and felt the cool of it, for I , too, stood close to the western doorway. And we could see each other. I'm sure of it. I saw eyes meet mine, and not just once or twice.

I stepped forward, then, to dance with them, but I fell—it seemed a long, slow fall—and as I fell, the sun was no longer in my eyes and I saw then my rocky ground and my dried-up streambed.

After I got up, I felt extraordinarily lucid. As though I had drunk from the ice-cold river. Clearheaded and happy—happier than I'd been in a long time (though I've not been unhappy digging here. On the contrary). I didn't want to go home and rest—I felt so powerful—but I forced myself. I had hardly eaten all day, and most important, if I tried to dig in the dark I might miss something. I might toss away a stone like my important librarian and not see what it really was.

When I got home that night I found that someone had been at my stones. They were all, all gone. I was so happy about my little librarian that I didn't notice it at first. It wasn't until I went to put her on my night table (I wanted her to be close to me as I slept) that I noticed there were no other stones there, not a single one. I knew right away what had happened. My daughters had decided that I'm being crowded out by stones. They think—because *they* would feel that way—that it must be uncomfortable to live like this. But I was brought up on stones, don't they remember that? I had geodes. I had chunks of amber. I had a cairngorm set in silver. Still have it somewhere, unless they took that off for safekeeping. They think I will lose it out there. Well, perhaps I already have, but if I did, it's been worth it many times over. And now even my hanging baskets of stones, gone, and stones from every surface, every shelf, all gone. Thank goodness I carry my most important ones with me in my vest pockets.

All these old stones. Mother wouldn't have appreciated them either. The work, yes, the care I've taken, the effort—she did appreciate effort and would have praised me for that, but she had no understanding of science and its slow, laborious unfolding. The care, the cataloging, she would have praised, but perhaps not when all this work involves merely stones. Back in those days she didn't even like my geodes (especially those that had not been opened yet). It can't be hoped that she would have liked my little naked librarian. Also, Mother disapproved of nakedness of any sort. I, on the other hand, want to stress the importance of childbearing librarians and so the importance of the bodies of the librarians, and so all the glory of their old-lady sexuality. (And I have seen it at the local library...the woman in charge sitting with her breasts against the table.)

Coming in like that, then, and no stones, my little librarian in hand, I couldn't possibly sleep. I was both too happy and too upset. I sat down instead to draw my new find. If I am, someday in the future, to be judged for this work by someone who really knows what it's all about, I don't want to make any mistakes that will spoil the scientific accuracy of the study. I labeled all the parts: these slits, eyes; that slit, the opening to the womb. (The look on her face was intelligent and self-sufficient.)

I hid the drawings under my socks. (Who knows what my daughters will think worth nothing?) I put the librarian in the top breast pocket of the vest, where tomorrow she will rest over my heart. Then I checked all the other pockets with my most important stones (all there, thank goodness) and went to bed. It was nearly morning.

Even so, the next day I woke still extraordinarily clearheaded. I fairly jogged out to my site. Worked hard all day but found nothing, saw nothing.

Once or twice I did think I heard the sound of flutes and perhaps some drumming, but I knew that was just my imagination plus the beat of my own heart in my ears. I always hear that on hot days when I lean over too much or get up too fast.

When I got home I sensed, again, a change. (Why do they always come in the daytime when I'm not here? Why are they afraid to face me?) I couldn't see the changes this time, but I knew they'd been there and I knew things were gone. I checked my closet first, and yes, those few dresses I have that I hardly ever wear weren't there. Also the suitcase that I keep at the back on the closet floor. A pair of walking shoes were gone, and my best dressy shoes. Also a white sweater my daughters gave me but that I never wear, except to please them once in a while to make them think I like it. Then, in the drawers, I found half my underwear gone and my jewelry, such as I have. (Probably my cairngorm. I didn't see it there.)

They have already packed me up and taken my things off somewhere, and I think I know where. From the looks of what they thought I'd need there— dresses, jewelry, stockings—I knew what it would be like: Dress for dinner, sit on porches, play cards, watch TV, sing, entertainment every Saturday night. Did they think I was so senile I wouldn't notice what was going on? I knew it wouldn't be long before they'd come for me, and I wondered exactly when that would be. Perhaps very early in the morning, before I was up and out at my dig. Well, I would just have to go back out there right away. The thing was, I wasn't ready yet. Now I would have to make something happen before I really understood anything. Before I went out, though, I thought I would sit down, have a cup of tea, and let my left hand write a bit. I thought it might have something to tell me.

Why not why not lie down and in the cool sanctuary of the library why not come cool all night and see the shores of the sky.

(My daughters have never been interested in libraries nor in anything they can't put their finger on nor anything they can't understand the first time they see it.)

Take a white string long and measure and dig in the center of the library a place to lie down with quilts and pillows.

Nothing much else to do that I could think of right then. I didn't wait. I did as they said, got white cord and quilt and pillow. I didn't bring a flashlight. The night was clear, stars out but no moon. I could see well enough to find the center of the library. I dug a shallow grave just my size and lay down there, facing up, looking at the constellation Swan. I kept my eyes on that. It took effort, but everything worth doing takes effort. Effort is what makes it all worthwhile, so I held my eyes open and on the Swan, her wings stretched out, flying out there so high I knew I couldn't even conceive of the distance. I forced myself not to sleep. Pretty soon the Swan seemed to move and wobble and then began to swoop about the sky. My God, I'd never seen anything so strange and wonderful as that swooping Swan of stars. And then I heard— faintly at first—that *clack, clack, clack* of stones that meant all the librarians were there around me. I didn't see them, but I knew they were there. I was afraid to turn my eyes away from the Swan. Nor did I want to by then. I liked watching it loop and tumble and glide. And then it whizzed by directly over my head so close I felt the rush of the air. And after that, there was the fat red Venus, life-size, sitting right beside me. "Sanctuary," she said, but she didn't need to say it. I knew that. "Stay," she said, and all of a sudden I knew it was death, death now and had been death all along. But I thought, *I could be working in the sanctuary of the vegetable garden at the old ladies' home. Or I might even be sitting on the porch, but I'd be alive if only for a little longer...not much, but a little bit.* "No," I said. But she kept nodding, and now I couldn't have turned away even if I wanted to, and the *clack, clack* of stones was loud and painful and right over my head.

"Why not later?"

"It's now or never."

I knew this *was* what I wanted, but suddenly it seemed too easy. I could hear, by now, not only *clacks,* but the rush and rustle of the great river nearby. I even heard the sound of a boat, the bump of wood on wood as a skiff came up to the dock. I heard the thump of stone tablets being placed upon the shore, and I knew they were full of women's thoughts...women's writings...women's good ideas. Even old women's good ideas. Then the old women danced toward me with flowers, and suddenly I was standing up on my white quilt and I was wearing my old white nightgown, which I know I had not put on to come out here in. (I know better than to walk around at night in nothing but that.) And I worried because I wondered what had happened to my vest with all my best finds in it. But the Venus read my mind. "If you give us up," she said, "you have to give up those, too. You have to give up the proof that there were some little germs of sanity to what you were doing." All the old women came one by one and looked me right in the eye then and smiled; and all their eyes were blue, every one of them, the exact same blue. I could see that they wanted me as much or more than I wanted them and that we would talk and it would be my kind of talk. I knew that my left hand would write, then, many books on stones.

"And they will be found here," the Venus said, "and will be deciphered and all in less than five years from now."

"Otherwise?" I said.

"Otherwise, nothing. No library, no books, no mirror, no Venus."

"I'll take nothing," I said, and the Swan swooped down and knocked me over. I fell, clutching feathers, and I thought. *They lied to me. I'm dying right now. They lied to me and took me anyhow.*

But it wasn't dying. I woke up to voices and to the sound of a van and my daughters and two men. They don't have to say anything. I know where they're taking me, and I know that I chose it myself. I will go silently and with dignity. I will walk like a queen. I'm thinking that I'll find something there to make an effort for. I'll find something so I can "do." I'll not just "be."

Odd thing, though. I pick up my vest lying there all torn. It's as though it had been attacked in anger. There's hardly an inch of it without a tear. I check what's left of the pockets. Everything is gone, just as they said it would be—every single smooth, white stone and all the other things—and I'm standing here like a crazy woman, bare feet, nightgown (I feel sure I didn't come out here like this). And I am surrounded by feathers...white feathers. When I move they float out all around me. When I shake my head they flutter down.

Reason Seven

Barry N. Malzberg

For over twenty years Barry Malzberg has been writing daring, different stories of science fiction, fantasy, and any other sort that will hold his brilliant imagination. He has won critical acclaim for novels such as *Beyond Apollo, The Remaking of Sigmund Freud*, and the story cycle *Galaxies*. Malzberg's fiction is frequently intensely personal, as is his book of criticism, *The Engines of the Night*. His stories have been collected in *The Best of Barry Malzberg, Malzberg at Large*, and *The Man Who Loved the Midnight Lady*.

"Reason Seven" came out of a prolific period of paranoid/relationship stories by Malzberg. It was published May 1985.

Reason Seven

Barry N. Malzberg

I prepare "captured secret documents." A smattering of Russian, hints of Spanish, *un peu* French, some Chinese; it is not important that I be fluent in these languages as long as I can provide what might be called their *flavor*. The "documents" are intended to read as translations anyway, which excuses many limitations in style. They contain polemics about the need for world conquest, interspersed with statistics so dull that they must chill: feed grains, diseased chickens, pastures, coal mines, resources. The style is horrifying, but that is the agency's problem, not my own. I merely conform to established rules. I follow format.

    This job—and I regard it solely as a job; I have no delusions of grandeur here—cost me a promising relationship recently. It is of this that I wish to speak—however hesitantly—for the files. I have been instructed to do this. Otherwise it is not to be discussed outside of context. Francine, however, was disingenuous, and me—I knew less then—I was also a little bit of a patriot and proponent (fool!) of relative openness in affairs. So I told her, more or less, what I did. It took Francine a while to grasp the context, but when she did, her reaction was one of disgust. "You're a functionary," she said, "a *clerk*. Don't all of the lies sicken you?"

    "They are not lies. I choose to believe they reflect a higher truth in the endless battle between the Soviet bloc and the Western forces of light."

    "We've heard that rationalization for half a century," Francine said. She was really quite angry. I am doing a poor job, I sense, of conveying her outrage. (My prose is more keyed toward the smoothly bureaucratic. It is all a matter of training.) "This is crazy," she said. "You mean you write this stuff so that when

105

the troops come in they plant the documents and then those documents become what are supposed to be captured from somebody's files?"

"*Secret* documents," I pointed out. "Transcripts and writings that were supposed to have been destroyed or taken away and were instead left behind by the enemy in their headlong flight. Captured *public* documents would be another division."

"Are you trying to tell me you just sit in front of a typewriter and make up this stuff? That's horrifying."

Well, perhaps it is, considered in that way; I had never done so before. I gather that I am being rather light on characterization. Characterization and her handmaiden, description, are not to be neglected in certain prose documents.

Francine was five feet four, with a certain severity of mouth and cheekbones, perhaps a consequence of her upbringing in the mine country of Pennsylvania but more likely associated with the fact that she was a master of arts in nursing administration and had seen a good deal in her time, not the least of which was the interior of my apartment, if not my unrevealed psyche. (Me, I had seen little and had been nowhere; travel, in the viewpoint of my mentors, not being conducive to that free flow of the imagination needed to produce fine secret documents.) Breasts two, eyes blue, ass nicely formed, and so on, and I would go into further particulars of appearance and physical relationship if they were relevant under any circumstance. They are not relevant.

"This is bizarre," Francine said. "I've never heard of anything like it. Why are you telling me all this?"

"You said you wanted a sharing relationship, Francine."

"But this is crazy."

"Crazy?" I said, and added an agency dictum. "In war nothing is crazy, and we are in deadly combat. We make up everything, yes, but only in a tight format. There's a style sheet, there's rigid schematization of the voicing, and there are lists of facts, all of which must be included in a certain fashion. Actually," I emphasized, "it's a very demanding job, fully deserving of its GS-eighteen rank, and we're thinking about making a formal appeal for reclassification."

"Who are 'we'?"

"All of us in the branch, of course."

"You mean, there's a whole little disgusting army of clerks. Of captured secret document preparers."

"Our official classification is *informational writer*," I said, "but I wouldn't really object to your label."

"Well, I object to every aspect of it," Francine said.

And so on and so forth. It was a difficult argument in a difficult time, and it is not, perhaps, worthwhile to extend this transcript. I have included this much only to indicate that I am well aware (so are all of us on this level) of the contempt that my occupation incites in some quarters. I am not unaware of pain, nor unacquainted with grief. Looking at this objectively (and objectivity is the grand, sad curse of the century), there is something futile, something indeed *clerkly*about preparing crude drafts, in uncertain language, of materials that will never be read other than by a skeptical smattering of the public. There is something awful about justifying troop actions that are, perhaps, unjustifiable, led by interests who are, to some, unspeakable. But I am no politician.

Politics and the civil service are kept separate by fiat. Insulated by the Career & Salary Plan, I minimize implication.

Someone, after all, has to prepare the captured secret documents; reporters are persistent, the times insist upon evidence for everything, and I have learned to do my work as well as anyone could under the circumstances. Me and my army of clerks. (Army? There is none such; Francine had it wrong. There are only a dozen of us, and we are, of course, kept separate not only by area of expertise but by anonymity. My colleagues have never been identified to me. I learned we were a dozen only through captured secret documents.)

A note on human vanity and folly: In the adjoining room of this apartment—I work and sleep in the windowed partition, do my wooing there as well—lies the library of my collected works. As every writer must have his pride and bibliography, so must I have mine. Lined up in uniform binders are the output of all my years at the agency: original drafts of documents captured in Beirut, the Antilles, Cairo, San Miguel de Allende, and other places. Most of these bear the mark of the haste and pressure under which they were written (deadlines are pressing in this business), but in every one of them will be at least a page and sometimes two of prose that I consider to bear my own personal impress, prose that sings or at least moves to a certain inner rhythm. *Eighty-six knives to the oppressors, an arcing bullet for the American swine, hold the temple inviolate*—this one of my favorite phrases (unearthed by the liberating troops in Port-au-Prince). *A four-year plan past folly, a hole in the tent of American domain*—there is another. Most of these documents, of course, are written in a prose of the most stale and ponderously bureaucratic sort, this to grant the counsel of realism, but every now and then—as I insisted to Francine, as I insist to you—personal voice must extrude. A man must have his pride. A man must, after all, have his individuality.

They understand this in the agency, and as long as it does not interfere with the essentials, they have even been known to encourage this approach.

There is more compassion, greater understanding within these corridors than outsiders could ever understand. This is not a dehumanizing business; it breeds great feeling.

So that other room—my library, the collected works— is inviolate, stark but for the shelves and the thin fluorescence with which the carefully stacked binders are illuminated. It is that place (I like to feel) in which all purpose resides, a repository, I think, and an *hommage* to larger purposes. For there are not, I have come to know, merely the six reasons cited in the Career & Salary brochure for the advantages of this employment, but a seventh reason, too. And it's the most important of all: giving testimony, to change the face of the earth a little. All of us who would be artists, who would use the medium of words or paint or song, are driven by this need to alter, however slightly, that terrain upon which we have found ourselves. And my alteration, stacked floor to ceiling in the spackled, glowing binders that contain not only statistics but a kind of poetry...my alteration, it has to be understood, *is very important to me;* it matters, it is not trival. I must make this clear, this is not insignificant material, not hackwork but testimony. That seventh reason portends: *to make a difference.*

And a difference has been made; my captured documents have given justification where such did not before exist. I have shifted the balance of popular opinion away from loathing, and I have the evidence to cite. But this is not a document of sheer exposition, as we would call it at the agency; this is a narrative of some dimension and dramatic weight. I come before you not only with a postion to cite but a story to tell. And I come to explain not only Francine (although she has a part in this) but to explain much that goes past her, Francine being ultimately only a symbol. "I'm going to write to all of the newspapers," she said toward the conclusion of the discussions to which I have already alluded. "Do you understand that? I'll publish in the letters-to-the-editor columns, and I won't stop there. I'll write my congressman, I'll send communications to action-news-drama center. Someone will believe me. Someone will at last accept this bizarre truth: that there are roomfuls of little clerks like yourself making up captured documents to justify our disgusting adventures and equations, our rotten entrepreneuring. I'll make them believe it, I swear I will, and it will never be the same for you again. Just you wait and see."

"Francine," I said, "you are overreacting. It's merely a *job,* Francine. It's employment like any other, it can become as routine as those facets of anguish—melanoma, termination, helplessness, suffering—to which you are exposed every day in your own work. It is necessarily impersonal. You can get used to it, believe me."

"I'll never become numb to it," she said. "*I'm* not a clerk, not a functionary. That's why I got the master's; I had to get off the floor. I couldn't look at their eyes anymore, lie to the relatives, watch them as they stared out the windows at the sun in the late autumn. I had to indulge some separation, open up distance, stop lying, find a way to get away from it. But not you, you would be there at this moment, holding their hands and telling them that remissions were common in their situation."

I should explain—lest Francine seem unduly unsympathetic at this point, so reprehensible that a sensible reader might ask, "Why is a person like you even involved with her anymore?"—that it was not necessarily always this way.

On our very first date, arranged by a video-computer service, Francine and I had sexual relations and enjoyed one another enormously, and it was only after some time (and after the initiation of conversation) that matters moved to this state of relative collapse. Francine, I learned, is one of those who rejects *anonymous, sustaining relationships* and wants *real human contact.* This is terrific for arguments but not so good for sex. Agency employ or not, I am a normal American male, heterosexual to the core, thirty-four years driven and necessitous, and I would far rather get laid (*especially* anonymously) than become involved in discussions like this. I feel justified, powerfully so.

"This is unbelievable," she said, pointing to the binders. This argument was taking place in the library. I had made the mistake of taking her into the library. "You *save* all of this stuff? You're proud of it?"

She reached up, took a binder, opened it, and stared at it. "This is full of *French,*" she said, "and strange-looking letters. You know these languages?"

"Cyrillic," I said, "for the Russian language. This gives it authenticity. Keep on going though, you'll find something that you can read if you just give it time." I maintained a sense of pride in my work. Even then, I only wanted a reading.

She turned some pages. "Running dog," she read, "imperialist swine will fall within the mark, and the penitentiary of the century will not, cannot, wholly enclose them."

"Dominican Republic. 1988," I said rather pompously.

"Praise the keepers, for the keepers will set us free; know the truth, and the truth will cut our shackles."

"Yes," I said. "Isn't that good?"

"You wrote that?"

"Every word of it."

"And you're proud of this?"

"I'm not ashamed, Francine, if that's what you're asking me to say. I have nothing to be ashamed of."

She hurled the binder on the floor. "I can't tell you how angry this makes me," she said. "This then, *this* is the face of the enemy, the liars who have turned this country into the nightmare of the century. You serve the forces of this lie, and yet you're a *clerk,* just a functionary!" She reached, took another binder from the shelf, threw this down unopened. "This is terrifying," she said, "it's absolutely terrifying. I can't believe that you've told me all this."

"You're causing disorder."

"I'm what?"

"You're causing disorder, Francine, and I won't have it. So please, I'm asking you to stop."

"*I'm* causing disorder," she said fiercely. "Oh my—"

"This is my library. I'm proud of it. I worked hard to put it together. My *writings* are here. I don't want them disturbed, and I don't want to argue over them anymore."

She opened the binder, clawed out a sheet. "This says something about steel quotas," she said, rolled it into a ball, threw it at me. She ripped out another sheet, scanning it hurriedly.

"I mean it. I said stop it, Francine," I said. I felt myself beginning to flush. I knew arrhythmia would shortly follow. I am quite serious about my collected works. Some aspect of permanence and history is important to me. This is testimony. Call it evidence if you like. Call it the evidence of the century. "Please don't do this."

"I'm going to dismantle your library piece by piece, you disgusting little clerk. Then I'll call everyone I know and expose you. See if *I'm* afraid of the CIA."

"It's not the CIA."

"I'm not afraid of *anything!*" Francine said. "You people hide in the dark, you make your little threats. But when you're exposed, you're nothing—"

Who would have thought there to be so much passion in her? Three dates, three casual fucks, some dinners, a walk on the piers, one concert, an unfortunate confession, and then all of this. She had reacted as if I were an assassin.

"It must be being surrounded by all of the dying," I said to her, trying to be reasonable. "Yes, that would explain it, that would explain the rage. But I'm just a victim, too, Francine. I do what they tell me."

"That's the great line of our age: 'Don't bother me, I just work here.' "

She seized *two* binders this time and kicked one across the room. The heavy impact of her little shoe caused the reinforcement to break. Pages spewed from a height, settled unevenly on the floor like nestling birds. I endeavored up to this point—as must be clear—to be reasonable. I am a reasonable man.

But I am afraid that at this moment I lost control of myself.

A description of the events of the next hour or so is not necessary. That description would be too painful, albeit truly humbling, but I can say that I was brought to realize the inner, substantial truth of that which I had written in a group of documents to be found in a warehouse in Amman during the invasion of 1991: "One truly does not know the measure of the man until one has been tested by the invader. One truly does not know the running of the beast, the stalking of all the steps, until one has heard the heartbeat of the self. One never truly knows, then, until one *knows,* and not an instant before."

It was a formative experience, let me say that, also quite painful. At length I found myself at the desk of my supervisor. It was an emergency appointment, but the agency makes it clear in the Career & Salary Plan manual: Normal procedures may be overridden in case of serious difficulty. I was in serious difficulty. One must never operate conventionally in our terrain, not after what I had done. *What I had done.* I am afraid that I was rather out of control. I sobbed. I wrung my hands . The supervisor listened quietly to the recapitulation and coda, then made a call. "We will have operatives there immediately," he said. "Are you sure the scene was absolutely secure?"

"It was when I left."

"Stop your sniveling. You know that won't get you anywhere. You are positive that there were no witnesses? No one around."

"Yes," I said, sighing deeply, heaving. "Yes, I am quite sure."

"And it was accomplished just as quietly as you say? There were no undue sounds?"

"No, there were not." I tried to hold back the sobbing but could not. "I did care for her," I said. "She was very nice at the beginning. I thought we had a real relationship. I felt that I could tell her things. Maybe it will because she worked with dying people. It was only later that it got dreadful. I made a mistake."

"Oh, yes, you did," the supervisor said. "Oh, yes indeed, you did." I would engage in characterological description here, but like all of them, like me on the job, he was masked. His voice was without affect. It is important to remember that there is nothing personal in all of this. "You made a terrible, a stupid mistake," he said, "but now you'll know better, won't you?"

"Oh, yes."

"You understand why these jobs must be confidential?"

"Oh, yes," I said, "I know that now."

His eyes were kindly but nonetheless cold. Impenetrable even. Something like the agency prose itself. "Yes," I said, "I understand that now and much else."

"You were really quite stupid, and you will have to pay the price for that stupidity."

"My job?"

The supervisor stared at me. "The *job?*" he said. "That's the last thing. We wouldn't even ask your life."

"I want my job."

"The situation, however, is manageable. It's a little tricky, but we've had worse. You knew her fairly well, of course?"

"Of course. Except that I misjudged her terribly at the end."

"It's too late to think of that. Draft a statement, then."

"A statement?"

"Right here and now. A credible suicide note that can be found with a corpse. Don't worry about the strangulation; cyanosis can occur for lots of reasons, and there are ways around it. But then there's the note. It has to be *right*. I assume you can take care of it. There isn't much time."

"I can take care of it," I said gratefully, seeing for the first time (but I could have deduced it earlier!) a way out. "Yes, that shouldn't be too hard."

"It's Sunday," the supervisor said, "and also I would prefer to play this very close. I would prefer to keep it in the family. I would prefer *not* to call in the domestic division."

There are seven reasons, and of them all only the seventh counts: to take testimony, to leave testimony, to make a difference. Hence the library and hence the note to be left beside you, my love.

I am sorry, Francine. Had you but understood, it could have been different. Had I but understood, you might have been with me yet. We do what we must do, and we know none other. The secret, the document itself, is my life.

Fire Catcher

Richard Kadrey

Richard Kadrey lives in San Francisco, California. His first novel,*Metrophage,* was published as part of the revived Ace Special series in 1988. His second, *Kamikaze L'Amour,* is expanded from his story "Horse Latitudes," (*Best Omni Science Fiction One*) and will be published by St. Martin's Press in 1995. Kadrey has written for *The Mississippi Review, The San Francisco Chronicle, Interzone, Omni*, and the anthology *Semiotext(e) SF*. He has also authored *Covert Culture Sourcebook. Covert Culture Sourcebook 2.0* is in the works and will be published this fall.

"Fire Catcher" is about a man under a type of pressure no human should have to endure. It was originally pulbished in *Interzone,* the British science fiction magazine, and in an unusual circumstance, was reprinted in the August 1986 issue of *Omni.*

Fire Catcher

Richard Kadrey

Preston promises himself that when this bottle is empty, he will stop taking the pills.

The black market barbiturates are strong, much more potent than the sleeping pills he used to get from the Army infirmary in town. (But why call a dozen T-shacks, barracks, and a million tons of rubble a town?)

Even so, without the booze to wash the pills down, Preston knows he would never get to sleep.

Once, Preston took some of the pills to an Army lab and had them analyzed. It turned out that each pill was completely different, a crazy-quilt combination of whatever the manufacturers had lying around: Thorazine, MDA, Megaludes, Nembutal. Sometimes Preston purchases small amounts of raw opium. This he mixes with vodka to produce his own crude version of laudanum. At times all of this effort strikes him as amusing. He is well aware that any of the drugs combined with all the alcohol he drinks could kill him. And what would General Bower say then? How would he explain to the European high command that he had let the best assassin in the American Occupation Army drug himself to death?

Within a half hour it becomes clear that the pills are not working. The blinking cursors on a dozen computer terminals are about to drive him crazy. Preston takes two more pills and gulps them down with vodka from a plastic cup. He goes to the bedroom to get his coat but pauses to close the door of his wife's empty closet.

Four A.M., Berlin time. Outside the computer bunker a metallic-smelling fog drifts through the city. Preston needs a drink. Six pills to the wind, and he

115

isn't even drowsy yet. The beam of his flashlight plays over the unlit ruins. Each day the Army busies itself clearing the streets, pushing pulverized buildings back onto the blasted foundations from which they have fallen.

Jumbled concrete blocks and twisted wires abut each other in long rows until the residential blocks begin to resemble one vast and continuous block.

Preston moves the beam of his flashlight over the empty buildings, hoping for some romantic sense of connection with the ruins, as if among the shattered stones might lie the antidote to all his unnamed fears. He finds a pair of sunglasses, some sheets of scorched piano music, and the acid fog.

It has only been a few days since she left, but already he has forgotten her face, what he said to her, what she said to him. She is gone; that is the only truth. He watched her cross the tarmac; watched her board the military transport for New York.

He had tamed the most complex computer systems in the world, yet he could not stop his wife from leaving.

When she was walking up the boarding ramp to the plane and Preston was standing on the other side of a barbed-wire fence, he screamed out her name. Just once. Everybody on the airstrip turned to stare at him. Preston hurried back to his bunker and got drunk. Later, when he was sober, he discovered gashes on his hands where he had gripped the barbed wire.

Back in the computer bunker, Preston turns his attention to the monitor where the pharmacy codes for the state hospital in Leningrad are displayed. He begins typing, changing a number here, a number there. A white wave of interference shimmers across the screen, washing out the display. A bad connection? Preston gets up and checks his fiberoptic leads. He cracked the pharmacy system just a few minutes before and is anxious not to call attention to his presence.

Reflexively his hands move over the cables, testing connections and solder points. He pours himself some vodka and drains the cup. As the interference sudsides, he begins to work quickly.

Finding the room number is easy. High Party officials are always given special accommodations and kept well away from the general hospital population. Locating the proper drugs, however, is another matter. In the state hospitals, paranoia reigns. All of the drugs are listed either by complex chemical codes or by obscure euphemisms that mean virtually nothing to Preston, an outsider. He works his way through the drug catalog, a page at a time, occasionally shifting to another system when his LED alarm flashes, indicating that someone at the hospital is trying to access the pharmacy listings.

Finally Preston finds the chemical symbols he is looking for. After that, it is a matter of a few seconds to reprogram the nursing drones and change the Party official's daily vitamin B shot to a lethal dose of succinylcholine.

Before he exits the system, Preston dumps the contents of a slave disk throughout the hospital's patient records. The disk contains approximately a million words of English pornography (with pictures) and ten digitized hours of American rock music.

The Army told him to dump the porn. The music Preston added himself.

He takes two more hits of speed. From his seat at the console, Preston can see the unmade bed across the hall. He has not slept in the bed since his wife left. He has not slept at all. He is, in fact, afraid of the room. The contours of the rumpled sheets, the stark geometry of the empty closet imply an end a thousand times more terrifying than all the rubble overhead.

They call him the Fire Catcher because he once held the nuclear blaze in his hands, and he snuffed it out.

1996: Alone, Preston hacked his way into the nexus of the Soviet nuclear-missile system. He sliced through the data web; boiled through 3-D grids; smashed time vectors, system checks, fail-safes. Preston the Visigoth, the madman, the cybernetic assassin, had breached the Russian program, and it had yielded up its prize.

On the eve of World War III, Preston had locked the Soviet missiles in their silos. A day later American and French paratroopers landed in Vladivostok and began shooting their way west. A Soviet submarine, *The People's Victorious Liberator,* torpedoed the British naval base at Gibraltar.

Preston returned to the United States. There the President gave him a medal, calling Preston a great humanitarian.

Preston married an anthropologist named Nina Abreu, and they settled in New York. Preston continued his research on developing intelligent security programs for computer systems.

Fought with conventional weapons, the war Preston had helped shape seethed back and forth across Europe for twelve years without a winner.

National boundaries were liquid, flowing in and around interregnum war states. New countries appeared and disappeared overnight. In the first two years of the war, twenty million people died.

Preston sips some of his homemade laudanum while he completes his report on the Party official's death. When the report is done, he queues it into

117

General Bower's private security file. Above the console a bank of red and green LEDs flash a warning. Preston checks out his lines. The CIA is monitoring him again. He switches on the slave disk and jams the Agency lines with the same porn he dumped on the Soviets.

Taped to the side of the slave drive is a wallet-size hologram of Preston's wife. He rips the rectangle of plastic from the drive and holds his lighter to it. In the wedge of flame the hologram melts, his wife's face twisting, turning in on itself, liquefying, and finally fading completely as the hologram drips away.

Later Preston goes to the base infirmary and stares through blue-gray bulletproof glass at the Soviet flier who had been shot down a few days earlier. There he reflects on the nature of sweet circumstance. Over forty million dead, and the small woman with the Red Star and serial number tattooed on her forearm is only the second war casualty Preston has ever seen. The first was his wife.

Preston wonders if the flier is awake, if she is aware of the burns that have blackened her skin, if she can sense that the interrogations will soon begin.

Looking at the soot the burning hologram left on his fingertips, Preston begins to cry. In a few minutes an embarrassed guard asks him to leave.

They gave Preston a long list of names when he was recalled to Europe. To the base he was the Fire Catcher, but officially he became known as Project Earwig. An earwig is an insect that will sometimes burrow into the body of an animal, lay its eggs, and then continue through the animal's body, eating its way out. When the earwig's young are born they repeat the pattern, often destroying the host animal.

Preston carried out his first assassination a week before he cracked the Soviet database. His victim was a key official in the Transportation Ministry. Preston simply entered the Party records and erased all traces of the man. After that the man's official State Access Card would no longer function. He could not enter his home, retrieve his car, buy food. His comrades refused his panicked calls; assuming a new purge was under way, they avoided him.

The man was found a few weeks later, frozen stiff to a bench at a bus stop in his hometown of Gorki.

Preston was a methodical worker. He made backup disks of all his work. He had records of every system he had ever cracked, from his high-school records code (he had manipulated other students' files for a fee) to the Soviet missile system. It was easier than recracking the system each time he went in.

He kept the disks in a lead-lined floor safe under his bed. Besides the disks, the safe contained a .45 caliber pistol, sleeping pills, and an emergency bottle of vodka.

* * *

His system clear again, Preston enters a military override code into the lines for the United States and clears a data path straight to New York. Then he enters the phone company's lines and accesses his wife's phone, transmitting a playback signal to the CIA tap he had discovered there months before.

His wife's voice, thin and shot through with static, crackles out of a tiny speaker over his console.

Her conversation is nothing; it is ordinary. She is speaking with a friend whose name Preston remembers as being something like Judy or Julie. He fast-forwards the tape. The conversation is the same. The mundane life of the city. The price of eggs, the refugees from Europe who crowd the subways, a day on the beach at Coney Island. Preston listens for his name, but no one mentions him. He plays the whole thing through again before shutting down the override. Something burns in Preston's throat. A sudden wave of drowsiness engulfs him, but it's too late. He does not want the pills to work. Preston stumbles to his dresser, pulls out a bottle of amphetamines, downs a handful. In a few minutes he vomits the whole thing back up, but he is no longer sleepy.

When he is alone, Preston goes through his papers, emptying his desk and collecting reams of printouts. Spreading the papers around himself, he sits on the floor and reads, reconstructing his past with hard data. He keeps lists—things like his mother's maiden name, computers he has owned, and the color of his first car—which he tapes to the walls of the bunker. When he is working and can't concentrate, the lists form a sort of mantra for him: Boyle, IBM, NEC, red Riviera, and Nina's eyes.

Love is a dangerous concept. People do strange things for love, but Preston is well aware of this. Love of a spouse, love of a country, an ideology. Love as strength, as power, as fear.

"Murder," Preston once told his wife, "is the American moral equivalent of enlightenment. The ultimate expression of the *self*."

In the first two years of World War III, twenty million people died. The President once gave Preston a medal. Preston was well aware of the symbol implicit in the decoration: He was a hero, he was loved. Preston's wife married him for love. A victim of circumstance, he knew that she had left him for love, too. In the next eleven years of World War III, forty million people died, all victims of circumstance.

There are terrifying mathematical possibilities in the dimensions of empty closets and vacant dresser drawers. The sheets of an unmade bed reveal clues to a whole landscape of conflict; the crease in a blanket, the trajectory of shadows on a pillow imply the flow of armies in the shapes left by two bodies moving together.

All of this, Preston is aware, has something to do with the price of eggs and the feel of wind at the beach, but he has trouble making the connections.

Preston touches the rigid face of the Soviet pilot. Her skin is dry and coarse, delicate as rice paper. She stirs for a moment and opens her eyes. Preston has never seen such fear on a human face before.

Her eyes are wide and gray, sunk deep in the immobile black mask of her ruined face. Lightly Preston touches his fingers to her lips. "Don't be afraid," he says. "Everything is going to be alright."

A dying guard stares at Preston from the floor; on the guard's chest, a red orchid of blood widens, seeping through his knotted fingers. Preston sets his pistol on the bedside table. From his pocket he pulls a remote trigger switch. Before he left the bunker, Preston went to his safe and removed one of the backup disks. Sitting next to the flier on the bed, he punches in a code that loads the program.

A thousand miles away, Klaxon horns sound. Underground doors, rusted and full of grit, slide, screaming and groaning, open to the night.

The Fire Catcher opens his hands, and flame takes the sky.

Preston offers the dying guard a glass of water. "Don't worry," he tells the guard, "I'm supposed to be here."

Turning to the pilot, Preston almost tells her he loves her, but he knows that is not true. He loves what she might have been, what she could have been, under different circumstances. But none of that matters now. Preston thinks of unmade beds and empty closets. The foolish icons of love. It occurs to Preston vaguely, for the first time, that he, too, might be a victim. He thinks of this and can almost smell his wife's body but they are all burned away before he can recall her face.

Dead Run

Greg Bear

Greg Bear came to prominence in the late seventies, primarily as a hard science fiction writer. He has won both the Hugo and Nebula Awards. Bear is the author of the novels *Eon, Blood Music,The Forge of God, Queen of Angels,* the short novel *Heads,* and, most recently, *Moving Mars.* In addition to his hard science novels and stories, Bear is also a terrific fabulist, having authored some memorable fantasies—"Petra," "Sleepside Story," and "Dead Run" (April 1985). His stories have been collected in *The Wind From a Burning Woman* and *Tangents.*

"Dead Run" is a wry story about truckdrivers in Hell.

Dead Run

Greg Bear

There aren't many hitchhikers on the road to Hell.

I noticed this dude from four miles away. He stood where the road is straight and level, crossing what looks like desert except it has all these little empty towns and motels and shacks. I'd been on the road for about six hours, and the folks in the cattle trailers behind me had been quiet for the last three—resigned, I guess—so my nerves had settled a bit, and I decided to see what the dude was up to. Maybe he was one of the employees. That would be interesting. Truth to tell, once the wailing settled down, I got bored.

The dude was on the right hand side of the road, thumb out. I piano-keyed down the gears, and the air brakes hissed and squealed at the tap of my foot. The semi slowed, and the big diesel made that gut-deep dinosaur belch of shuddered downness. I leaned across the cab as everything came to a halt and swung the door open.

"Where you heading?"

He laughed and shook his head, then spit on the soft shoulder. "I don't know," he said. "Hell, maybe." He was thin and tanned, with long, greasy black hair and blue jeans and a vest. His straw hat was dirty and full of holes, but the feathers around the crown area were bright and new looking—pheasant, if I was any judge. A fob hung out of his vest going into his watch pocket. He wore old Frye boots with the toes turned up and soles thinner than my spare's retread. He looked an awful lot like I did when I hitchhiked out of Fresno, broke and unemployed, looking for work.

"Can I take you there?"

"Sho'." He climbed in and eased the door shut behind him. He took out a kerchief and mopped his forehead, then blew his long nose and stared at me with bloodshot, sleepless eyes. "What you hauling?" he asked.

"Souls," I said. "Whole shitload of them."

"What kind?" He was young, not more than twenty-five at the most. He wanted to sound nonchalant, but I could hear nerves in his tone.

"Usual kind," I said. "Human. Some Hare Krishnas this time. Don't look too close anymore."

I pushed the truck along, coaxing and manipulating, wondering if the engine was as bad as it sounded. When we were up to speed—eighty, eighty-five, no smokies on *this* road—he asked, "How long you been hauling?"

"Two years."

"Good pay?"

"It'll do."

"Benefits?"

"We're union like everybody else."

"I heard about that," he said. "In that little dump about two miles back."

"People live there?" I asked. I didn't think anything lived along the road.

"Yeah. Real down folks. They said teamsters bosses get carried in limousines when they go."

"Don't really matter how you get there, I suppose. The trip's short, and the time after is long."

"Getting there's all the fun?" he asked, trying for a grin. I gave him a shallow one.

"What're you doing out here?" I asked a few minutes later. "You aren't dead, are you?" I'd never heard of dead folk running loose or looking quite as vital as he did, but I couldn't imagine anyone else being on the road. Just dead folks and drivers.

"No," he said. He was quiet for a bit. Then slow, as if it embarrassed him, "I came to find my woman."

"Yeah?" Not much surprised me, but that was a new twist. "There ain't no returning, you know."

"Sherill's her name, spelled like *sheriff* but with two *l*'s."

"Got a cigarette?" I asked. I didn't smoke, but I could use it later. He handed me the last three in a crush-proof pack and didn't say anything.

"Haven't heard of her," I said. "But then, I don't get to converse with everybody I haul. And there are lots of trucks, lots of drivers."

"I know," he said. "But I heard about them benefits."

He had a crazy kind of sad look in his eye when he glanced at me, and that made me angry. I tightened my jaw and stared straight ahead.

"You know," he said, "I heard some crazy stories. About how they use old trains for China and India, and in Russia there's a tramline. In Mexico it's old buses along roads, always at night—"

"Listen. I don't use all the benefits," I said. "I know some do, but I don't."

"Sure, got you," he said, nodding that exaggerated goddamn young folks' nod his whole neck and shoulders moving along, it's all right, everything's cool.

"How you gonna find her?"

"I don't know. Do the road, maybe ask the drivers."

"How'd you get in?"

He didn't answer for a moment. "I'm going to be here when I die. It's not so hard for folks like me to get in before. And...my daddy was a driver. He told me the route. By the way, my name's Bill."

"Mine's John," I said.

"Glad to meet you."

We didn't say much to each other after that for a while. He stared out the right window, and I watched the desert and faraway shacks go by.

Soon the mountains came looming up—space seems compressed on the road, especially once past the desert—and I sped up for the approach. There was some noise from the back.

"What do you do when you get off work?" Bill asked.

"Go home and sleep."

"Nobody knows you're on the run?"

"Just the union."

"That's the way it was for Daddy, until just before the end. Look, I didn't mean to make you mad or nothing. I'd just heard about the perks, and I thought—" he swallowed, his Adam's apple bobbing. "Thought you might be able to help. I don't know how I'll ever find Sherill. Maybe back in the Annex...."

"Nobody in their right mind goes into the yards by choice," I said. "And you'll have to look through everybody that's died in the last four months. They're way backed up."

Bill took that like a blow across the face, and I was sorry I'd said it. "She's only been gone a week," he said. "She don't belong here."

I couldn't help but grin.

"No, I mean, I belong here but not her. She was in this car wreck a couple of months back, got pretty badly messed up. I'd dealt her dope at first and then fell in love with her, and by the time she landed in the hospital she was, you know, hooked on about four different things."

My arms stiffened on the wheel.

"I tried to tell her when I visited that it wouldn't be good for her to get anything, no more dope, but she begged me. What could I do? I loved her."

He wasn't looking out the window now. He was looking down at his worn

125

boots and nodding. "She begged me, man. So I brought her stuff. I mean, she took it all when they weren't looking. She just took it *all*. They pumped her out, but her insides were just gone. I didn't hear about her being dead until two days ago, and that really burned me. I was the only one who loved her, and they didn't even tell me. I had to go up to her room and find her bed empty. Jesus. I hung out at Daddy's union hall. Someone talked to someone else, and I found her name on a list. The Low Road."

"I don't use any of those perks," I said, just to make it clear I couldn't help him. "Folks in back got enough trouble without me. I think the union went too far there."

"Bet they felt you'd get lonely, need company," Bill said quietly, looking at me. "It don't hurt the folks back there. Maybe give them another chance to, you know, think things over. Give 'em relief for a couple of hours, a break from the mash—"

"Listen, a couple of hours don't mean nothing in relation to eternity. I'm not so sure I won't be joining them someday, and if that's the way it is I want it smooth, nobody pulling me out of a trailer and putting me back in."

"Yeah," he said. "Got you, man. I know where that's at. But she might be back there right now, and all you'd have to—"

"Bad enough I'm driving this rig in the first place." I wanted to change the subject.

"Yeah. How'd that happen?"

"Couple of accidents, my premiums went up to where I couldn't afford payments and premiums, and finally they took my truck."

"You coulda gone without insurance."

"Not me," I said. "Anyway, some bad word got out. No companies would hire me. I went to the union to see if they could help. Told me I was a dead-ender, either get out of trucking or—" I shrugged—"this. I couldn't leave trucking. It's bad out there, getting work. Lot of unemployed. Couldn't see myself pushing a hack in some big city."

"No, man," Bill said, giving me that whole-body nod of his again. He cackled sympathetically.

"They gave me an advance, enough for a down payment on my rig." The truck was grinding a bit but maintaining. Over the mountains, through a really impressive pass like from an old engraving, and down in a very rugged rocky valley, was the City.

"I don't think I'd better go on," Bill said. "I'll hitch with some other rig, ask around."

"Well, I'd feel better if you rode with me back out of here. Want my advice?" Bad habit. "Go home."

"No," Bill said. "Thanks anyway. Not without Sherill." He took a deep breath. "I'll try to work up a trade. I stay, she goes to the High Road. That's the way the game runs down here, isn't it?"

At the top of the pass I pulled the rig over and let him out. He waved at me, I waved back, and we went our separate ways.

The City looks a lot like a county full of big, white cathedrals. Casting against type. High wall around the perimeter, stretching as far as my eye can see. No horizon but a vanishing point, the wall looking like an endless highway turned on its side. As I geared the truck down for the decline, the noise in the trailers got irritating again. They could smell what was coming, I guess, like pigs stepping up to the man with the knife.

I pulled in to the disembarkation terminal and backed the first trailer up to the holding pen. Employees let down the gates and used some weird kind of prod to herd them.

These people were past mortal pain, and I didn't want to think about what the employees used to stimulate them.

They unhooked the first trailer, and I backed in the second. I got down out of the cab, and an employee came up to me, a big fellow with red eyes and brand-new coveralls. "Good ones this load?" he asked. His breath was like the end of a cabbage, bean, and garlic dinner.

I shook my head and held a cigarette out for a light. He pressed his fingernail against the tip. The tip flared and settled down to a steady glow. He looked at it with pure wanting in his eyes.

"Listen," I said. "You had anyone named Sherill through here?" I spelled it for him.

"Who's asking?" He grumbled, still eyeing the cigarette. He started to walk away.

"Just curious. I heard you guys knew all the names."

"So?" He stopped. He had to walk around, otherwise his shoes melted the asphalt a bit and got stuck. He came back and stood, lifting one foot, twisting a bit, then putting it down and lifting the other.

"Couple of Cheryls. No Sherills," he said. "Now—"

I handed him the cigarette. They loved the things. "Thanks," I said. He popped it into his mouth and chewed, bliss pushing over his seamed face. Tobacco smoke came out of his nose, and he swallowed. "Nothing to it," he said, and walked on.

I took the empties back to Baker. Didn't see Bill. Eight hours later I was in bed, beer in hand, paycheck on the bureau, my eyes wide open.

Shit. My conscience was working. I'd thought I was past that. But then I didn't use the perks, and I wouldn't drive without insurance. I wasn't really cut out for the life.

The next trip it was cool dusk, and the road crossed a bleak flatland of skeletal trees, all the same uniform gray as if cut from paper. When I pulled over to catch a nap—never sleeping more than two hours at a stretch—the shouts of the damned in the trailers bothered me even more than usual. They said silly things like:

"You can take us back, Mister! You really can!"

"Can he?"

"Shit no, mo'fuck pig."

"You can let us out! We can't hurt you!"

That was true enough. Drivers were alive, and the dead could never hurt those alive. But I'd heard what happened when you let them out. There were about ninety of them in back, and in any load there was always one who'd make you want to use your perks.

I scratched my itches in the narrow bunk, looking at the Sierra Club calendar hanging just below the fan. The Devil's Postpile. The load became quieter as the voices gave up, one after the other. There was one last shout— some obscenity—then silence.

It was then I decided to let them out and see if Sherill was there or if anyone knew her. They mingled in the Annex, got their last socializing before the City. Someone might know. Then if I saw Bill again—

What? What could I do to help him? He had screwed Sherill up royally, but then she'd had a hand in it too, and that was what Hell was all about. Poor stupid sons of bitches.

I swung out of the cab, tucking in my shirt and pulling my straw hat down on my crown. "Hey!" I said, walking alongside the trailers. Faces peered at me from the two inches between each white slat.

"I'm going to let you out. Just for a while. I need some information."

"Ask!" someone screamed. "Just ask, goddammit!"

"You know you can't run away, can't hurt me, you're all dead. Understand?"

"We know," said another voice, quieter.

"Maybe we can help."

"I'm going to open the gates one trailer at a time." I went to the rear trailer

128

first, took out my keys, and undid the Yale padlock. Then I swung the gates open, standing back a little like there was some kind of infected wound about to drain.

They were all naked. But they weren't dirty or unhealthy. Dead, they couldn't be. But all had some sort of air about them indicating what brought them to Hell; not anything specific, but subliminal.

Like the three black dudes in the rear trailer, first to step out. Why they were going to Hell was all over their faces.

"Stupid ass mo'fuck," one of them said, staring at me beneath thin, expressive eyebrows. He nodded and swung his fists, trying to pound the slats from the outside, but the blows hardly made them vibrate.

An old woman crawled down, hair white and neatly coiffed. I couldn't be certain what she had done, but she made me uneasy. Then the others, young, old, mostly old. Quiet. They looked me over, some defiant, most just bewildered.

"I need to know if there's anyone here named Sherill," I said, "who happens to know a fellow named Bill."

"That's my name," said a woman hidden in the crowd.

"Let me see her." I waved my hand at them. The black dudes came forward. A funny look got in their eyes, and they backed away. The others parted, and a young woman walked out. "How do you spell your name?" I asked.

She got a panicked expression. She spelled it, hesitating, looking to see if she was connecting, making the grade. I felt horrible already. She was a Cheryl.

"Not who I'm looking for," I said.

"Maybe not specifically," she said, real soft. She was very pretty, with medium-size breasts, hips like a teenager's, legs not terrific but nice. Her black hair was clipped short, and her eyes were almost Oriental.

"You can walk around a bit," I told them. "I'm letting out the first trailer now." I opened the side gates on that one, and the people came down. They didn't smell of anything, didn't look hungry; they just all looked pale.

"Woman named Sherill," I repeated. No one stepped forward. Then I felt someone close to me, and I turned. It was the Cheryl woman. She smiled. "I'd like to sit up front for a while," she said.

"So would we all, sister," said the white haired old woman. The black dudes stood off separate, talking low.

I swallowed, looking at her. Other drivers said they were real unsubstantial except at one activity. That was the perk. And it was said the hottest ones always ended up in Hell.

"No," I said. I motioned for them to get back into the trailers.

It had been a dumb idea all around. They went back, and I returned to the cab, wondering what had made me do it. I shook my head and started her up. Thinking on a dead run was no good. "No," I said, "goddamn," I said, "good." Cheryl's face stayed with me.

Cheryl's body stayed with me longer than the face.

There is always something that comes up on a life to lure a man onto the Low Road, not driving but riding in the back. We all have something. I wondered what reason God had to give each of us that little flaw, like a chip on a crystal soul. You press the chip hard enough, everything splits up crazy.

I returned hauling empties and found myself this time outside a small town called Shoshone. I pulled my truck into the café parking lot. The weather was cold, and I left the engine running. It was about eleven in the morning, and the café was half full. I took a seat at the counter next to an old man with maybe four teeth in his head attacking French toast with downright solemn dignity. I ordered eggs and hash browns and juice, ate quickly, and went back to my truck.

Bill stood next to the cab. Next to him was an enormous young woman with a face like a bulldog. She was wrapped in a filthy piece of plaid fabric, looking like it had been snatched from a trash dump somewhere. "Hey," Bill said. "Remember me?"

"Sure."

"I saw you pulling up. Wanted you to meet Sherill. I got her out of there." The woman stared at me with all the expression of a brick. "It's all screwy back there. Like a power failure or something. We just walked out on the road, and nobody stopped us."

Sherill could have had any number of weirdnesses beneath her formidable looks and gone unnoticed by ordinary folks, but I didn't have any trouble picking out the biggest thing wrong with her. She was dead. I looked around to make sure that I was in the World, and I was, and he wasn't lying. Clearly something serious was happening on the Low Road.

"Trouble?" I asked.

"Lots of escapes." He grinned at me. "Pan-demon-ium."

"That can't happen," I said, knowing I was wrong. Sherill was trembling now, hearing my voice.

"He's a *driver*, Bill," she said. "He's one takes us there. We got to git out of here." She had that soul-branded air and the look of a pig that's just escaped the slaughter seeing the butcher again. She took a few steps backward. Gluttony, I thought. Gluttony and buried lust and a real ugly way of seeing life, inner eye pulled all out of shape by her bulk.

"Tell me more," I said.

"There's these folks running all over down there, holing up in them towns, devils chasing them—"

"Employees," I corrected.

"Yeah, every which way."

Sherill tugged insistently on his arm. "We got to go, Bill."

"We got to go," he echoed. "Hey, man, thanks. I found her!" He pointed at Sherill and nodded his whole-body nod, and they were off down the street, Sherill's plaid wrap dragging in the dirt.

I drove back to Baker, parked in front of my little house, and sat inside with a beer while it got dark, checking my calendar for next day's run and feeling very cold. Next day I was scheduled to pick up another load at the Annex. Nobody called. If there was trouble, surely the union would let me know.

I showed up at the Annex early morning. The crossover from World to work was as usual; I followed the route, and the sky muddied from blue to solder color, and I was on the first leg of the road that leads to the Annex. I backed the rear trailer up to the yard's gate and unhitched it, then placed the forward trailer at the ramp, all the while keeping my ears tuned to pick up interesting conversation. The employees who worked the Annex look quite human. I took my bill of lading from a red-faced, billiard-ball-eyed old guy. He spit smoking saliva on the pavement, returned my querying look slantwise, and said nothing. Maybe it was all settled. I hitched up both full trailers and pulled out.

It was the desert again this time, only now the towns and tumbledown houses looked bomb-blasted, like something big had come through, flushing out game with a howitzer.

No nevermind. Keep your eyes on the road. Push that rig.

Four hours in I came to a roadblock. Nobody on it, no employees, just big carved-lava barricades cutting across all lanes and beyond them a wall of yellow smoke, which, the driver's unwritten instructions advised, meant absolutely no entry.

I got out. The load was making noises. I suddenly hated them. Least they could do was go with dignity and spare me their misery. I stood by the truck, waiting for instructions or some indication of what I was supposed to do. The load got quieter after a while, but I heard noises off the road, screams mostly and far away.

"There isn't anything," I said to myself, lighting up one of Bill's cigarettes even though I don't smoke and dragging deep, "*anything* worth this shit." Not job or dignity or anything. I vowed I'd quit after this run.

I heard something come up behind the trailers, and I edged closer to the cab steps. High wisps of smoke obscured things at first, but a dark shape four or five yards high plunged through and stood with one hand on the top slats of the rear trailer.

It made little grunting noises. It was covered with naked people, crawling all over, biting and scratching and shouting obscenities. It fell to its knees, then stood again and lurched off the road.

I'd never seen an employee so big before, or in so much trouble. The load began to wail like banshees. I threw down my cigarette and ran after it.

Workers will tell you. Camaraderie extends even to those on the job you don't like. If they're in trouble, it's part of the mystique to help out. Besides, the unwritten instructions were very clear on such things, and I've never knowingly busted a job rule—not since getting my rig back—and couldn't see starting now.

Through the smoke and across great ridges of lava, I ran until I spotted the employee about ten yards ahead. It had shaken off the naked people and was standing with one in each hand. Its shoulders smoked, and scales stood out at all angles. They'd really done a job on the bastard. Ten or twelve of the dead were picking themselves off the lava, unscraped, unbruised. They saw me.

The employee saw me.

Everyone came at me, grabbing. I turned and ran for the truck, stumbling over outstretched arms and legs. My hair stood on end. People pleaded for me to haul them out, whining like whipped dogs.

Then the employee got hold of me and swung me up high out of reach. Its hand was cold and hard like iron tongs kept in an ice-cream freezer. It grunted and ran toward my truck, opening the door wide and throwing me roughly inside. It made clear with wild gestures that I'd better turn around and go back, that there was no way through.

I started the engine and turned the rig around. I rolled up my window and hoped the dead weren't substantial enough to scratch paint or tear up slats.

All rules were off now.

I headed back down the road.

My load screamed like no load I'd ever had before. I was afraid they might get loose, but they didn't. I got near the Annex, and they were quiet again, too quiet for me to hear over the diesel.

The yards were deserted. The long, white-painted cement platforms and whitewashed wood-slat loading ramps were unattended. No souls in the pens. The sky was an indefinite gray, and an out-of-focus yellow sun gleamed faintly off the white walls of the employees' lounge. I stopped the truck and swung down to investigate.

There was no wind, only silence. The air was frosty without being particularly cold. What I wanted to do most was unload and get out of there, go back to Baker or Barstow or Shoshone.

I hoped that was still possible. Maybe all exits had been closed. Maybe the overseers closed them to keep any more souls from getting out.

I tried the gate latches and found I could open them. I did so and returned to the truck, swinging the rear trailer around until it was flush with the ramp. Nobody made a sound. "Go on back," I said. "Go on back. You've got more time here. Don't ask me how."

"Hello, John." That was behind me. I turned and saw an older man without any clothes on. I didn't recognize him at first. His eyes finally clued me in.

"Mr. Martin?" My high-school history teacher. I hadn't seen him in maybe twenty years. And I'd never seen him naked.

"This is not the sort of job I'd expect one of my students to take," Martin said. He laughed the smooth laugh he was famous for, the laugh that seemed to take everything he said in class and put it in perspective. "The cat's away, John. The mice are in charge now. I'm leaving, if I can."

"How long you been here?" I asked.

"I died a month ago, I think."

"You can't go," I said. The ice creeped up my throat.

"Team player," Martin said. "Still the screwball team player, even when the team doesn't give a damn what you do."

I wanted to explain, but he walked away toward the Annex and the road out. Looking back over his shoulder, he said, "Get smart, John. Things aren't what they seem." I last saw him shaking his head as he rounded the corner of the Annex.

The dead in my load had pried loose some of the ramp slats and were jumping off the rear trailer. Those in the forward trailer were screaming and carrying on, shaking the whole rig.

Responsibility, shit, I thought. As the dead followed after Mr. Martin I unhitched both trailers. Then I got in the cab and swung around away from the Annex onto the incoming road. "Sure as anything," I said, "I'm going to quit."

The road out seemed awfully long. I was taking a route that I'd never been on before, and I had no way of knowing if it would put me where I wanted to be. But I hung in there for two hours, running the truck dead-out on the flats.

The air was getting grayer, like somebody turning down the contrast on a TV set. I switched on the high beams, but they didn't help. By now I was shaking in the cab and saying to myself, *nobody deserves this. Nobody deserves going to Hell no matter what they did.* I was scared. It was getting colder.

Three hours, and I saw the Annex and yards ahead of me again. The road had looped back. I swore and slowed the rig to a crawl. The loading docks had been set on fire. Dead were wandering around with no idea what to do or where to go. I sped up and drove over through the few that were on the road. They'd come up, and the truck's bumper would hit them and I wouldn't feel a thing, like they weren't there. I'd see them in the rearview mirror, getting up after being knocked over. Just knocked over. Then I was away from the loading docks, and there was no doubt about it this time.

I was heading straight for Hell.

The disembarkation terminal was on fire, too. Buy beyond it the City was bright and white and untouched. For the first time I drove past the terminal and took the road into the City. It was either that or stay on the flats with everything screwy. Inside, I thought, maybe they'd have things under control.

The truck roared through the gate between two white pillars, maybe seventy or eight feet thick and as tall as the Washington Monument. I didn't see anybody, employees or dead. Once I was through the pillars, and it came as a shock—

There was no City, no walls, just the road winding along and countryside in all directions, even behind.

The countryside was covered with shacks, houses, little clusters and big clusters. Everything was tightly packed, people working together on one hill, people sitting on their porches, walking along paths, turning to stare at me as the rig barreled on through. No employees—no monstrosities of any sort. No flames. No bloody lakes or rivers.

This must be the outside part, I thought. Deeper inside it would be worse.

Another hour of driving through that calm landscape, and the truck ran out of fuel. I coasted to the side and stepped down from the cab, very nervous.

I lit up my last cigarette and leaned against the fender, shaking a little. But the shaking was running down, and a tight kind of calm was replacing it.

The landscape was still condensed, crowded, but nobody looked tortured. No screaming, no eternal agony. Trees and shrubs and grass hills and thousands and thousands of little houses.

It took about ten minutes for the inhabitants to get around to investigating me. Two men came strolling over to my truck and nodded cordially. Both of them were middle-aged and healthy looking, just like they were alive. I nodded back.

"We were betting whether you're one of the drivers or not," the first, a black-haired fellow, said. He wore a simple handwoven shirt and pants. "That so?"

"I am."

"You're lost then."

I agreed. "Maybe you can tell me just where I am?"

"Hell," said the second man, younger by a few years and just wearing shorts. The way he said it was like you might say you came from Los Angeles or Long Beach. Nothing big, nothing dramatic.

"We've heard rumors there's been problems outside," a woman said, coming up to join us. She was about sixty and skinny. She looked like she should be twitchy and nervous but she acted rock-steady. They were all rock-steady.

"There's some kind of strike," I said. "I don't know what it is, but I'm looking for an employee to tell me."

"They don't usually come this far in," the first man said. "We run things here. Or rather, nobody tells us what to do."

"You're alive?" the woman asked, a curious hunger in her voice. Others were coming around to join us, a whole crowd. They didn't try to touch. They stood their ground and stared and talked.

"I can't take you back," I said. "I don't know how to get there myself."

"We can't go back," the woman said. "That's not our place. Maybe you could just listen to us, you know?"

More people were coming, and I was getting nervous again. I stood my ground, trying to seem calm, and the dead gathered around me, looking at one another and then at me, looking eager.

"I never thought of anybody but myself," one said. Another interrupted with, "Man, I fucked my whole life away, I hated everybody and everything. I was burned out—"

"I thought I was the greatest. I could pass judgment on everybody—"

"I was the stupidest goddamn woman you ever saw. I was a sow, a pig. I farrowed kids and let them run wild, without no guidance. I was stupid and cruel, too. I used to hurt things—"

"Never cared for anyone. Nobody ever cared for me. I was left to rot in the middle of a city, and I wasn't good enough not to rot."

"Everything I did was a lie after I was about twelve years old—"

"Listen to me, Mister, because it hurts, it hurts so bad—"

I backed up against my truck. They were lining up now, getting organized, not like any mob. I had crazy thought they were behaving better than any people on Earth, but these were the damned.

An ex-cop told me what he did to people in jails. An ex-Jesus freak told me that knowing Jesus in your heart wasn't enough. "Because I should have made it, man, I should have made it."

135

"A time came and I was just broken by it all, broke myself really. Just kept stepping on myself and making all the wrong decisions—"

They confessed to me, and I began to cry. Their faces were so clear and so pure, yet here they were, confessing, and except maybe for specific things—like the fellow who had killed Ukrainians after the Second World War in Russian camps—they didn't sound any worse than the crazy sons of bitches I called friends who spent their lives in trucks or bars or whorehouses.

They were all recent. I got the impression the deeper into Hell you went, the older the damned became, which made sense; Hell just got bigger, each crop of the damned got bigger, with more room on the outer circles.

"We wasted it," someone said. "You know what my greatest sin was? I was dull. Dull and cruel. I never saw beauty. I saw only dirt. I loved the dirt, and the clean just passed me by."

Pretty soon my tears were uncontrollable. I kneeled down beside the truck, hiding my head, but they kept coming by and confessing. Hundreds must have passed, orderly, talking quietly, gesturing with their hands.

Then they stopped. Someone had told them to back away, that they were too much for me. I took my face out of my hands, and a young-seeming fellow stood looking down on me. "You all right?" he asked.

I nodded, but my insides were like broken glass. With every confession I had seen myself, and with every tale of sin I had felt an answering echo.

"Someone's going to be taking me here soon," I mumbled. The young fellow helped me up to my feet, and he cleared a way around my truck.

"Yeah, but not yet," he said. "You don't belong here yet." He opened the door to my cab, and I got back inside.

"I don't have any fuel," I said.

He smiled that sad smile they all had and stood on the step, up close to my ear. "One of the employees is bound to get around to you after they take care of the disturbances." He seemed a lot more sophisticated than the others. I looked at him maybe a little queerly, like there was some explaining in order.

"Yeah, I know all that stuff," he said. "I was a driver once. Then I got promoted. What are they all doing back there?" He gestured up the road. "They're really messing things up now, aren't they?"

"I don't know," I said, wiping my eyes and cheeks with my sleeve.

"You go back, and tell them all that this revolt on the outer circles, it's what I expected. Tell them Charlie's here and that I warned them. Word's getting around."

"Word?"

"About who's in charge. Just tell them Charlie knows and I warned them."

I closed my eyes. Some shadow passed over. The young fellow and everybody else seemed to recede. I felt rather than saw my truck being picked up like a toy.

In the cab in the parking lot of a truck stop in Bakersfield, I jerked awake, pulled my cap away from my eyes, and looked around. It was about noon. There was a union hall in Bakersfield. I checked, and my truck was full of diesel, so I started her up and drove to the union hall.

I knocked on the door of the office. I went in and recognized the old dude who had given me the job in the first place. I was tired, and I smelled bad, but I wanted to get it all done with now.

He recognized me but didn't know my name until I told him. "I can't work the run anymore," I said. "I'm not the one for it. I don't feel right driving them when I know I'm going to be there myself, like as not."

"Okay," he said, slow and careful, sizing me up with a knowing eye. "But you're out. You're busted then. No more driving, no more work for us, no more work for any union we support. It'll be lonely."

"I'll take that kind of lonely any day," I said.

"Okay." That seemed to be that. I headed for the door and stopped with my hand on the knob.

"One more thing," I said. "Why there's so much trouble in the outer circles. I met Charlie. He says to tell you word's getting around about who's in charge, and that's why."

The old dude's knowing eye went sort of glassy. "You're the fellow ended up inside?"

I nodded.

"You wait a minute. Out in the office."

I waited and heard him talking on the phone. He came out and was smiling and put his hand on my shoulder.

"Listen, John, I'm not sure we should let you quit so easy. Word is, you stuck around and tried to help when everyone else ran. The company appreciates that. You've been with us a long time, reliable driver, maybe we should argue with you a bit, know what I mean? Give you some incentive to stay. I'm sending you to Denver to talk with a fellow, an important fellow."

The way he said it, I intuited there wasn't too much choice and I'd better not fight it. You work union long enough and you know when to keep your mouth shut and go along with them.

They put me up in a motel and fed me, and by late morning I was on my way to Denver. I was in a black union car with a silent driver and air conditioning and some *Newsweek*s to keep me company.

Saturday morning, bright and early, I stood in front of a very large corporate building with no sign out front and with a bank on the bottom floor. I went past the bank and up to the very top.

A secretary met me, pretty but with her hair done up very tight and her jaw grimly square. She didn't like me. By her looks she'd be friendly only to insurance salesmen and visiting preachers. She let me into the next office, though.

I'd seen the fellow before, I wasn't sure where. He wore a narrow tie and a tasteful but conservative, small-checked suit. His shirt was pastel blue, and there was a big Rembrandt Bible on his desk, sitting on the glass next to an alabaster penholder. He shook my hand firmly and perched on the edge of the desk.

"First, let me congratulate you on your bravery. We've had some reports from the...uh...field, and we're hearing nothing but good about you." He smiled like that fellow on TV who's always asking the audience to give him some help. Then his face got sincere and serious. I honestly believe he was sincere; he was also very well trained in dealing with not-very-bright people.

"I hear you have a report for me. From Charlie Frick."

"He said his name was Charlie." I told him the story. "What I'm curious about, what did he mean, this thing about who's in charge?"

"Charlie was in the organization until last year. He died in a car accident. I'm shocked to hear he got the Low Road."

He didn't look shocked. "To tell the truth, he was bit of a troublemaker here. Maybe I'm shocked but not surprised."

He smiled brightly again, and his eyes got large, and there was a little too much animation in his face. He had on these MacArthur wire-rimmed glasses too big for his eyes.

"What did he mean?"

"John, I'm proud of all our drivers. You don't know how proud we all are of you folks down there who are stuck doing the dirty work. Hauling in sinners."

"What did Charlie mean?"

"The abortionists and pornographers, the hustlers and muggers and murderers. Atheists and heathens and idol worshippers. Surely there must be some satisfaction in keeping the land clean. Sort of a giant sanitation squad, you people keep the scum away from the good folks, the good and obedient workers. Now we know that driving's maybe the hardest job we have in the company, and that not everyone can stay on the Low Road indefinitely. Still, we'd like you to stay on. Not as a driver—unless you really wish to continue, for the satisfaction of a tough job. No, if you want to move up—and you've earned it by now, surely—we have a place for you here. A place where you'll be comfortable and—"

"I've already said I want out. You're acting like I'm hot stuff, and I'm just shit. You know that, I know that. Down there they all started confessing to me like they was Ancient Mariners or something. What is going on?"

His face hardened on me.

"It isn't so easy up here either, buster." The "buster" bit got me. I pushed up from the chair. When I stood, he held up his hand conciliatory-like and pursed his lips as he nodded.

"Sorry. There's incentive, there's certainly a reason why you should want to work here. If you're so convinced you're on your way to the Low Road, you can work it off, you know."

"How can you say that?"

Bright smile. "Charlie told you something about who's in charge here."

Now it was getting dangerous. I could smell it, like with the union boss.

"He said that's why there's trouble."

"It comes every now and then. We put it down gentle. I tell you we really need good people, compassionate people. People who listen to even the damned. We need them to help with the choosing."

"Choosing?"

"Surely you don't think the Boss does all the choosing directly?"

I couldn't think of a thing to say.

"Listen, the Boss—let me tell you. A long time ago, the Boss decided to create a new kind of worker, with more decision-making abilities. You and me and all the rest of mankind." Smile. Fable time, kiddies. "Some of the supervisors disagreed, especially when the Boss said we'd be around for a long, long time. We'd have immortal souls. When the Boss got his program going strong, giving us the freedom to choose between good and evil, it was inevitable that a few would choose evil. You could think of it as waste—nuclear waste. There are benefits to the program—good people, hard workers. And there's garbage, too; poison, toxic garbage. The garbage builds up after a time—those we don't want to go along, not good workers, you might say.

"A few turn out to be...chronically unemployable. Can't find it in themselves to go along with the program. Get out of line. What do you do with them? Can't dispose of them by just making them go away; the rule is, they're immortal. Poison, but they last forever. So—"

"Chronically unemployable?" He was being mighty clever. *And what do you do with nuclear waste? You shit-can it. Put it in the biggest, deepest shit can....*

139

"The damned. You're a union man. Think of what it must feel like to be out of work...forever. The Boss's work is very important, there's no denying that. He's got big plans for us all, and if the Boss can't use you, then nobody can."

I knew the feeling, both the way he meant it and the reality behind the comparison. *What do you do with the chronically unemployable? You put them on welfare...forever.* So what was Hell, shit can or welfare dump? I got the impression this fellow considered it a shit can.

But a good union man knows there isn't anybody who can't do some sort of work, can't be persuaded to be useful some way. Only management thinks of shit-canning or welfaring. Only management thinks in terms of human waste.

"The Boss feels the project half succeeded, so He doesn't want to dump it completely. But He doesn't want to be bothered with all the pluses and minuses, the bookkeeping."

"You're in charge," I said, my blood cooling quickly.

And I knew where I had seen him before.

On television.

God's right-hand man.

And human. Flesh and blood.

We ran Hell.

He nodded. "Now, that's not the sort of thing we'd like to get around."

"You're in charge, and you let the drivers take their perks on the loads, you let—"

I stopped, instinct telling me that if I didn't, I would soon be on a rugged trail with no turnaround.

"I'll tell you the truth, John. I have only been in charge here for a year, and my predecessor let things get out of hand. He wasn't a religious man, John, and he thought this was a job like any other, where you could compromise now and then. I know that isn't so. There's no compromise here, and we'll straighten those inequities and bad decisions out very soon. You'll help us, I hope. You may know more about the problems than we do."

"How do you qualify for a job like this?" I asked. "And who offered it to you?"

"Not the Boss, if that's what you're getting at, John. It's been kind of traditional. You may have heard about me. I'm the one, when there was all this talk about after-death experiences and everyone was seeing bright light and beauty, I'm the one who wondered why no one was seeing the other side. I found people who had almost died and had seen Hell, and I turned their lives around. The management in the company decided a fellow with my ability could do good work here. And so I'm here. And I'll tell you, it wasn't easy. I sometimes wish we had a little more help from the Boss, a little more guidance, but we don't, and somebody has to do it." Again the smile.

I put on my mask.

"Of course," I said. I hoped that a gradual increase in piety would pass his sharp-eyed muster.

"And you can see how this all makes you much more valuable to the organization."

I let light dawn slowly.

"We'd hate to lose you now, John. Not when there's security, so much security, working for us. I mean, here we learn the real ins and outs of salvation."

I let him talk at me until he looked at his watch, and all the time I nodded and considered and tried to think of the best ploy. Then I eased myself into a turnabout. I did some confessing until his discomfort was stretched too far—I was keeping him from an important appointment—and made my concluding statement.

"I just wouldn't feel right up here," I said. "I've been a driver all my life. I'd just want to keep on, doing my bit wherever I'm best suited."

"Keep your present job?" he said, tapping his shoe on the side of the desk.

"Lord, yes," I said, grateful as could be.

Then I asked him for his autograph. He smiled real big and gave it to me, God's right hand man, who had prayed with presidents.

I'm on the road again. I'm talking to people here and there, being real cautious. Maybe I'll get caught.

When it looks like things are getting chancy, I'll take my rig back down the road. Then I'm not sure what I'll do.

I don't want to let everybody loose. But I want to know who else is ending up on the Low Road who shouldn't be. People unpopular with God's right-hand man.

My message is simple.

The crazy folks are running the asylum.

Maybe I'll start hauling trucks back out instead of in. Christ was supposed to be the last person to do that. He went to Hell and rescued the righteous...*harrowed* Hell, that's what they had always called it in my Bible school classes.

If I don't make it, if they're too powerful and too sly, then I'll end up riding in back, not in front.

But until then, I'm doing my bit. It's not as if I'm asking for help by telling you this. But you're a union man, aren't you? We could shut it down, you know. Truck drivers harrowing Hell. Isn't that a thought?

Adeste Fideles

Frederik Pohl

Frederik Pohl has been one of the genre's shaping forces—as writer, editor, agent, and anthologist—for more than fifty years. He was the founder of the *Star* series, science fiction's first continuing anthology series, and was the editor of the *Galaxy* group of magazines form 1960 to 1969. He has won several Nebula and Hugo Awards, as well as the American Book Award and the Prix Apollo. His novels include *Gateway, Man Plus, Beyond the Blue Event Horizon, Mining the Oort,* and *The World at the End of Time.* His short fiction has been collected in several collections, the most recent of which are *Planets Three, Pohlstars,* and *BiPohl.*

"Adeste Fideles" is a moving off-planet Christmas story featuring an unlikely hero.

Adeste Fideles

Frederik Pohl

A Christmas was only an abstraction on Mars, even for Henry Steegman. The calendars didn't match; Earth's winter solstice had nothing to do with Martian timekeeping. But they kept to the twelve familiar months, to make it easier to count up how long before they could leave for the slow-orbit return trip. As the calendar crept past November and Thanksgiving and crawled toward the holiday, Steegman thought more and more about wrapping paper and Christmas cards and, above all, Christmas trees.

The Christmas before, the community had pulled itself together and made an effort. Most of them were still alive then, and even fairly healthy; so they flanged together something tree-shaped—sort of tree-shaped—out of foam plastic and transparent piping. After it was sprayed, it did at least look green. It didn't smell like a tree. But once they had hung it with bright red and green micromatrices from the spare-parts bins and festooned it with instrument lights, it did cheer up the common room. They went further than that, too. They had even made a Santa Claus suit out of somebody's red flannel long johns, stuffed with somebody else's sweaters and bearded with some other body's curly wig. It made Santa Claus's beard platinum blond rather than white, but that was the least of the incongruities. Santa Claus had very few gifts to give them. For most of them, not even the gift of survival.

Henry Steegman was not an important member of his community of Mars explorers. He was neither a xenoanthropologist nor a xenobiologist, nor did he have any of the special skills that made the lives of the survivors fairly tolerable—or almost—like food chemist, power technician, or medic. Steegman was a construction engineer. That is, he drove tractors. He drove interesting

145

kinds of tractors: a nuclear one that crawled through the Martian rock and melted out tunnels, as well as two or three solar-powered ones that leveled and shaped the surface of the planet, twenty meters up from where they lived. He didn't usually drive any of them in person. The places where his tractors went were not very hospitable to human beings. When his services were needed, which was less and less often, as the captain and the council decided that there was really no more need ever to build new domes and explore new anomalies the gravitometers pointed out for them, he sat before a television screen and commanded his tractors by remote control.

That was more or less Christmassy, too. It was like having the world's biggest—anyway, Mars's biggest—set of electric trains to play with.

It was about that useful, too, for a community of thirty-eight, once two hundred and four, mostly sick human beings.

Since there was no necessity for much activity of any kind anymore, Steegman was encouraged to play with his toys whenever he wanted to. It kept him out of the way, and it cost nothing. It didn't cost the community valuable working time, because there wasn't a whole lot Steegman was able to do. Radiation sickness in his case had attacked the nerves. He was likely to spasm when he tried anything very demanding. Since the diggers were nine-tenths automatic he couldn't do much harm there. But he couldn't be trusted with anything as delicate as, say, changing bedpans for the dying. And it certainly didn't cost any more than they could afford in power. As long as the photovoltaic cascades were given plenty of time to recharge, they provided plenty of power for the surface tractors. For the tunneler there were stocks far beyond any reasonable expectation of need of fuel rods, salvaged from the wreck of the slave rocket. The instrumentation it bore was all mangled, but there's not much you can do to stubby, heavily clad rods of radionuclides. There was also plenty of food, water, heat, and light.

The community was really only short of three things. People. Purpose. And hope.

Hope had gone for the most of them, along with purpose, when the slave rocket crashed. The expedition was there to conduct scientific investigations. When the drone toppled off its axis of thrust, it split open, blew its fuel tanks, wrecked every delicate part of the instruments, which was most of their parts, and drenched the surface with radionuclides. The misguidance of the rocket wasn't the only thing that went wrong. Someone, unforgivably, in the frantic rush to salvage what they could, had brought hot piping down into the cavern; someone else had hooked it into the water recirculators; it had simmered there, seeping powdery fission products into their drinking water for more than a day before someone else thought to put a dosimeter to his coffee cup.

By then, of course, it was all contaminated. They couldn't live without water. They drank it, glumly watching the dosimeters go into the black. As soon as they could, they began to melt water out of the permafrost under the Martian polar ice cap, only a dozen kilometers away; but by then the people began to get sick. The dosage was not terribly high. Just enough to kill, but not very quickly.

There was one other bad effect.

NASA's vast and powerful public relations machine fought for them most courageously, but the odds were too much. No matter how many tearjerker TV interviews NASA ran with weeping wives and children, no matter what presidential proclamations and prayers, the public image of the expedition was robust against propaganda. *Bunch of clowns,* the public thought. *Busted their rocket ship. Ruined their equipment. Got themselves killed.*

Fortunately for the American spirit, there was a new black American tennis player who won the Wimbledon that year, and a TV star who actually wrestled grizzly bears in his spare time.

The public found new heroes.

And thought rarely, if at all, about the spoiled heroes on Mars.

So on what the calendars said was the twenty-first of December Henry Steegman got out of his bunk, felt his gums to see if they were bleeding, and went to the common room for a leisurely breakfast. He peered in first to make sure Captain Seerseller wasn't up unusually early. He wasn't. The only other person there was Sharon bas Ramirez, the biochemist, and when Henry had picked his almost-hash out of the freezer and passed it through the microwave, he joined her. Sharon bas Ramirez was one of the few survivors who treated Steegman like a worthwhile human being, no doubt because it was Steegman who had brought back samples of organic-contaminated rock for her. "Life on Mars!" their dispatch had read, and they had hoped for a wonderful rebirth of excitement back home. But it wasn't really anything alive, only chemicals that might once have been. And besides, that day the TV star had wrestled a female grizzly with cubs.

"Henry," said Sharon bas Ramirez, "do me a favor, will you? See if you can bring back some better samples."

She was looking very tired. He ate his almost-hash slowly, studying her: black patches under her eyes, fatigue in the set of her jaw.

"What kind of samples?" he asked.

She shrugged wearily. "You cook them with the heat of the drill," she complained, "so the structure gets degraded."

"I tried cold rock drills, Sharon! I even went out myself! I even swiped some blasting powder and a detonator and—"

"Don't get excited, Henry," she said sharply, reaching over to wipe some spilled hash off his coverall. He muttered an apology, calming himself down. "Maybe you can find a fissure somewhere," she said. "Try, anyway? Because I'm a biochemist, not a candy striper, and I get real tired of feeding the sick ones because I don't have anything more important to do."

"I'll try," he promised, and thought hard about how he could keep that promise, all the way to his handler room.

He took the deep tunneler this time, pondering how he could oblige Sharon bas Ramirez. He pushed it through deep Martian rock, twenty kilometers north of the camp. He was not paying strict attention to what he was doing. He was humming "Adeste Fideles," part of his mind thinking about Sharon bas Ramirez, part of it worrying about the latest one to begin to lose blood rapidly—sickly, pale little Terry Kaplan—when the instruments revealed a temperature surge before the nose of the borer.

He shut the machine down at once and palped the rock ahead with sonic probes. The dials showed it was very thin. The sonar scan showed a lumpy, mostly ball-shaped patch, quite large, filled with white-traced, shadowy shapes.

Henry Steegman grinned. A cavern! Even better than a fissure in the rock! He could break in at one end, let it cool, bring the borer back home, get in it himself, and ride back to collect all the samples Sharon could want, uncooked. He started the drill again on low power and gentled the tunneler another meter along its course.

The instruments told him that he had broken through.

Steegman shut the tunneler down and thought for a minute.

Good practice required that he let the rock cool for half an hour before opening the shutters over the delicate and rarely used optical system. He could do that. Or he could start it back without looking and then go in person, which would take two or three hours anyway.

He shrugged and stretched and leaned back, waiting for time to pass, with a smile on his face. Sharon was going to be real pleased! Especially if there turned out to be anything organic in the rock of the cavern—though of course, he cautioned himself, that wasn't guaranteed. Was pretty damn rare, actually. The crust of the planet Mars was very cold and very lifeless; it was only in a few places, where a vagrant stirring of deep-down heat made a patch minutely warmer than what was around it, that you could say it was anything capable of supporting a microbe, anyway. Still, they were well under the polar cap with the digger now. There would at least be residual water, here and there...

When the time was up he looked, and in the searchlight beam, he saw that the cavern was there, all right, but it wasn't exactly empty. It wasn't natural, either. It was a great bubble laced with what might have been catwalks and what looked like balconies, and all about it were what seemed to be shelves and what could be called tables. Some of them had things on them.

Henry Steegman didn't know what it was he had found, but it had a funnily suggestive look to it. He didn't make the connection for nearly twenty minutes, though. By then his yells had brought others into the control room.

They began to yell, too. Captain Seerseller ordered Henry back out of the way because they were all afraid, naturally, that he would get too excited and knock something over or push the wrong button, but he could catch glimpses of what was on the screen and hear what everyone was shouting to each other. He heard perfectly when Marty Lawless yelled, "You know what it is? It's a Martian Macy's!"

By the time Steegman had painfully inched his drill out of the way, he was almost alone at the base. Not quite alone. The walking sick, Terry Kaplan and Bruce DeAngelis and one or two others who were well enough to look but far from well enough to make the trip to the cavern, were wheezing and gasping behind him, but everyone else was gone.

The tunnel from the base camp to the "department store" was thirty-three kilometers and a bit, the last five still unlined. Wheeled vehicles couldn't go down the unlined part, but no one was willing to wait for lining. So the first two parties drove, six or eight at a time in the big-wheeled tunnel buggies, as far as the surfaced section of the tunnel went.

Then they walked, in air masks and backpacks, because the department store was by light-years the most astonishing discovery the expedition had made on Mars, and therefore the thing that most nearly justified the loss of nearly all their lives.

They *almost* all went, all but the ones too sick...and Henry Steegman. The discoverer of the department store was not allowed to enter it.

It wasn't just that he was needed to get the big borer out of the tunnel so people could clamber through. Captain Seerseller's last order had made that clear. It was, "You stay here, Steegman, you understand? No matter what."

So for the first ten minutes Steegman and his hovering casualties saw nothing on the screen but the sonar scan, reporting on what sorts of rock the drill tractor was nibbling through. Then Steegman turned it off and switched channels to the portable cameras in the first buggy. "Is that it?" little Terry Kaplan asked, hoarding breath to speak. "It looks...looks"—she took a deep breath —"looks different."

"It's only the tunnel," Steegman said absently, watching as the field of view swung dizzingly around. Then the first party was inside, and whoever was carrying that camera was glad to set it down on automatic scan. So Steegman watched jealously as the others piled into the wonderland he had found for them, each one more excited than the other. Marty Lawless, six feet six and fifty years old, pulled his spidery body in and out of prism-shaped structures inside the great hollow bubble and cried, "It really is a store! Kind of a store! Like an enclosed market? Like a great big shopping mall, where you can find almost anything."

"It could be a warehouse," objected Manuel Andrew Applegate, senior surviving archaeologist, annoyed at the presumption of someone who actually was a communications engineer.

"There's nothing on most of the shelves, Manny-Anny," Captain Seerseller pointed out.

Lawless answered that one, too. "The perishables have perished, of course," he cried. "God knows how old this is! But it's a store, all right. A suq. A bazaar!"

And back in the control booth Terry Kaplan whispered to Steegman, with what sounded like the last of her breath, "It really is a Macy's, Henry. Oh, how Morton is going to love this!"

And no one answered, because Terry was a widow. Morton Kaplan had died more than three months before.

And so the expedition began to live again—as much as it could with most of its people already buried under the Martian soil. Pictures, samples, diagrams, data of all kinds—everyone wanted to put his speciality to work at once, no, not after the archaeological team made its inventories, but now, me first! Not only were they thrilled at what they had found, they were actually getting signs of real interest from Earth, for the first time in many months.

It didn't happen right away. The round-trip travel time for talking to NASA Command was less than thirty minutes, but no one at NASA Command was paying attention when the first excited messages came in. Hours later, some no-doubt-bored comm specialist decided he might, after all, earn his day's pay by looking over the last batch of accumulated tapes. And did. And boredom vanished.

It was a good time for Earth to take an interest in Mars again. The movie star had lost his last bout with a grizzly, terminally; and there was a new Czechoslovakian kid burning up the tennis courts. So the network news carried the pictures, and there were special half-hour reports every night after the late news, and NASA's P.R. people were in heaven. Send us more, they begged. Not just some crummy old archaeological drawings and photographs. Personalities! *Interviews!*

Interviews with, most of all, that one hero of the expedition, whoever he was, who had first discovered the Martian Macy's.

Since the captain was well and truly NASA trained, he saw his duty and did it. They co-opted Sharon bas Ramirez away from her delightful duties of studying moldering samples of definitely organic substances from the store and put her to work patching Henry Steegman's old tunic; the one surviving surgeon was taken off the wards of the dying to cut Henry's hair and shave him; and they put him in front of the TV camera.

Captain Seerseller, of course, did the interview himself—he remembered *all* of his training. They found the two best-looking chairs in the colony and planted them before a camera, with a table containing a bizarre sort of unrusted metal implement between them. It was the most spectacular piece the archaeologists had so far allowed them to bring in.

Then the captain gestured the camera to himself. When it was on, he smiled directly into the lens. "Hello, my friends," he said. "Mars reporting. Under my leadership the expedition has continued to survey this old planet, on its surface and under, and we have just made the most wonderful discovery in human history. Under my direction Henry Steegman was extending our network of exploratory tunnels. He broke through into a sealed underground chamber of approximately twenty thousand cubic meters volume. It is divided into five levels. All levels are built over with triangular prism-shaped structures. Each triangular 'booth' contains a different kind of item. Our specialists have made a preliminary inspection, on my orders, and have reached the tentative conclusion that the objects are merchandise and that the cavern itself was the equivalent of a Martian department store. This object," he said, picking up the gleaming thing, "was perhaps a scientific instrument or possibly even a household utensil. Of course, most of the contents of this 'store' are rusted, decayed, or simply vanished—they have been there for a long, long time. So I have ordered our archaeologists to exercise extreme care in their handling so that no valuable data might be lost."

The camera focus had pulled back to show the stand the object had come from, and also Henry Steegman, digging into one ear with a finger while he was listening in fascination to the captain. Steegman was not at all sure what he was supposed to be doing. His instructions had been, Just relax. But it was hard to relax with the captain's occasional frosty, sidelong looks. He was feeling that funny, buzzy sensation that meant his ruined nervous system was being overstimulated again; he closed his eyes and breathed deeply.

"Now," said the captain, with an edge in his voice, "I want to introduce to you the man who, carrying out my directions, made the first penetration of this Martian marvel, Henry Steegman."

Steegman jerked his eyes open and blinked at the camera. He didn't like having it look at him; his eyes wavered away but only onto the monitor, which was worse. He could see that he was shaking. He tried to control it, which made it worse. "Henry," said the captain, "tell us how you felt when you broke through into the cavern."

Steegman thought for a moment and then said uncertainly, "Real good?"

"Real good! Well, we all did that, Henry," said the captain with audible forbearance. "But when you completed this task I had assigned you and saw for the first time proof that there had once been life on Mars—even civilized life!— were you surprised? Excited? Happy? Did it make you want to laugh? Or cry? Or both at once?"

"Oh, I see what you mean," Henry said, pondering. "Pretty much that kind of thing, I guess."

"And did it make you realize that all the great sacrifices of blood and treasure—the lives of so many of us, and the wonderful support the people have given in making this venture possible—did it make you think it was all worthwhile?"

Henry had figured out a safe response. He said promptly, "I don't exactly remember that, Captain."

The captain swallowed a sigh and motioned to Mina Wandwater, the best looking of the surviving women, who came forward into camera range with a champagne bottle and a glass. "This is for you, Henry," said the captain, leaning forward to stay in range of the camera as Mina poured. "It's your just reward for carrying out my instructions so successfully!"

Henry held the glass carefully while Mina filled it, curtsied prettily to him and the captain, and withdrew. He looked at the captain for instructions.

The captain said tightly, "Drink it!"

"Right, Captain," Henry said. He stared at the glass, then suddenly jerked it to his lips. He slobbered half the contents over himself and the floor. Then— because the bottle was champagne but the contents weren't; they were something bubbly the chemists had cooked up to refill the empty—Steegman sputtered and choked. He twitched and dropped the glass and then sat there, gaping dumbly into the television camera.

It was not only a lot of trouble to keep up the morale back home, it sometimes didn't work at all. The captain gave the camera a great smile and said,

"That concludes our interview with Henry Steegman, who under my—what is it, Henry?" he asked irritably. Steegman had stopped dabbing at the mess on his tunic long enough to wave frantically at the captain.

"I just wanted to say one more thing," he pleaded. "You folks at home? I know it's a little early, but—Merry Christmas!"

They made Steegman take another physical after that, which kept him in the ward overnight, among the immobile and the dying. The surgeon studied his tests and plates and told Henry matter-of-factly, "You're going, I'm afraid. A few more weeks. Your myelin sheaths are rotted away. It's going to get worse pretty soon—that's a nice haircut, though, isn't it?"

When Henry went to the captain's office, the captain wasn't there. Neither was the surgeon, but his report had already come over the net, and the executive officer was studying it on her screen.

"You want what, Henry?" she asked. "You want to go into the *cavern?* Good lord, no! Captain Seerseller would never permit it. The surgeon's report makes it very clear, your motor reflexes are too untrustworthy, that's very delicate stuff in there, and we don't want it wrecked."

"I wouldn't hurt anything," he protested, but she wasn't listening anymore. She just waved him out.

Nobody else wanted to listen, either, though some of them tried to make it more palatable. "You wouldn't want to spoil your own discovery, would you?" Mina Wandwater asked.

"I wouldn't hurt anything," Steegman pleaded.

"Of course you wouldn't *mean* to. No," she said kindly, "you just stay out of there, okay? We just can't afford any more accidents on our record, you know."

She was gone before Steegman remembered to point out that he wasn't the one who had crashed the instrument rocket or let the fission products into the water. Sharon bas Ramirez was kinder but also busier. She looked up from the tubes of samples long enough to say, "I really can't talk to you now, Henry, but don't worry. They'll let you in sooner or later, you know."

But if it weren't sooner, it couldn't be later. Steegman said absently, "You know it's Christmas Eve?"

"Oh. So it is. Merry Christmas, Henry," she said, turning back to her lab bench.

Steegman limped back to his control booth and activated his tunneler. Then he sat moping before the screen without sending it forward. Sometimes he got pleasure out of executing circles and figure eights under the surface of Mars, drilling the old planet hollow, lacing it with wormholes and channels the likes of which it had never known. Would never know again, most likely, but would also never forget. The Martian crust was too cold to squeeze itself seamless again. The arteries Steegman gouged would stay there forever.

He turned it off and thought about the surface tractors. But he didn't like working on surface much. Oh, in those first weeks after landing—in spite of the deaths and the doom that hung over most of the survivors—what a thrill it had been! He had delighted in bulldozing ageless, eternally untrodden Martian sand and gravel into flat bases for the huge dish transmitter that sent their signals back to Earth, or in roaming out fifty or a hundred kilometers to pick up samples and bring them back for testing. Just seeing the dwarfed, distant sun was a thrill. The tiny points of hot light that were the stars were a delight. The queerly close horizon was an astonishment—they were marvels, all of them, all the time. Over every hummock there was the mystery of what Mars was all about. What would they find? A city? An oasis? A...*Martian?*

Or, as hopes for any of those dwindled, a tree?

Or a bush?

Or a thin patch of moss on a rock?

And they had found none of them. There was nothing. There was always nothing except the same sterile sand and rock or sandy ice at the beginning of the cap. Even the tiny sun and the white-hot stars weren't exciting anymore.

Steegman kicked against the rock wall under his control desk.

Then he brightened.

It was, after all, Christmas Eve!

So Henry Steegman made the long trek back to the captain's office again, pausing on the way in his own chamber. The Santa Claus suit was still there in the locker under his cot! He pulled out a knapsack, stuffed the suit in, and hurried down the corridor. Captain Seerseller was not there, and Lieutenant Tesca was not encouraging. "He's at Macy's" she said, "and really very busy, and so am I—I'm going there myself. What, a Christmas party? No, no, I can't authorize that—really, Henry," she said fairly patiently. "I don't think you understand what finding this means to us. We just don't have time for nonsense right now."

But she let Steegman hitch a ride with her. The big-wheeled buggy slid smoothly down the tunnel until they reached the unlined part; then the executive officer jumped out and left rapidly for the last kilometers. Steegman toiled patiently behind. His gait was getting worse all the time, he knew. His knees were wobbly—not painful, just sort of loosely put together, so that he was never sure his leg would support him at any stride—and his calves were beginning to ache from the unaccustomed strain on the muscles caused by his awkward foot placement. It took him an hour, but by the time he passed the side shaft where he had left the tunneler, he could already hear voices up ahead.

The loudest voice was Captain Seerseller's. He was arguing with Manuel Andrew Applegate at the entrance to the cavern. Beyond them Steegman could see the interior of the cavern as he had never seen it before. A score of bright lights had been put in place all around it, throwing shadows, illuminating bright colors and pastels, clusters of long-rusted-away metal things and heaps of heaven knew what, rotted into black grit. When the captain caught sight of Steegman he turned and blazed, "What are you doing here? I've told you to stay out of this place!"

"I wasn't coming in, Captain," Henry said humbly. "I just wanted to ask if we were going to have a Christmas party this year."

"Christmas?" the captain repeated, and Applegate next to him said, "What about Christmas? We don't have time for that, Henry. Everybody's too busy!"

"I'm not too busy, Manny-Anny," Steegman said, and the captain snorted, "Then get busy! Dig something useful!"

"I've already dug six of everything we could ever use."

"Then make some of the things bigger."

"But I've already—" Steegman began, shifting position to back away from the captain—and in the process sliding on the rubble of loose talus where the drill had broken through. He lurched against the captain.

"Oh, sorry," he said, "but nothing needs enlarging. Not even the grave-yards."

"*Go,*" snarled the captain. And Steegman went. He hesitated at the tunnel buggy, casting a look at the captain. But the captain was once again in deep argument with Manny-Anny Applegate.

Steegman sighed and started the long, limping walk back to the dome. He could not, after all, just take the buggy and leave those people marooned.

But a dozen meters down the tunnel his face brightened, his stride quickened, and he turned off into the shaft where he had left the digger. He could drive himself home! Not in that tunnel, of course. But there was nothing to stop him from making a new one.

Steegman pressed against the scarred metal of the tunneler, just where it rounded into the straight flank. He found the recessed catch. It had rock chips in it, of course; but he patiently worked them free, opened the hatch, climbed in, and made his way to the driver's seat.

The quarters were cramped, and the cabin was still uncomfortably hot from the last spate of digging. But it was his own. He pulled the Santa Claus suit out of his knapsack and rolled it up behind his head. Then he leaned back and closed his eyes.

He didn't sleep.

After a while he sat up straight, turned the idling circuits on, checked his instruments. The tunneler had communications as well as control circuits to the campsite, and Steegman considered calling back to let anyone who might care know where he was. He thought he might leave a message about how he felt too, because in fact he was beginning to feel very peculiar.

Since very few persons would really care, Steegman decided against it. He cut the communications system out entirely. Then he advanced the control for the drills and engaged the tractor motors.

There was a racketing roar of noise. The cab, and the whole tunneler, shook in short, sharp shocks. It began to move forward, down into virgin Martian rock.

Twenty minutes later Steegman began to throw up for the first time. Fortunately, he was expecting it. The pounding motion of the tunneler was enough to make anyone queasy, even if he hadn't been drinking the colony's water; and Steegman had found a receptacle—actually, it was a case for one of the fuel rods—to throw up. When he was through he was sweating and lightheaded, but peaceful.

He advanced the speed of the tunneler a bit and bored on.

He had no particular objective in mind except to go on. He liked having no objectives. It was how you found unexpected things. At the head of the borer, where the immense, terribly hard, tough teeth ground into the rock, were two flush-mounted poppers. Every second each of them emitted a shattering pistol crack of sound, the frequencies just different enough from each other, and sufficiently unlike any of the spectrum of noises the chewing of the borer itself produced, to be distinguishable by the sonar receivers inside the shell. Every second they reached out and felt for flaws or faults or soft spots and displayed the results on the screen before Steegman. Steegman didn't have a windshield, of course. There was no glass strong enough to fit the shell of the tunneler, and generally nothing to see if there had been. But the screen was as good.

Steegman leaned back, watching the patterns change before him. What he was looking for, mostly, were soft spots in the rock ahead—an intrusion of lighter rock, maybe, or a lens of clathrate, the ice-and-solids mix that was the principal Martian source of liquid water.

Or—perhaps!—another cavern...

It was a pity, Steegman reflected, that he was going to die soon.

It was not a horror. The first shock of that sort of realization had long worn calloused. He had known for a year that his life would be short and had been certain almost that long that he would not survive to the liftoff, much less through the endless return to low Earth orbit and home. So there were pleasures he would never have again. Item, he would never see clouds in a blue sky. Item, he would never swim. Item, he would never get a chance to see the marvels he had not got around to—Niagara Falls, Stonehenge, the Great Wall of China. Never again a full moon or a rainbow or a thunderstorm; never hail a taxi on a city street; never walk into a movie theater with a pretty woman; never—

Never any of those things. On the other hand, he comforted himself, there was hardly anyone who would ever see the things he had seen on Mars!

Even what he was seeing now on the screen, why, it was wonderful! He was kilometers beyond the "department store" now, far under the thin smear of dry ice and water ice that was the North polar cap. The false-color images on the screen formed pretty patterns, constantly changing as the tunneler moved forward and the sonars got better information on what was before them. If there was any tectonic activity at all on Mars, it lay not far from here, where echo sounders had indicated an occasional plume of warmer, lighter, softer matter— even liquid water in a few sparse, small places. Peter Braganza, the head geologist, had likened some of them to the white smoke/black smoke fountains at the bottom of some of the earth's seas, slow upwellings of warmth from the tiny residual core heat of the old planet.

It was from plumes like those that Steegman had brought back the samples that thrilled Sharon bas Ramirez. Organics! It was almost certainly organic matter, she thought, at least—but the heat of the tunneler had boiled the water out of the minerals and had cooked the carbon compounds as well. If they had just had some of the instruments they should have had, the nuclear magnetic resonance scanner in particular, she could have been sure...but the NMR equipment had been on the crashed rocket.

Steegman leaned forward, peering at the screen.

A gray blob on the lower right-hand corner had changed to pale blue as the sonars got a better reading on it. Clathrate? Not exactly. Liquid water? Perhaps. Steegman couldn't get a temperature reading that meant anything while the drills were going, but things did warm up a little as one approached the plumes. It was quite possible that water could be liquid here. He was humming "Silent Night" to himself as he studied the screen.

It was unusually pretty now. It was almost a hologram, or at least it gave the illusion of depth. What the poppers scanned, the sonar computers examined and analyzed and sculpted into the scene before him.

What they displayed was almost always more intricate and beautiful than anything he would have seen drilling through the crust of the earth. Even the most homogeneous of earthly rock shows differences of texture and density. On Mars, where the crust had been almost all cold for almost forever, there were countless splits and cracks and fault lines to make a pleasing tracery of color streaks and blobs.

It was funny, Steegman thought, that they didn't look really random.

He had to pause for another seizure of vomiting, holding the canister close to his lips against the cruelly sharp lurches of the tunneler. When he was through he put it aside, still staring at the screen. He tried to make sense of what he was seeing.

Almost ahead, a little below the level he was drilling through, there was a prism-shaped tubular structure that was displayed in golden yellow. Not clathrate! Not even liquid water. It stretched off to the left and away as far as the sound probe could reach in one direction. In the other, for a hundred meters or so back toward the "department store" he had long ago passed, until it came up against a hard new—geologically new—intrusion.

Smiling to himself in pleasure, Steegman inched the nose of the borer down and around to intersect it.

When it was huge before him, there was a lurch, and the cutting nose spun madly.

That was a surprise! There were not many caverns under the Martian surface. Steegman quickly shut the blades off. On the tractor treads alone, dead slow, the tunneler shoved its way through a few crumbling edges of rock. When it was free, he turned everything off and paused to consider the situation.

He was really very tired, he realized. Although he was glad that the painful jolting of the tunneler had stopped, he was still very queasy. He cautiously allowed himself a few sips of water from the tunneler's supplies. When he did not immediately throw them up again, he felt more cheerful.

He thought for a moment of opening the communications link again to report his find. The geologists would surely want to investigate this unusual structure....

But Steegman wanted to investigate it himself.

He pulled on his air mask and, with less strength than he had expected, was finally able to force the front hatch open against the gravel that had accumulated outside it. It was hot.

When he stepped cautiously out onto the talus, it burned his feet. He hopped back into the tunneler, rubbing one foot and looking around for what he needed. Lights. There was a shoulder pack of batteries and a hand lamp.

Clothing, too, because apart from the rock that had been heated by the drill the tunnel was quite cold.

He grinned to himself, took the garments from the back of the seat, and pulled them on, even the platinum-blond beard.

He engaged the tractor treads and inched forward, past the rubble where he had broken through, as far as he could until the motionless drill teeth crunched against the far wall.

Then he stepped out onto the smooth, flat floor of the tunnel, which was no geologic feature at all.

Although his vision was blurring and his breathing had become painful, Steegman was sure of that. The tunnel was as much an artifact as the "department store." Crystalline walls, undimmed by the millennia, bounced back the light of his hand lamp. The cross section of the tunnel was triangular, with rounded corners. Natural formations did not come in such shapes.

What price Niagara Falls now! Steegman laughed out loud in triumph. His duty was clear. He should jump back into the tunneler and tell the rest of the expedition what he had found. They would want to come rushing, to explore this tunnel, to see what it led to—

But so did he.

Without looking back he turned left, settled his battery pack better on his shoulder straps, and began limping down the tunnel. When he had his next spasm of vomiting he had no handy canister to fill. (On the other hand, there was not much left in him to throw up, so the mess was minimal.) When at last he could walk no longer he sat down, his fingers fumbling with crumbled bits of what might have been broken porcelain or might have been some kind of stone.

He closed his eyes, perfectly happy.

It was a long time before he opened them again, and he wouldn't have, except that he felt as though his old dog were nuzzling at his fingers.

When he woke, the sensation remained. Something was nuzzling at his hand. It wasn't a dog. When he stirred, it flinched away from the light, but with the last of his vision he got a good look at it. More than anything else, it looked like one of those baby harp seals the fur hunters clubbed, only with skinny, stiltlike legs. "Merry Christmas," Henry Steegman whispered, and died.

When at last anyone noticed that Steegman was missing, the captain ordered Manuel Andrew Applegate to follow the new tunnel and retrieve the borer itself, at least—whether Steegman were retrieved or not, he declared, he didn't at all care.

When Applegate reached the borer and saw what it had broken into, his almost incoherent message back brought half the colony there on as close to a run as they could manage.

When finally they saw the dimming glow of Steegman's hand lamp, far down the corridor, and hurried toward it, they saw that Steegman was not alone.

He was dead, propped against the wall in his Santa Claus suit. Even under the fake beard they could see he was smiling; and around him, whistling in distress as they tried to avoid the harsh glare of the approaching lights, were eight unbelievably, wholly unexpectedly, unarguably living and breathing Martians.

And when at last the few survivors of the expedition came home to a presidential reception and a New York ticker-tape parade, Broadway was not renamed Captain Seerseller Avenue for the occasion. It was called Henry Steegman Boulevard.

The Lions Are Asleep This Night

Howard Waldrop

Howard Waldrop was born in Mississippi and has been living in Austin, Texas, for many years. He is the author of three novels: *The Texas-Israeli War,* in collaboration with Jake Saunders, *Them Bones,* and *A Dozen Tough Jobs.* He is better known, though, for his brilliant, quirky short stories. Waldrop popularized the alternate history and famous person sub-genre and is still the best practitioner of both. His stories are collected in *Howard Who?*, *All About Strange Monsters of the Recent Past,* and *Night of the Cooters.* He has been a regular contributor to *Omni* since 1982, when we published "Ike at the Mike."

"The Lions Are Asleep This Night" is about a boy living in an alternate Africa who has a deep interest in Elizabethan revenge drama. It was published August 1986.

The Lions Are Asleep This Night

Howard Waldrop

The white man was drunk again. Robert Oinenke crossed the narrow, graveled street and stepped up on the boardwalk at the other side. Out of the corner of his eye he saw the white man raving. The man sat, feet out, back against a wall, shaking his head, punctuating his monologue with cursing words.

Some said he had been a mercenary in one of the border wars up the coast, one of those conflicts in which two countries had become one; or one country, three. Robert could not remember which. Mr. Lemuel, his history teacher, had mentioned it only in passing.

Since showing up in Onitsha town the white man had worn the same khaki pants. They were of a military cut, now torn and stained. The shirt he wore today was a dashiki, perhaps variegated bright blue and red when made, now faded to purple. He wore a cap with a foreign insignia. Some said he had been a general; others, a sergeant. His loud harangues terrified schoolchildren. Robert's classmates looked on the man as a forest demon. Sometimes the constables came and took him away; sometimes they only asked him to be quiet, and he would subside.

Mostly he could be seen propped against a building, talking to himself. Occasionally somebody would give him money. Then he would make his way to the nearest store or market stall that sold palm wine.

He had been in Robert's neighborhood for a few months. Before that he had stayed near the marketplace.

Robert did not look at him. Thinking of the marketplace, he hurried his steps. The first school bell rang.

* * *

163

"You will not be dawdling at the market," his mother had said as he readied himself for school. "Miss Mbene spoke to me of your tardiness yesterday."

She took the first of many piles of laundry from her wash baskets and placed them near the ironing board. There was a roaring fire in the hearth, and her irons were lined up in the racks over it. The house was already hot as an oven and would soon be as damp as the monsoon season.

His mother was still young and pretty but worn. She had supported them since Robert's father had been killed in an accident while damming a tributary of the Niger. He and forty other men had been swept away when a cofferdam burst. Only two of the bodies had ever been found. There was a small monthly check from the company her husband had worked for, and the government check for single mothers.

Her neighbor Mrs. Yortebe washed, and she ironed. They took washing from the well-to-do government workers and business people in the better section.

"I shan't be late," said Robert, torn with emotions. He knew he wouldn't spend a long time there this morning and be late for school, but he did know that he would take the wide route that led through the marketplace.

He put his schoolbooks and supplies in his satchel. His mother turned to pick up somebody's shirt from the pile. She stopped, looking at Robert.

"What are you going to do with two copybooks?" she asked.

Robert froze. His mind tried out ten lies. His mother started toward him.

"I'm nearly out of pages," he said. She stopped. "If we do much work today, I shall have to borrow."

"I buy you ten copybooks at the start of each school year and then again at the start of the second semester. Money does not grow on the breadfruit trees, you know?"

"Yes, Mother," he said. He hoped she would not look in the copybooks, see that one was not yet half-filled with schoolwork and that the other was still clean and empty. His mother referred to all extravagance as "a heart-tearing waste of time and money."

"You have told me not to borrow from others. I thought I was using foresight."

"Well," said his mother, "see you don't go to the marketplace. It will only make you envious of all the things you can't have. And do not be late to school one more time this term, or I shall have you ever ironing."

"Yes, Mother," he said. Running to her, he rubbed his nose against her cheek. "Good-bye."

"Good day. And don't go near that marketplace!"

"Yes, Mother."

The market! Bright, pavilioned stalls covering a square Congo mile of ground filled with gaudy objects, goods, animals, and people. The Onitsha market was a crossroads of the trade routes, near the river and the railway station. Here a thousand vendors sold their wares on weekedays, many times that on weekends and holidays.

Robert passed the great piles of melons, guinea fowl in cages, tables of toys and gewgaws, all bright and shiny in the morning light.

People talked in five languages, haggling with each other, calling back and forth, joking. Here men from Senegal stood in their bright red hats and robes. Robert saw a tall Wazir, silent and regal, indicating the prices he would pay with quick movements of his long fingers, while the merchant he stood before added two more each time. A few people with raised tattoos on their faces, backcountry people, wandered wide-eyed from table to table, talking quietly among themselves.

Scales clattered, food got weighed, chickens and ducks rattled, a donkey brayed near the big corral where larger livestock was sold. A goat wagon delivered yams to a merchant, who began yelling because they were still too hard. The teamster shrugged his shoulders and pointed to his bill of lading. The merchant threw down his apron and headed toward Onitsha's downtown, cursing the harvest, the wagoners, and the food cooperatives.

Robert passed by the food stalls, though the smell of ripe mangoes made his mouth water. He had been skipping lunch for three weeks, saving his Friday pennies. At the schoolhouse far away the ten-minute bell rang. He would have to hurry.

He came to the larger stalls at the far edge of the market where the booksellers were. He could see the bright paper jackets and dark type titles and some of the cover pictures on them from fifty yards away. He went toward the stall of Mr. Fred's Printers and High-Class Bookstore, which was his favorite. The clerk, who knew him by now, nodded to Robert as he came into the stall area. He was a nice young man in his twenties, dressed in a three-piece suit. He looked at the clock.

"Aren't you going to be late for school this fine morning?"

Robert didn't want to take the time to talk but said, "I know the books I want. It will only be a moment."

The clerk nodded.

Robert ran past the long shelves with their familiar titles: *Drunkards Believe the Bar is Heaven; Ruth the Sweet Honey That Poured Away; Johnny, the Most-Worried Husband; The Lady That Forced Me to Be Romantic; The Return of Mabel, in a Drama on How I Was About Marrying My Sister,* the last with a picture of Miss Julie Engebe, the famous drama actress, on the cover, which Robert knew was just a way to get people to buy the book.

Most of them were paper covered, slim, about fifty pages thick. Some had bright, stenciled lettering on them, others drawings; a few had *photographios.* Robert turned at the end of the shelf and red the titles of others quickly: *The Adventures of Constable Joe; Eddy, the Coal-City Boy; Pocket Encyclopedia of Etiquette and Good Sense; Why Boys Never Trust Money-Monger Girls; How to Live Bachelor's Life and a Girl's Life Without Too Many Mistakes; Ibo Folktales You Should Know.*

He found what he was looking for: *Clio's Whips* by Oskar Oshwenke. It was as thin as the others, and the typefaces on the red, green, and black cover were in three different type styles. There was even a different *i* in the word *whips.*

Robert took it from the rack (it had been well thumbed, but Robert knew it was the only copy in the store). He went down two more shelves, to where they kept the dramas, and picked out *The Play of the Swearing Stick* by Otuba Malewe and *The Raging Turk, or Bajazet II* by Thomas Goffe, an English European who had lived three hundred years ago.

Robert returned to the counter, out of breath from his dash through the stall. "These three," he said, spreading them out before him.

The clerk wrote figures on two receipt papers. "That will be twenty-four new cents, young sir," he said.

Robert looked at him without comprehension. "But yesterday they would have been twenty-two cents!" he said.

The clerk looked back down at the books. Then Robert noticed the price on the Goffe play, six cents, had been crossed out and eight cents written over that in big, red pencil.

"Mr. Fred himself came through yesterday and looked over the stock," said the clerk. "Some prices he raised, others he liberally reduced. There are now many more two-cent books in the bin out front," he said apologetically.

"But...I only have twenty-two new cents." Robert's eyes began to burn.

The clerk looked at the three books. "I'll tell you what, young sir. I shall let you have these three books for twenty-two cents. When you get two cents more, you are to bring them *directly* to me. If the other clerk or Mr. Fred is here, you are to make no mention of this matter. Do you see?"

"Yes, yes. Thank you!" He handed all his money across. He knew it was borrowing, which his mother did not want him to do, but he wanted these books so badly.

He stuffed the pamphlets and receipts into his satchel. As he ran from the bookstall he saw the nice young clerk reach into his vest pocket, fetch out two pennies, and put them into the cashbox. Robert ran as fast as he could toward school. He would have to hurry or he would be late.

Mr. Yotofeka, the principal, looked at the tardy slip.

"Robert," he said, looking directly into the boy's eyes, "I am very disappointed in you. You are a bright pupil. Can you give me one good reason why you have been late to school three times in two weeks?"

"No, sir," said Robert. He adjusted his glasses, which were taped at one of the earpieces.

"No reason at all?"

"It took longer than I thought to get to school."

"You are thirteen years old, Robert Oinenke!" His voice rose. "You live less than a Congo mile from this schoolhouse, which you have been attending for seven years. You should know by now how long it takes you to get from your home to the school!"

Robert winced. "Yessir."

"Hand me your book satchel, Robert."

"But I..."

"Let me see."

"Yessir." He handed the bag to the principal, who was standing over him. The man opened it, took out the schoolbooks and copybooks, then the pamphlets. He looked down at the receipt, then at Robert's records file, which was open like the big book of the Christian Saint Peter in heaven.

"Have you not been eating to buy this trash?"

"No, sir."

"No, yes? Or yes, no?"

"Yes. I haven't."

"Robert, two of these are pure trash. I am glad to see you have bought at least one good play. But your choices are just, just...You might have well poured your coppers down a civet hole as buy these." He held up *Clio's Whips*. "Does your mother know you read these things? And this play! *The Swearing Stick* is about the kind of primitive superstitions we left behind before independence. You want people to believe in this kind of thing again? You wish blood rituals, tribal differences to come back? The man who wrote this was barely literate, little more than just come in from the brush country."

"But..."

"But me no buts. Use the library of this schoolhouse, Robert, or the fine

167

public one. Find books that will uplift you, appeal to your higher nature. Books written by learned people, who have gone to university." Robert knew that Mr. Yotofeka was proud of his education and that he and others like him looked down on the bookstalls and their books. He probably only read books published by the universities or real books published in Lagos or Cairo.

Mr. Yotofeka became stern and businesslike. "For being tardy you will do three days' detention after school. You will help Mr. Labuba with his cleaning."

Mr. Labuba was the custodian. He was large and slow and smelled of old clothes and yohimbé snuff. Robert did not like him.

The principal wrote a note on a form and handed it to Robert. "You will take this note home to your hardworking mother and have her sign it. You will return it to me before *second* bell tomorrow. If you are late again, Robert Oinenke, it will not be a *swearing* stick I will be dealing with you about."

"Yes, sir," said Robert.

When he got home that afternoon Robert went straight to his small alcove at the back of the house where his bed and worktable were. His table had his pencils, ink pen, eraser, ruler, compass, protractor, and glue. He took his copybooks from his satchel, then placed the three books he'd bought in the middle of his schoolbook shelf above the scarred table. He sat down to read the plays. His mother was still out doing the shopping as she always was when he got out of school.

Mr. Yotofeka was partly right about *The Play of the Swearing Stick*. It was not a great play. It was about a man in the old days accused of a crime. Unbeknownst to him, the real perpetrator of the crime had replaced the man's swearing stick with one that looked and felt just like it. (Robert knew this was implausible.) But the false swearing stick carried out justice anyway. It rose up from its place on the witness cushion beside the innocent man when he was questioned at the chief's court. It went out the window and chased the criminal and beat him to death. (In the stage directions the stick is lifted from the pillow by a technician with wires above the stage and disappears out the window, and the criminal is seen running back and forth yelling and holding his head, bloodier each time he goes by.)

Robert really liked plays. He watched the crowds every afternoon going toward the playhouse in answer to the drums and horns sounded when a drama was to be staged. He had seen the children's plays, of course—*Big Magic, The Trusting Chief, Daughter of the Yoruba*. He had also seen the plays written for European children—*Cinderella, Rumpelstiltskin, Nose of Fire*. Everyone his age had—the Niger Culture Center performed the plays for the lower grades each year.

But when he could get tickets, through the schools or his teachers, he had gone to see real plays, both African and European. He had gone to folk plays for adults, especially *Why the Snake Is Slick,* and he had seen Ourelay the Congo playwright's *King of All He Surveyed* and *Scream of Africa.* He had seen tragedies and comedies from most of the African nations, even a play from Nippon, which he had liked to look at but in which not much happened. (Robert had liked the women actresses best, until he found out they weren't women; then he didn't know what to think.) But it was the older plays he liked best, those from England of the early 1600's.

The first one he'd seen was *Westward for Smelts!* by Christopher Kingstone, then *The Pleasant Historie of Darastus and Fawnia* by Rob Greene. There had been a whole week of old English European plays at the Culture Hall, at night, lit by incandescent lights. His school had gotten free tickets for anyone who wanted them. Robert was the only student his age who went to all the performances, though he saw several older students there each night.

There had been *Caesar and Pompey* by George Chapman, *Mother Bombey* by John Lyly, *The Bugbears* by John Jeffere, *The Tragicall History of Romeus and Juliet* by Arthur Broke, *Love's Labour Won* by W. Shaksper, *The Tragedy of Dido, Queen of Carthage* by Marlow and Nash, and on the final night, and best of all, *The Sparagus Garden* by Richard Brome.

That such a small country could produce so many good playwrights in such a short span of time intrigued Robert, especially when you consider that they were fighting both the Turks and the Italians during the period. Robert began to read about the country and its history in books from the school library. Then he learned that the Onitsha market sold many plays from that era (as there were no royalty payments to people dead two hundred fifty years). He had gone there, buying at first from the penny bin, then the two-cent tables.

Robert opened his small worktable drawer. Beneath his sixth-form certificate were the pamphlets from Mr. Fred's. There were twenty-six of them: twenty of them plays, twelve of those from the England of three hundred years before.

He closed the drawer. He looked at the cover of Thomas Goffe's play he had bought that morning—*The Raging Turk, or Bajazet II.* Then he opened the second copybook his mother had seen that morning. On the first page he penciled, in his finest hand:

MOTOFUKO'S REVENGE:
A Play in Three Acts
By Robert Oinenke

* * *

After an hour his hand was tired from writing. He had gotten to the place where King Motofuko was to consult with his astrologer about the attacks by Chief Renebe on neighboring tribes. He put the copybook down and began to read the Goffe play. It was good, but he found that after writing dialogue he was growing tired of reading it. He put the play away.

He didn't really want to read *Clio's Whips* yet; he wanted to save it for the weekend. But he could wait no longer. Making sure the front door was closed, though it was still hot outside, he opened the red, green, and black covers and read the title page:

CLIO'S WHIPS: The Abuses of Historie
by the White Races
By Oskar Oshwenke

"So the Spanish cry was Land Ho! and they sailed in the three famous ships, the *Nina,* the *Pinta,* and the *Elisabetta* to the cove on the island. Colon took the lead boat, and he and his men stepped out onto the sandy beach. All the air was full of parrots, and it was very wonderful there! But they searched and sailed around for five days and saw nothing but big bunches of animals, birds, fish, and turtles.

"Thinking they were in India, they sailed on looking for habitations, but on no island where they stopped were there any people at all! From one of the islands they saw far off the long lines of a much bigger island or a mainland, but tired from their search, and provendered from hunting and fishing, they returned to Europe and told of the wonders they had found, of the New Lands. Soon everyone wanted to go there."

This was exciting stuff to Robert. He reread the passage again and flipped the pages as he had for a week in Mr. Fred's. He came to his favorite illustration (which was what made him buy this book rather than another play). It was the picture of a hairy elephant, with its trunk raised and with that magical stuff, snow, all around it. Below was a passage Robert had almost memorized:

"The first man then set foot at the Big River (now the New Thames) of the Northern New Land. Though he sailed for the Portingals, he came from England (which had just given the world its third pope), and his name was Cromwell. He said the air above the Big River was a darkened profusion of pigeons, a million and a million times a hundred hundred, and they covered the skies for hours as they flew.

"He said there were strange humped cattle there (much like the European wisents) that fed on grass, on both sides of the river. They stood so thickly that you could have walked a hundred Congo miles on their backs without touching the ground.

"And here and there among them stood great hairy mammuts, which we now know once lived in much of Europe, so much like our elephant, which you see in the game parks today, but covered with a red-brown hair, with much bigger tusks, and much more fierce-looking.

"He said none of the animals were afraid of him, and he walked among them, petting some, handing them tender tufts of grass. They had never seen a man or heard a human voice, and had not been hunted since the beginning of time. He saw that a whole continent of skins and hides lay before European man for the taking, and a million feathers for hats and decorations. He knew he was the first man ever to see this place, and that it was close to Paradise. He returned to Lisboa after many travails, but being a good Catholic, and an Englishman, he wasn't believed. So he went back to England and told his stories there."

Now Robert went back to work on his play after carefully sharpening his pencil with a knife and setting his eraser close at hand. He began with where King Motofuko calls in his astrologer about Chief Renebe:

MOTOFUKO: Like to those stars which blaze forth overhead, brighter even than the seven ordered planets? And having waxed so lustily, do burn out in a week?
ASTROLOGER: Just so! Them that awe to see their burning forget the shortness of their fire. The moon, though ne'er so hot, stays and outlasts all else.
MOTOFUKO: Think you then this Chief Renebe be but a five month's wonder?
ASTROLOGER: The gods themselves do weep to see his progress! Starts he toward your lands a blazing beacon, yet will his followers bury his ashes and cinders in some poor hole 'fore he reaches the Mighty Niger. Such light makes gods jealous.

Robert heard his mother talking with a neighbor outside. He closed his copybook, put *Cilo's Whips* away, and ran to help her carry in the shopping.

During recess the next morning he stayed inside, not joining the others in the playground. He opened his copybook and took up the scene where Chief Renebe, who has conquered all King Motofuko's lands and had all his wives and (he thinks) all the king's children put to death, questions his general about it on the way to King Motofuko's capital.

171

RENEBE: And certaine, you, all his children dead, all his warriors sold to the Moorish dogs?

GENERAL: As sure as the sun doth rise and set, Your Highness. I myself his children's feet did hold, swing them like buckets round my conk, their limbs crack, their necks and heads destroy. As for his chiefs, they are now sent to grub ore and yams in the New Lands, no trouble to you forevermore. Of his cattle we made great feast, his sheep drove we all to the four winds.

This would be important to the playgoer. King Motofuko had escaped, but he had also taken his four-year-old son, Motofene, and tied him under the bellwether just before the soldiers attacked in the big battle of Yotele. When the soldiers drove off the sheep, they sent his son to safety, where the shepherds would send him far away, where he could grow up and plot revenge.

The story of King Motofuko was an old one any Onitsha theatergoer would know. Robert was taking liberties with it—the story of the sheep was from one of his favorite parts of the *Odyssey,* where the Greeks were in the cave of Polyphemus. (The real Motofene had been sent away to live as hostage-son to the chief of the neighboring state long before the attack by Chief Renebe.) And Robert was going to change some other things, too. The trouble with real life, Robert thought, was that it was usually dull and full of people like Mr. Yotofeka and Mr. Labuba. Not like the story of King Motofuko should be at all.

Robert had his copy of *Cilo's Whips* inside his Egyptian grammar book. He read:

"Soon all the countries of Europe that could sent expeditions to the New Lands. There were riches in its islands and vast spaces, but the White Man had to bring others to dig them out and cut down the mighty trees for ships. That is when the White Europeans really began to buy slaves from Arab merchants, and to send them across to the Warm Sea to skin animals, build houses, and to serve them in all ways.

"Africa was raided over. Whole tribes were sold to slavery and degradation; worse, wars were fought between black and black to make slaves to sell to the Europeans. Mother Africa was raped again and again, but she was also traveled over and mapped: Big areas marked "unexplored" on the White Man's charts shrank and shrank so that by 1700 there were very few such places left."

Miss Mbene came in from the play yard, cocked an eye at Robert, then went to the slateboard and wrote mathematical problems on it. With a groan, Robert closed the Egyptian grammar book and took out his sums and ciphers.

172

* * *

Mr. Labuba spat a stream of yohimbé-bark snuff into the weeds at the edge of the playground. His eyes were red and the pupils more open than they should have been in the bright afternoon sun.

"We be pulling at grasses," he said to Robert. He handed him a big pair of gloves, which came up to Robert's elbows. "Pull steady. These plants be cutting all the way through the gloves if you jerk."

In a few moments Robert was sweating. A smell of desk polish and eraser rubbings came off Mr. Labuba's shirt as he knelt beside him. They soon had cleared all along the back fence.

Robert got into the rhythm of the work, taking pleasure when the cutter weeds came out of the ground with a tearing pop and burst of dirt from the tenacious, octopuslike roots. Then they would cut away the runners with trowels. Soon they had made quite a pile near the teeter-totters.

Robert was still writing his play in his head; he had stopped in the second act when Motofuko, in disguise, had come to the forgiveness-audience with the new King Renebe. Unbeknownst to him, Renebe, fearing revenge all out of keeping with custom, had persuaded his stupid brother Guba to sit on the throne for the one day when anyone could come to the new king and be absolved of crimes.

"Is he giving you any trouble?" asked the intrusive voice of Mr. Yotofeka. He had come up and was standing behind Robert.

Mr. Labuba swallowed hard, the yohimbé lump going down chokingly.

"No complaints, Mr. Yotofeka," he said, looking up.

"Very good, Robert, you can go home when the tower bell rings at three o'clock."

"Yes, sir."

Mr. Yotofeka went back inside.

Mr. Labuba looked at Robert and winked.

MOTOFUKO: Many, many wrongs in my time. I pray you, king, forgive me. I let my wives, faithful all, be torn from me, watched my children die, while I stood by, believing them proof from death. My village dead, all friends slaves. Reason twisted like hemp.

GUBA: From what mad place came you where such happens?

MOTOFUKO: (*Aside*) Name a country where this is not the standard of normalcy. (*To Guba*) Aye, all these I have done. Blinded, I went to worse. Pray you, forgive my sin.

GUBA: What could that be?

MOTOFUKO: (*Uncovering himself*): Murdering a king. (*Stabs him*)

GUBA: Mother of gods! Avenge my death. You kill the wrong man. Yonder— (*Dies*) (*Guards advance, weapons out.*)

MOTOFUKO: Wrong man, when all men are wrong? Come dogs, crows, buzzards, tigers. I welcome barks, beaks, claws and teeth. Make the earth one howl. Damned, damned world where men fight like jackals over the carrion of states! Bare my bones then; they call for rest.

(*Exeunt, fighting. Terrible screams off. Blood flows in from the wings in a river.*)

SOLDIER (*Aghast*): Horror to report. They flay the ragged skin from him whole!

"But the hide and fishing stations were hard to run with just slave labor. Not enough criminals could be brought from the White Man's countries to fill all the needs.

"Gold was more and more precious, in the hands of fewer and fewer people in Europe. There was some, true, in the Southern New Land, but it was high in the great mountain ranges and very hard to dig out. The slaves were worked underground till they went blind. There were revolts under those cruel conditions.

"One of the first new nations was set up by slaves who threw off their chains. They called their land Freedom, which was the thing they had most longed for since being dragged from Mother Africa. All the armies of the White Man's trading stations could not overthrow them. The people of Freedom slowly dug gold out of the mountains and became rich and set out to free others, in the Southern New Land and in Africa itself....

"Rebellion followed rebellion. Mother Africa rose up. There were too few white men, and the slave armies they sent soon rebelled too and joined their brothers and sisters against the White Man.

"First to go were the impoverished French and Spanish dominions, then the richer Italian ones, and those of the British. Last of all were the colonies of the great German banking families. Then the wrath of Mother Africa turned on those Arabs and Egyptians who had helped the White Man in his enslavement of the black.

"Now they are all gone as powers from our continent and only carry on the kinds of commerce with us which put all the advantages to Africa."

ASHINGO: The ghost! The ghost of that dead king!

RENEBE: What! What madness this? Guards, your places! What mean you, man?

174

ASHINGO: He came, I swear, his skin all strings, his brain a red cawleyflower, his eyes empty holes!

RENEBE: What portent this? The old astrologer, quick. To find what means to turn out this being like a goat from our crops.

(*Alarums without. Enter astrologer.*)

ASTROLOGER: Your men just now waken me from a mighty dream. Your majesty was in some high place, looking over the courtyard at all his friends and family. You were dressed in regal armor all of brass and iron. Bonfires of victory burned all around, and not a word of dissent was heard anywhere in the land. All was peace and calm.

RENEBE: Is this then a portent of continued long reign?

ASTROLOGER: I do not know, sire. It was *my* dream.

His mother was standing behind him, looking over his shoulder.

Robert jerked, trying to close the copybook. His glasses flew off.

"What is that?" She reached forward and pulled the workbook from his hands.

"It is extra work for school," he said. He picked up his glasses.

"No, it is not." She looked over his last page. "It is wasting your paper. Do you think we have money to burn away?"

"No, Mother. Please..." He reached for the copybook.

"First you are tardy. Then you stay detention after school. You waste your school notebooks. Now you *have lied* to me."

"I'm sorry, I..."

"What is this?"

"It is a play, a historical play."

"What are you going to do with a play?"

Robert lowered his eyes. "I want to take it to Mr. Fred's Printers and have it published. I want it acted in the Niger Culture Hall. I want it to be sold all over Niger."

His mother walked over to the fireplace, where her irons were cooling on their racks away from the hearth.

"What are you going to *do*!!?" he yelled.

His mother flinched in surprise. She looked down at the notebook, then back at Robert. Her eyes narrowed.

"I was going to get my spectacles."

Robert began to cry.

She came back to him and put her arms around him. She smelled of the marketplace, of steam and cinnamon. He buried his head against her side.

"I will make you proud of me, Mother. I am sorry I used the copybook, but I had to write this play."

She pulled away from him. "I ought to beat you within the inch of your life, for ruining a copybook. You are going to have to help me for the rest of the week. You are not to work on this until you have finished every bit of your schoolwork. You should know Mr. Fred nor nobody is going to publish anything written by a schoolboy."

She handed him the notebook. "Put that away. Then go out on the porch and bring in those piles of mending. I am going to sweat a copybook out of your brow before I am through."

Robert clutched the book to him as if it were his soul.

RENEBE: O rack, ruin, and pain! Falling stars and the winds do shake the foundations of night itself! Where my soldiers, my strength? What use taxes, tribute if they buy not strong men to die for me?

(*Off*): Gone. All fled.

RENEBE: Hold! Who is there? (*Draws*)

MOTOFENE (*Entering*): He whose name will freeze your blood's roots.

RENEBE: The son of that dead king!

MOTOFENE: Aye, dead to you and all the world else, but alive to me and as constant as that star about which the groaning axle-tree of the earth does spin. (*Alarums and excursions off.*)

Now hear you the screams of your flesh and blood and friendship, such screams as those I have heard awake and fitfully asleep these fourteen years. Now hear them for all time.

RENEBE: Guards! To me!

MOTOFENE: To you? See those stars which shower to earth out your fine window? At each a wife, child, friend does die. You watched my father cut way to bone and blood and gore and called not for the death stroke! For you I have had my Vulcans make you a fine suit. All iron and brass, as befits a king! It you will wear, to look out over the palace yard of your dead, citizens and friends. You will have a good high view, for it is situated on cords of finest woods. (*Enter Motofene's soldiers*) Seize him gently. (*Disarm*) And now, my former king, outside. Though full of hot stars, the night is cold. Fear not the touch of the brass. Anon you are garmented, my men will warm the suit for you.

(*Exeunt and curtain.*)

Robert passed the moaning white man and made his way down the street, beyond the market. He was going to Mr. Fred's Printers in downtown Onitsha.

He followed broad New Market Street, being careful to stay out of the way of the noisy streetcars that steamed on their rails toward the center of town.

He wore his best clothes, though it was Saturday morning. In his hands he carried his play, recopied in ink in yet another notebook. He had learned from the clerk at the market bookstall that the one sure way to find Mr. Fred was at his office on Saturday forenoon, when the Onitsha *Weekly Volcano* was being put to bed.

Robert saw two *wayway* birds sitting on the single telegraph wire leading to the relay station downtown. In the old superstitions one *wayway* was a bad omen, two were good, three a surprise.

"Mr. Fred is busy," said the woman in the *Weekly Volcano* office. Her desk was surrounded by copies of all the pamphlets printed by Mr. Fred's bookstore, past headlines from the *Volcano* , and a big picture of Mr. Fred, looking severe in his morning coat, under the giant clock, on whose face was engraved the motto in Egyptian: TIME IS BUSINESS.

The calendar on her desk, with the picture of a Niger author for each month, was open to October 1894. A listing of that author's books published by Mr. Fred was appended at the bottom of each page.

"I should like to see Mr. Fred about my play," said Robert.

"Your play?"

"Yes. A rousing historical play. It is called *Motofuko's Revenge*."

"Is your play in proper form?"

"Following the best rules of dramaturgy," said Robert.

"Let me see it a moment."

Robert hesitated.

"Is it papertypered?" she asked.

A cold chill ran down Robert's spine.

"All manuscripts must be papertypered, two spaces between lines, with wide margins," she said.

There was a lump in Robert's throat. "But it is in my very finest book-hand," he said.

"I'm sure it is. Mr. Fred reads everything himself, is a very busy man, and insists on papertypered manuscripts."

The last three weeks came crashing down on Robert like a mud-wattle wall.

"Perhaps if I spoke to Mr. Fred..."

"It will do you no good if your manuscript isn't papertypered."

"Please. I..."

177

"Very well. You shall have to wait until after one. Mr. Fred has to put the *Volcano* in final form and cannot be disturbed."

It was ten-thirty.

"I'll wait," said Robert.

At noon the lady left, and a young man in a vest sat down in her chair.

Other people came, were waited on by the man or sent into another office to the left. From the other side of the shop door, behind the desk, came the sound of clanking, carts rolling, thumps, and bells. Robert imagined great machines, huge sweating men wrestling with cogs and gears, books stacked to the ceiling.

It got quieter as the morning turned to afternoon. Robert stood, stretched, and walked around the reception area again, reading the newspapers on the walls with their stories five, ten, fifteen years old, some printed before he was born.

Usually they were stories of rebellions, wars, floods, and fears. Robert did not see one about the burst dam that had killed his father, a yellowed clipping of which was in the Coptic Bible at home.

There was a poster on one wall advertising the fishing resort on Lake Sahara South, with pictures of trout and catfish caught by anglers.

At two o'clock the man behind the desk got up and pulled down the windowshade at the office. "You shall have to wait outside for your father," he said. "We're closing for the day."

"Wait for my father?"

"Aren't you Moletules's boy?"

"No. I have come to see Mr. Fred about my play. The lady..."

"She told me nothing. I thought you were the printer's devil's boy. You say you want to see Mr. Fred about a play?"

"Yes, I..."

"Is it papertypered?" asked the man.

Robert began to cry.

"Mr. Fred will see you now," said the young man, coming back in the office and taking his handkerchief back.

"I'm sorry," said Robert.

"Mr. Fred only knows you are here about a play," he said. He opened the door to the shop. There were no mighty machines there, only a few small ones in a dark, two-story area, several worktables, boxes of type and lead. Everything was dusty and smelled of metal and thick ink.

A short man in his shirtsleeves leaned against a workbench reading a long, thin strip of paper while a boy Robert's age waited. Mr. Fred scribbled something on the paper, and the boy took it back into the other room, where several men bent quietly over boxes and tables filled with type.

"Yes," said Mr. Fred, looking up.

"I have come here about my play."

"Your play?"

"I have written a play, about King Motofuko. I wish you to publish it."

Mr. Fred laughed. "Well, we shall have to see about that. Is it papertypered?"

Robert wanted to cry again.

"No, I am sorry to say, it is not. I didn't know..."

"We do not take manuscripts for publication unless..."

"It is in my very best book-hand, sir. Had I known, I would have tried to get it papertypered."

"Is your name and address on the manuscript?"

"Only my name. I..."

Mr. Fred took a pencil out from behind his ear. "What is your house number?"

Robert told him his address, and he wrote it down in the copybook.

"Well, Mr.—Robert Oinenke. I shall read this, but not before Thursday after next. You are to come back to the shop at ten A.M. on Saturday the nineteenth for the manuscript and our decision on it."

"But..."

"What?"

"I really like the books you publish, Mr. Fred, sir. I especially liked *Clio's Whips* by Mr. Oskar Oshwenke."

"Always happy to meet a satisfied customer. We published that book five years ago. Tastes have changed. The public seems tired of history books now."

"That is why I am hoping you will like my play," said Robert.

"I will see you in two weeks," said Mr. Fred. He tossed the copybook into a pile of manuscripts on the workbench.

"Because of the legacy of the White Man, we have many problems in Africa today. He destroyed much of what he could not take with him. Many areas are without telegraphy; many smaller towns have only primitive direct current power. More needs to be done with health and sanitation, but we are not as badly off as the most primitive of the White Europeans in their war-ravaged countries or in their few scattered enclaves in the plantations and timber forests of the New Lands.

It is up to you, the youth of Africa of today, to take our message of prosperity and goodwill to these people, who have now been as abused by history as we Africans once were by them. I wish you good luck.

Oskar Oshwenke,
Onitsha, Niger, 1889"

Robert put off going to the market stall of Mr. Fred's bookstore as long as he could. It was publication day.

He saw that the nice young clerk was there. (He had paid him back out of the ten Niger dollar advance Mr. Fred had had his mother sign for two weeks before. His mother still could not believe it.)

"Ho, there, Mr. Author!" said the clerk. "I have your three free copies for you. Mr. Fred wishes you every success."

The clerk was arranging his book and John-John Motulla's *Game Warden Bob and the Mad Ivory Hunter* on the counter with the big starburst saying: JUST PUBLISHED!

His book would be on sale throughout the city. He looked at the covers of the copies in his hands:

The TRAGICALL DEATH OF KING
MOTOFUKO
and HOW THEY WERE SORRY
a drama by Robert Oinenke
abetted by
MR. FRED OLUNGENE
"The Mighty Man of the Press"
for sale at Mr. Fred's High-Class Bookstore
300 Market, and the *Weekly Volcano*
Office, 12 New Market Road
ONITSHA, NIGER
price 10¢ N.

On his way home he came around the corner where a group of boys was taunting the white man. The man was drunk and had just vomited on the foundation post of a store. They were laughing at him.

"Kill you all. Kill you all. No shame," he mumbled, trying to stand.

180

The words of *Clio's Whips* came to Robert's ears. He walked between the older boys and handed the white man three Niger cents. The white man looked up at him with sick, gray eyes.

"Thank you, young sir," he said, closing his hand tightly.

Robert hurried home to show his mother and the neighbors his books.

The Dragon Seed

Kate Wilhelm

Kate Wilhelm lives in Eugene, Oregon. She began publishing in 1956, and is widely regarded as one of the best of today's writers—outside the genre as well as in. She and her husband, writer Damon Knight, ran the Milford Writer's Conference for many years and are still deeply involved in the operation of the Clarion Workshop for new writers. Her fiction has won the Hugo and several Nebulas.

Equally at ease in several genres, Wilhelm has published mysteries, mainstream thrillers, and comic novels, as well as science fiction. Her novels include *Margaret and I, Where Late the Sweet Birds Sang, Juniper Time, Welcome, Chaos, Death Qualified, Justice For Some,* and *The Best Defense,* the sequel to *Death Qualified,* which is about to come out from St. Martin's Press. Her more recent story collections are *The Infinity Box, Listen Listen, Children of the Wind,* and *And the Angels Sing.*

"The Dragon Seed" could be considred a mainstream story and both Wilhelm and her agent questioned me when I planned to publish it in *Omni.* I responded that it was "weird enough" for me. The story was first published December 1985.

The Dragon Seed

Kate Wilhelm

Bruce Enfield has a seat on the aisle and nowhere to put his elbows or his feet. Next to him is a woman with squatter's rights to the armrest, and in the aisle the stewardesses are hurrying back and forth, pushing their heavy carts, delivering drinks and peanuts. He huddles into himself, hating it all, hating the rest of the day that will be just as bad with a two-hour wait in O'Hare, another cattle car in the sky to Portland, another two-hour delay, and finally the last lap, twenty minutes to Eugene.

He is troubled because he is not certain why he is going back. Not to see her, he tells himself again, and he wishes he had taken the slim Lucite piece from his pocket before he put his coat in the overhead bin. He will visit his parents and an old friend or two, sleep and relax, and on Sunday afternoon make the rest of the trip to San Francisco, his actual destination. He will not see Cory. There is no reason to look her up; he is married, settled, rising in his world.

He twists and struggles to extract his wallet from his pocket, gets a glare from his neighbor, and accepts his drink gratefully when the stewardess puts it before him. In his mind he is seeing Cory side by side with Beatrice, and that is embarrassing to him.

Cory in her jeans and heavy boots caked with mud, a man's flannel shirt over a sweater, an unbuttoned, olive rain jacket over it all, her pale hair pulled back carelessly with a string or a rubber band. And Beatrice, elegant in a navy blue dressmaker's suit, high heels, her nails and lips exactly the same shade of red, hair as soft and sweet as a baby's, kept in a style that flatters her face and draws attention to her wonderfully made-up eyes. Beatrice has the loveliest eyes in the world, he thinks, and he finds he cannot summon an image of Cory's eyes.

185

Pale lashes and brows, pale gray or blue eyes. The comparison of the two women is cruel, and again he feels embarrassed that he is making it. He gulps his scotch and thinks of the Lucite in his coat pocket, wishes he had it in his hand. He wants a cigarette although he has not smoked for almost a year. He thinks almost desperately that he has to have a cigarette, because in his head the comparison is continuing, and he cannot stop it. Beatrice with her quick intelligence, her humor, her easy grasp of everything she reads or hears; and Cory, cowlike, retarded, or so near that it makes little difference.

Whitman had put his ad in the paper on Sunday, and on Monday morning, when he opened his door before seven to start work, she was there on the back doorstep. Whitman was a large, muscular man in his late fifties, a widower for the last six years. To him Cory appeared an empty-faced child that bright morning.

"I've come for the job," she said.

"Worked in a nursery before?"

She shook her head. She was tall, strong enough, and the fact that she was there that early meant that she wanted to work, Whitman thought, studying her. "Where you live?" She told him, one of the subdivisions ten miles or more away. "How'd you get here?"

She pointed to a bicycle leaning against a tree, and he hired her.

He would have to teach her everything, but then he always did, and come fall, they always left to go back to school, and next year he had to do it all over again.

He showed her how to take chrysanthemum cuttings and how to space and plant the pieces and mark them for a fall crop of blooming plants. She watched him silently and then took over as if she had been doing it for years. He supervised for a short while before he went off to get his other tasks started; he came back from time to time to glance at her work. Neither of them spoke. At ten-thirty he told her she could have a break when she wanted it, that he didn't expect anyone to work straight through, he wasn't a slave driver. She listened as attentively as she had listened to his instructions about the cuttings, and he realized that she could not distinguish between kidding and the straight goods. The tone he invariably took with his employees was either a brusque directive or a banter that was meaningless; he knew no other way to address them. He stood looking at the girl kneeling in the bark mulch along the row of chrysanthemums, and he did not know how to speak to her. It was a mistake to hire her, he thought, and felt a stir of self-contempt as he realized he was shifting his own problem of noncommunicativeness to her shoulders.

"When you get tired," he said, trying to soften his voice, because she looked frightened, "go on over to the shed and get a drink. Rest a few minutes. Okay?"

She nodded and turned again to the chrysanthemums, began to cut fast.

"Cory, take it easy, girl. You're doing a fine job, the best of anyone I've hired starting as green as you. I don't expect you to finish all this in one day."

She looked at him again as if trying to measure his words, to test his truthfulness. And then she smiled, and he knew he had done right in hiring her. He walked away thinking about her smile, not that it made her pretty or anything, but it changed her. At first her face was immobile, guarded; then it began to soften, and very slowly, like the opening of a tight, hard bud, the softening, relaxing continued until her whole face was transformed and was not protected at all.

During her lunch hour he saw her wandering over the nursery grounds, and he remembered that he had meant to show her around when he had time. There was always too much to do, not enough good people to get it done. Don, his brother and partner in the business, kept telling him to hire a full time manager, but he resisted. He had tried that. No one else did anything his way, and his way was not the book way. He did things when they needed doing, not when the books said it was time. Only one man, Hank Valchak, might have worked out, but he had quit after a few years and opened his own nursery on the other side of Eugene. And meanwhile Whitman's Nursery was growing, business was expanding, and he, William Whitman, was a tired, overworked man. But at least the paperwork was Don's department. Payroll, taxes, ordering, inventory, advertising, all that he cheerfully left to his brother, who in turn never set foot in one of the greenhouses or the long rows of seedling trees and bushes and shrubs.

It was Don, filling in the employment records, who discovered that Cory had left home to go to school that day and instead had come to the nursery. She had dropped out, he said, and only in the tenth grade.

Whitman tried to see Cory sitting quietly at a desk, immersed in history lessons or math problems, and nothing came. He shrugged. "Her business," he said. But Don Whitman was concerned about it. He had three grown children, and he knew teenagers sometimes did things their parents were ignorant of until too late. He called Cory's mother that night and learned that Cory had a history of failing and that the school counselor had advised a training school for her. The brothers dropped the subject and never referred to it again.

Cory's mother liked to go to her daughter's room on her day off from the bakery and just sit quietly awhile. The room was not messy, the bed always neatly made; there was no scattering of books or records or clothes to offend the most fastidious housekeeper, but there were plants everywhere, in pots, coffee cans, milk cartons, rusty vegetable cans, Styrofoam cups....In here the light was soft and green, filtered through leaves at both windows.

A heavy rain was driving leaves from the trees, marshaling them in untidy heaps. Mrs. Davenport had come in wet and cold from the weekly shopping and now sat drinking coffee, thinking nothing, content to smell the green smells of growing plants instead of cinnamon and vanilla and yeast. When the kitchen buzzer sounded, she got up to make supper. One day Raymond had come home to find her sitting in there and had raged all night at her, and, of course, at Cory. Sometimes when Mrs. Davenport came out of Cory's room she found that she had been weeping with no memory of the tears or the cause. Now that Cory had a good job and was doing well at it, there was no longer any reason to worry or cry over her, but still there were times when she wept.

If only Raymond could accept her, she thought at those times, that would make the difference, but he could not look at Cory without a shadow passing over his face, without his eyes narrowing and a slight ridge forming along his cheek. Most times he avoided looking at her, and most times she stayed out of his way, out of his sight. Now that she was working, they never even ate at the same time. He got home at four-thirty and had his supper, and Cory got in at six-thirty, after he had settled in front of the television for the rest of the evening.

Raymond was a good man, she thought as she peeled carrots. He was a good man in all ways except with Cory. From the start there had been something in her that drew out the devil in him. Mrs. Davenport knew that one of those long, slow smiles from Cory was more important than hours of giggles from other girls, but Raymond had never learned that.

Tonight they would fight over their daughter, she knew, stirring the meat and vegetables. Cory needed things, a new sweater, new woolen socks, and he would act as if it were his money. Each week Cory's check went to him, to be deposited in the checking account, where he guarded it jealously.

"How many years did we provide everything, ask nothing in return?" he would yell. *"It's her turn to help. If she wants to keep her money, let her move out! Once she's gone, I don't give a damn what she does."*

Sometimes Mrs. Davenport fantasized about moving out with Cory, just the two of them sharing a small house with a garden for Cory to work in. It was a pleasant reverie, but it was frightening also, because she cared for Raymond: It was only where Cory was concerned that he became a cruel stranger. Sometimes Mrs. Davenport felt that someone had planted a sharp knife in her skull on the day of Cory's birth that day by day through the years had sliced downward a little at a time, neatly dividing her into halves. She imagined that the knife was even with her heart by now and that if she had to make the decision about leaving with Cory or driving Cory away to be able to live with Raymond, the knife would make the rest of the cut very fast.

Bruce Enfield has gone to the phone booth twice and each time has left it without placing the call to his friends in Chicago. He sits in a clattering coffee shop and stares out the window at fitful snow that looks dirty even before it hits the ground.

His friends would ask about Beatrice, and he does not want to talk about her. He sips his coffee, wishing he had gone to the bar; he hates coffee shops. The snow is stopping again; it is like the ash-fall they sometimes have in Savannah. He remembers standing at the glass wall of his house, close to Beatrice but not touching her as they watch the powdery ashes settle on the lawn, on the surface of the pool.

"Lovely," she says. "Your company?"

"No."

"Have you made an appointment with a doctor yet?" Still looking out the glass, pretending nonchalance, or actually feeling it—he no longer can tell which—she asks the question as if she were asking for the time.

"No."

A 747 rolls past the window, and he watches until it is at home in its bay and the caterpillar mouth has attached itself to the giant body.

He imagines the scene with the doctor: "You say you have nightmares, Mr. Enfield. About what?"

"Dragons. They are chasing me, breathing flames, and I can feel the heat touching me, spreading, consuming me."

"Dragons! Very interesting, Mr. Enfield." He lights a cigarette and watches the tip, the smoke curling slightly at first, then ascending in a column until a draft hits it. He stubs out the cigarette and is mildly surprised to see four others already in the ashtray, all three quarters intact.

Yesterday he changed his reservation, added this side trip to Eugene. Beatrice did not ask why. He wishes she would pretend to be interested but understands that she won't play that game with him. From the start she refused games, then it did not matter because there was no game to play. But now....He hears again her indifference when she asked how long he would be gone. He can't remember if she acknowledged his answer or even if he answered. It mattered so little, they both seemed to say.

"Tell me about your mother," the doctor says, trying to hide a smile.

"Not my mother. Not my father. It's Cory. And I can't tell you." Abruptly he stands up and snatches his check and hurries from the coffee shop. He can feel the hot breath on his back, and he does not dare turn and look for fear he will see the dragon in daylight. He knows when that happens, he will be lost.

One morning Whitman woke up before daylight, listening to sleet hit the roof. Drowsily he turned over, finding comfort in the steady pattering of icy feet while his own feet were warm. Then he sat up. Sleet. He switched on the radio before he reached for the light. They were already talking about the weather conditions: freezing rain throughout the valley, roads closed, schools closed.

He dressed, made coffee and eggs, and planned. He had to prune the two-year-old trees; he had it scheduled for early January, but they would break under a load of ice. And cover the evergreens. And the balled and burlapped trees, and if he had time, get to the year-old, dwarfed fruit trees....The radio was giving no comfort at all, not even trying to predict when the ice storm would pass, turn into ordinary rain, wash away the grief the ice always brought with it.

It was as dark as night when he was ready to go out and start what seemed to be a day of futile effort. The ice was already a quarter inch thick. For a moment he squinted in disbelief as he stared at the toolshed, brightly lighted. He hurried toward it; the gravel drive was already treacherous as ice smoothed out the irregularities.

"Cory! What the hell are you doing here?"

She ducked her head and mumbled, and he drew closer to her.

"How'd you get here?"

Her mother had brought her, she said, on her way to work. She had heard the rain and knew it would turn to ice. He stared at Cory for another moment, and then they went to work. Together they pruned the trees and covered the evergreens and got to the grafted trees.

By late afternoon they had it all done, everything they could do to protect the nursery stock. In exhaustion Whitman made his way to the house, motioning her to follow. He envied her young, strong body, her stamina, but even she was tired by then and hungry and half frozen. Their outer coats were covered with ice; ice was an inch thick on everything in sight. It had stopped falling an hour earlier, but the temperature had dropped throughout the day; there would be no thaw until the wind changed. At the door of the house Cory stopped and looked at the magic world, and she smiled her rare smile. Whitman nodded. It was truly beautiful, but he was too cold and tired to smile.

He made coffee and got steaks from the deep freeze and made a fire in the fireplace. They both sat very close to it, driven back gradually as the flames went from orange-yellow to blue. Neither talked. When Whitman felt himself drifting off in a doze, he roused and went out to make their dinner. The telephone lines were down, and the radio was nothing but chatter about the ice storm and its consequences. Nothing was moving. Whitman sighed. She would have to spend the night, he thought gloomily, and there might be talk. No one else had been able to get to the nursery that day, and he had not talked to his brother, who probably was iced in. Who would ever know? He pushed the thought aside and went about making dinner methodically, the way he did everything. And he wondered about Cory. She always knew about the weather; no matter what it did, she was dressed for it or had clothes to change into. Today she had brought rain pants and heavy enough clothes to get by on an Arctic expedition. When they had come in, she had gone into the bathroom and stripped off a layer or two and had come out dry and clean. She never lost plants to a drought or had them rot in a week of steady rain. She knew.

She could not handle money, or take an order, or talk to a customer. She seldom talked to the other employees; she managed to take her lunch break after the others were back at work. Sometimes in good weather, she took her sack lunch out under one of the walnut trees and ate there alone. She had not missed a day in a year and a half. Never had a cold, an ache, a complaint. In fact, he had had to tell her she could not work seven days a week; it was the only thing he ever had to tell her more than once. And when he had tried to pin her down about her vacation, she had said sullenly that she had nowhere else to go, nothing else to do, and if she couldn't work, she would just sit under the trees and watch.

A few days later, when everything was back to normal, he told his brother he was raising Cory's salary.

" Why? You know her father gets her money."

"You been telling me for years I should hire myself another Hank Valchak, another manager. I been realizing more and more that she's it. She does more than Hank ever did. And we set up a trust and don't tell her daddy. When this goes," he said, motioning vaguely toward the grounds, the greenhouses, everything, "what's going to become of a girl like her? Set it up, Don."

Don Whitman was sixty-three and had begun to talk about training his own replacement. William Whitman would be sixty in the fall of that year. Soberly they nodded at each other and it was done, the trust fund was established; Cory became the highest-paid employee of the enterprise.

Bruce Enfield tries to remember if he ordered chicken or the seafood casserole. He cannot tell by tasting. He is on a DC-10 this time, seated by a window in the smoking section. The plane is two-thirds filled, service is prompt and efficient; already he has had two drinks, and after he finishes his meal, there will be plenty of time for several more.

Beatrice travels more often than he does; she is an assistant buyer for a department store, and her trips are to New York, Paris, London, even Hong Kong.

The food is taken away, and presently a mellow voice suggests that the window-seat passengers pull down their blinds in order to view the movie. He pulls down his blind and closes his eyes and remembers when he went to work for Whitman.

His master's degree was assured by the spring break, and in the fall he would report to MIT for the eighteen-month grind toward his Ph.D. That was already assured also; his project had been accepted, the execution would be a matter of putting in the time it took to do the designing, the drawings, the mock-ups. He was a chemical engineer specializing in plant design; there was a great need for him and the too few others like him.

What he wanted for that summer was an outdoor job that required muscles and no mind. He found it at Whitman's. The old man asked few questions, put him and Frank Fredrickson to work the day they applied.

"Cory, show these two fellows how to ball up the roses," Whitman called. Across the drive, near a shed, a girl nodded and motioned to them to follow her. She was tall and could have passed for a young man, bundled up as she was in jacket and boots and gloves. It was a cold March day, misty, with more rain threatening any minute.

Bruce and Frank exchanged a glance and followed her. She went inside the shed and waited for them. Her directions were terse, almost mumbled, and she did not look at them directly.

Within a few minutes they all walked toward the rows of roses, pulling long wagons. On hers there was a box with labels, a stack of wooden flats, clipping shears, scissors; Bruce's had a stack of burlap squares, a large box of wet sawdust, a spool of wire, and wire cutters, and Frank's had the spade and fork. The work was mindless enough, Bruce decided quickly. Cory moved on ahead of them, pruning the roses that they then dug out and balled up in little bundles with the roots packed in dirt and sawdust. The roses came out easily; Bruce learned later that they had been root pruned twice to force them to make a compact root system, easy to dig, easy to transplant, almost guaranteed to suffer no shock when removed. He found himself watching the girl as she left them behind. Her hands were so quick it was hard to follow exactly what she was doing. First she seemed to feel the rosebush, and then she clipped it so fast that he could not tell what she looked for, how she determined what needed cutting, what needed saving. Some of the cuttings fell around the plants, to be cleaned up later by one of the younger boys; some of them she kept until she had a bundle that she tied together and labeled. Her cuttings always grew, he learned that spring and summer. The more she cut, the more plant stock they seemed to have.

After a while she came back to Bruce and Frank to inspect their work. She shook her head over several of the burlapped roses and pointed to one she had done. It was a plump little package, neatly tied off with a wire. The ones she singled out were thin, scrawny. She told them to do theirs over and returned to her own task.

Frank watched her walk away. "And how did you spend your day? Balling roses." He laughed. "I'm going to be in her pants within two weeks, wanna bet?"

"Her? But she's a ..."

"A dummy? Sure, she is. They make the best lays. They're grateful, you know? And they don't tell. They do what you want them to do. Two weeks. I'll let you know how she is. A side bet. She's a virgin. Am I on?"

Bruce was revolted by the idea of taking a girl like her, revolted by Frank's easy appraisal, his experienced air. That winter Bruce had met Beatrice Langley, and although he looked at other girls, she was the one he always saw. The thought of groping a tall, frozen-faced, slow-witted girl like Cory was sickening.

Somehow Cory kept eluding Frank all spring. She was not where he expected to find her, or a third person entered when he thought he had her alone, or something else happened. He told Bruce that he had the place picked out, back behind the last greenhouse, the one they call Cory's trial greenhouse. A grove of holly trees hid the spot Frank had in mind, and no one ever bothered Cory when she went back to her own greenhouse. That was where she got strange grafts to take, where she hand-pollinated flowers to get new colors, new varities. No one knew what she did there because no one ever asked.

"Leave her alone," Bruce said sharply. "She doesn't bother anyone."

But he knew she did bother Frank. A frown from her was enough to make anyone have to do a day's work over again, and her a dummy, second in charge of a million-dollar operation. Frank resented her; more, he feared her, because if a retard could go up like that in a couple of years, where did it leave someone like him? It wasn't right, he said; Whitman treated her like some kind of special royalty, excusing her from anything she didn't want to do, things she couldn't do that any normal eight-year-old could handle.

One day Frank grinned at Bruce and motioned for him to look at something. It was an envelope. Frank opened it carefully and showed Bruce.

"Seeds," he said triumphantly. "She can't talk about movies, or books, or television, or anything. All she knows is plants. I have the ultimate weapon, my friend."

"What are they?"

"Damned if I know. My old man brought them back from Africa ten, fifteen years ago. They've been around the house ever since. Last night I remembered them and knew I had her."

Bruce thought so, too. He had an impulse to knock the envelope out of Frank's hand, to grind the seeds into the earth, to yell out to Cory to hide, to run away. It was none of his business, he reminded himself, and went back to work.

It was late afternoon when Frank wandered over to Cory's greenhouse. Bruce watched him helplessly and slowly followed, knowing he would not interfere. He wished a storm would come up, lightning hit the greenhouse, set fire to the holly grove. At the screened door he stopped and listened.

"I knew you'd be the only one to plant them," Frank was saying. "See that black one? It's almost like a stone, isn't it? And those little ones in the glassine envelope, they're more like grains of dust than seeds. And that red one. That must be the dragon seed."

Her voice did not carry enough for Bruce to make out her words.

Frank laughed. "Sure they did. Where do you think dragons came from? Two ways: seeds like that and their own teeth. When you grow one, you save the teeth and plant them, too. They'll grow. You want to borrow my book about dragons?"

Bruce could no longer choose to move or not to move. He was as cold, as rigid as stone, without will as he listened to Frank's voice, then the wordless murmur that was her voice, Frank's voice again, like a snare drawing tighter and tighter before the victim ever had a chance to suspect its presence. He was moving her towards the back door, saying what a wonderful surprise she would have for Mr. Whitman when the seeds sprouted. Then he was talking about how much the seeds cost, how he had been willing to pay so much because he liked her. Bruce could imagine his hands on her now, her bewilderment.

"When a man likes a girl and she likes him, it's the most natural thing in the world to show each other."

Bruce never saw him coming, but suddenly Whitman was there, entering the greenhouse. "Cory, you run along home now." His voice was low and easy, the way he always spoke to her. She ran from the greenhouse clutching the envelope, ran to her bicycle and sped away. "You, you piece of shit! Get your gear and clear out and don't come back."

"You've got no right, Mr. Whitman. I wasn't going to hurt her."

"You say another word and I'm going to whip you. Get out!"

Frank came out blinking in the bright sunlight. He called over his shoulder, "She's got free will, doesn't she? I was going to give her a good time, a little fun, that's all."

Bruce hurried back to the new greenhouse, where he was supposed to be caulking windows.

The next day when he met Whitman, he saw contempt on the old man's face.

Bruce opens his eyes in order to stop seeing that look. It is still there.

August heat lay over the land like someone opened the door to hell, Whitman thought, pulling up in the driveway of the Davenport house. He was not sure what he would say to Mrs. Davenport, but he had to say something, let her know Cory was vulnerable. All summer he had worried about this, pondered what he should do, what he could do, and finally he had got in his truck and started out to do something, but he still did not know what.

Mrs. Davenport was slightly built, pretty; she looked frightened, the same look that Cory got now and then. "Is anything wrong?"

"No, I didn't mean to scare you like that. I just dropped in to...make sure they did a good job with the greenhouse. Been meaning to check it out for months. Too busy."

She relaxed and admitted him to the house. It was cooler inside than out; the drapes were closed, and a fan moved the air. Whitman had never been here before; he was surprised for a reason he could not put a name to. He had expected poverty, maybe, and this was middle-class nice. Cory dressed as if every penny had to be weighed. The house was clean without being antiseptic; there were bookshelves and a stereo and an oversize television. No plants, he noticed with disappointment.

In Cory's room he nodded; this was what he expected. The greenhouse had been built next to her room, a door led to it. A miniature rose in full bloom, each perfect yellow blossom smaller than a fingertip; half a dozen hanging orchids enclosed in plastic bags to conserve moisture during this hot dry weather; a bench covered with blooming flowers—lobelias, begonias, a bronze-leaved geranium in bud....

He looked at the joints of the greenhouse and peered at the lights, the heater, while Mrs. Davenport hovered in the doorway. There was room for only one in here.

"Looks fine," he said then. "Just fine. She's enjoying it, isn't she?"

"You've been awfully good to her," Mrs. Davenport said softly. "I've wanted to thank you, but..."

"She earned it," he said brusquely. "She saved my business last winter. She's a good worker, the best one I've got."

Mrs. Davenport nodded. "She's good with plants."

"With plants," he agreed, and now they looked at each other.

She knew he had come to tell her something, to ask her something, to warn her....She felt the knife in her chest come alive, waiting.

And he found he could not bring any more torment to this woman. He sighed. She had done the best she could. Maybe she had even talked to Cory about boys, about drugs, about sex. If she hadn't and if he brought up any of it now, she would know something had happened, something that forced him to come here. He took a deep breath and smiled at her and, using the voice he used with Cory, he said, "She's a good girl, Mrs. Davenport. You've done a good job with her."

The next day he talked to Cory himself. What he said, quickly, almost roughly, was, "If any guy around here bothers you, you come tell me first thing. Understand?" It was all he could do.

For his sixtieth birthday that fall Cory gave him the bronze-leaved geranium; it had yellow flowers. "I'll be damned!" he said huskily. "I'll just be damned!" They would have to name it, protect the seeds as if they were Christ's tears, see if they came true....He looked from the plant to Cory, and her smile brought tears to his eyes.

A steady rain is falling in Portland. Bruce stands before a glass wall and watches the water on the tarmac. Today is like a repeat of his last trip home: It was raining that day, too; he had the same flights, stood in this same spot. That day he wanted to sing and dance all through the terminal, tell every stranger that he had his Ph.D. and a job and a fiancée....The standing water has an oil swirl that twists and turns, separates, recombines; it has a violet sheen that changes to blue, green....

He drove to all the places he had known, hiked some muddy trails, swilled beer at the old bars, saw a couple of his old girlfriends—just for a drink or lunch, nothing more. He was too full of Beatrice for anything more. They were already living together, and in one month they would be married and move to Savannah.

He stands at the glass wall watching the rain, the uneasy standing water, fingering the Lucite piece in his pocket. If only this could be that day, the intervening time a bad dream. He remembers.

He had no intention of going into the greenhouses or onto the property;

196

it was simply an act of finishing up the past that took him to Whitman's that Saturday. He wanted to say good-bye to all the past, the good and the bad. He drove by slowly, waved, and left that part of his life for good.

A mile or two from the nursery he saw Cory pushing her bicycle on the shoulder of the road. He knew it was she as soon as the figure emerged from the rain and mist and became human, not just a shadow. He slowed down, passed her, then stopped on the shoulder and got out.

"Hey, Cory, remember me? I used to work at Whitman's."

She stopped, peered at him awhile, then came on toward him and said hello. She was encased in a long green poncho with a hood pulled down nearly to her eyes.

"What happened? You have an accident?" The rain was cold and steady, already soaking through his sweater, into his shoes. He remembered the day she had taught them how to ball up the roses; it had rained that afternoon.

She shook her head and pointed to the front tire, which was flat.

"Let's put the bike in the station wagon, and I'll give you a ride home."

As soon as he spoke, he was afraid she would remember that other day, connect him with Frank, but she did not hesitate. She nodded and wheeled the bicycle toward the station wagon. They put it in, she sat in the passenger seat, and he got in and started to drive, and he searched for something to talk about. "You'll have to direct me," he said, glancing at her. She looked ahead with no sign of unease.

She directed him, he assumed, the same way she rode her bike to work, through back streets, secondary roads with deep potholes and no traffic. Because she waited until they were at the corners where he was to turn, he slowed down again and then again. The wagon grated sickeningly as the left rear wheel sank into a hole.

Again he looked at Cory; she had not changed her position or expression. *Damn her eyes*, he thought, twisting the steering wheel hard, creeping along.

"You ever plant those funny seeds Frank gave you?" he asked.

She nodded.

He had to drag it out of her. One was a banana plant. There was a fuzzy bush that was too young to flower yet, maybe a tree, she didn't know. And one was a dragon plant, with a red dragon flower.

"You're kidding."

She remained silent until they had to turn again, and suddenly they were at her house. "You want to see it?" she asked.

He wanted to get away from her, never see her again, never think of her again, but he found himself nodding. She led him through the house; no one else was there, but lights were on, as if her parents would be back soon. She took him to her room, through it to the small greenhouse, and pointed to a bushy plant with a single red flower and many tiny buds.

He went closer and looked at it curiously, just a red flower. Pretty and unusual, but no more than that. The air in the greenhouse, in her bedroom, was spicy, sharp, and clean. Beyond the glass walls, over his head against the glass ceiling, the rain was beating, running down crazily; the world was gray, and in here the light was green, there was a stillness. He turned abruptly from the greenhouse and looked at Cory, who was standing inside the doorway of her room. He started to say it was just a flower, but he said nothing; he found he did not want to break the silence.

He reached out and touched her cheek, and a look of terror crossed her face. He wanted to shout, "For God's sake, you don't have to be afraid of me!" His hand left her cheek and went to her shoulder, and she was moving backward, he was following, now with his hands on both her shoulders, and he knew she was not going to stop him and he was not going to stop himself. He fumbled with her clothes and his own, and then he was atop her, and she was moaning, then keening. And he heard a voice crying, "Oh my God! Oh my God! Oh my God!..." and finally realized it was his own voice.

When it was over, he pushed himself away from her. She was staring dry eyed at the ceiling. He grabbed his jeans and ran to the bathroom he had seen on their way in. He slammed the door and leaned against it shaking, and again he heard his strange, thick voice: "Oh my God! Oh my God!"

When he returned to the bedroom she was not there. He looked in the greenhouse, but it was empty. He hesitated, then pulled the bloom from the dragon plant and left.

Sitting in the plane, waiting for takeoff, he watches the rain running crazily down the window, and he realizes at last what he has come back for. He has to give the dragon flower back to her. He has to face her and make her take it back. He looks at his hand and slowly opens it and stares at the Lucite slab with a red flower embedded in it. She has to take it back, he says to himself.

Mrs. Davenport had to tell him; she couldn't make such a terrible decision by herself. For days she put it off, trying to think her way out of it, trying to will Cory back to normal, but it was no use, and finally she knew she had to tell him. They could take Cory away for a week or two, a vacation, they would say, and have it aborted. People did it every day.

He turned ashen, and a low, wordless cry came from his tightly clamped lips. He rushed to Cory's room and banged the door closed. Mrs. Davenport heard crashes, glass breaking. She sat rocking back and forth on a kitchen chair, clutching her head, her arms tight over her ears. When Cory came home, he pulled Mrs. Davenport away from the door and stormed out to meet Cory at the back of the house, where she was parking her bicycle. He grabbed it in both hands and hurled it through the last standing wall of her greenhouse. Cory stared, then turned around and walked away. Raymond held Mrs. Davenport's arm and would not let her run after her daughter.

It was nearly ten when Cory knocked on Whitman's door. He opened it and stood back for her to come in.

"What is it, Cory? What happened?"

She told him, and they looked at each other. Whitman nodded and motioned for her to go into the living room. "You have anything to eat yet?" She shook her head, and he could see the fatigue hunching her shoulders, drawing lines under her eyes. "Sit down, Cory. I'll get something hot for you." She followed him to the kitchen and sat at the table while he heated up leftover pot roast. She was waiting for him to tell her what to do, where to go. They would have it aborted, he thought, and he knew they must not to do that, not to Cory.

It is only late afternoon when Bruce arrives at the nursery. It seems impossible for such a long day to go on and never turn into night, as this has done. Everything looks exactly the same, as if this little pocket of the universe knows nothing of time and change.

He sees Whitman crossing the drive between the toolshed and the boiler house, and he starts to go to him. He has to see Cory alone, have a private talk with her, maybe in Whitman's house. He cannot talk to her while she's on her knees pruning roses, or potting up marigolds, or some damn thing. He draws nearer to Whitman, who looks the same, maybe even more vigorous than before, less tired. Bruce starts to call him, then stops as a woman comes from around the potting shed, pulling one of the long wagons. A small boy is sitting on the wagon, trying to drag his feet on the ground. He is too short to reach.

"Cory!" he says; his voice is a whisper that no one can hear, but she stops and looks at him, and her smile vanishes, leaving him feeling chilled.

The boy jumps from the wagon and runs across the drive to the boiler house, yelling, "Hey, Dad, we've got to go in now. Momma says it's going to rain real hard."

"You always knew," Bruce whispers, looking at her. She has not moved. His legs are heavy, his feet leaden, as he stumbles back to the rented car and gets in.

199

The ran starts as he drives back to his parents' house. It is a hard, pounding rain that the windshield wipers cannot control. He is forced to pull off the road and wait for the rain to let up, he is driving blind.

Only after he stops does he realize that he is weeping. He puts his forehead on the steering wheel and listens to the rain. His son, the son that Beatrice will never have. He hears her voice throught the rain, "We can't go on like this, you know. If it isn't physical, it's psychological. It's that simple. You have to see a doctor."

"I have nightmares, Doctor. About dragons. Always about dragons. And it isn't fair. It worked out for her; she's happy."

"Mr. Enfield, now that you know she's happy, perhaps you won't need to torture yourself with guilt. Perhaps that is why you went back, to make amends, and you found none are needed." He groans and starts the car. He won't see a doctor, he knows. There is no way he can ever explain.

"Bruce, what happened? It used to be so good with us. What happened?"

Cory happened, he thinks, and he feels the breath of the dragon on his back, in his chest, in his loins.

From the shelter of the porch Whitman and the child in his arms watch as Cory reaches out one hand, palm up, and then the other to the first drops of rain.

She tilts her head back, and the rain falls onto her face as she turns in a slow dance, welcoming the rain.

Permafrost

Roger Zelazny

Roger Zelazny lives in New Mexico. While best known for his Amber fantasy series, his science fiction writing is vivid and hard-edged. Among his novels are *The Dream Master, This Immortal, Creatures of Light and Darkness,* and *Lord of Light.* His most recent novel is a horror/humor/mystery collaboration with Gahan Wilson called *A Night in the Lonesome October.* Zelazny has won three Nebula Awards and six Hugos, including one for "Permafrost." His short fiction is collected in *The Doors of His Face, The Lamp of His Mouth, Unicorn Variations,* and *Frost and Fire.*

"Permafrost" is a love story that takes place on a frozen world. It was originally published in April 1986.

Permafrost

Roger Zelazny

High upon the western slope of Mount Kilimanjaro is the dried and frozen carcass of a leopard. An author is always necessary to explain what it was doing there because stiff leopards don't talk much.

THE MAN. The music seems to come and go with a will of its own. At least turning the knob on the bedside unit has no effect on its presence or absence. A half-familiar, alien tune, troubling in a way. The phone rings, and he answers it. There is no one there. Again.

Four times during the past half hour, while grooming himself, dressing and rehearsing his arguments, he has received non-calls. When he checked with the desk he was told there were no calls. But that damned clerk-thing had to be malfunctioning—like everything else in this place.

The wind, already heavy, rises, hurling particles of ice against the building with a sound like multitudes of tiny claws scratching. The whining of steel shutters sliding into place startles him. But worst of all, in his reflex glance at the nearest window, it seems he has seen a face.

Impossible of course. This is the third floor. A trick of light upon hard-driven flakes: Nerves.

Yes. He has been nervous since their arrival this morning. Before then, even...

He pushes past Dorothy's stuff upon the countertop, locates a small package among his own articles. He unwraps a flat red rectangle about the size of his thumbnail. He rolls up his sleeve and slaps the patch against the inside of his left elbow.

The tranquilizer discharges immediately into his bloodstream. He takes

203

several deep breaths, then peels off the patch and drops it into the disposal unit. He rolls his sleeve down, reaches for his jacket.

The music rises in volume, as if competing with the blast of the wind, the rattle of the icy flakes. Across the room the videoscreen comes on of its own accord.

The face. The same face. Just for an instant. He is certain. And then channelless static, wavy lines. Snow. He chuckles.

All right, play it that way, nerves, he thinks. *You've every reason. But the trank's coming to get you now. Better have your fun quick. You're about to be shut down.*

The videoscreen cuts into a porn show.

Smiling, the woman mounts the man....

The picture switches to a voiceless commentator on something or other.

He will survive. He is a survivor. He, Paul Plaige, has done risky things before and has always made it through. It is just that having Dorothy along creates a kind of déjà vu that he finds unsettling. No matter.

She is waiting for him in the bar. Let her wait. A few drinks will make her easier to persuade—unless they make her bitchy. That sometimes happens, too. Either way, he has to talk her out of the thing.

Silence. The wind stops. The scratching ceases. The music is gone.

The whirring. The window screens dilate upon the empty city.

Silence, under totally overcast skies. Mountains of ice ringing the place. Nothing moving. Even the video has gone dead.

He recoils at the sudden flash from a peripheral unit far to his left across the city. The laser beam hits a key point on the glacier, and it falls away.

Moments later he hears the hollow, booming sound of the crashing ice. A powdery storm has risen like surf at the ice mount's foot. He smiles at the power, the timing, the display. Andrew Aldon...always on the job, dueling with the elements, stalemating nature herself, immortal guardian of Playpoint. At least Aldon never malfunctions.

The silence comes again. As he watches the risen snows settle he feels the tranquilizer beginning to work. It would be good not to have to worry about money again. The past two years have taken a lot out of him. Seeing all his investments fail in the Big Washout—that was when his nerves had first begun to act up. He has grown softer than he was a century ago—a young, rawboned soldier of fortune then, out to make his bundle and enjoy it. And he had. Now he has to do it again, though this time will be easier—except for Dorothy.

He thinks of her. A century younger than himself, still in her twenties, sometimes reckless, used to all of the good things in life. There is something vulnerable about Dorothy, times when she lapses into such a strong dependence that he feels oddly moved. Other times, it just irritates the hell out of him. Perhaps this is the closest he can come to love now, an occasional ambivalent response to being needed. But of course she is loaded. That breeds a certain measure of necessary courtesy. Until he can make his own bundle again, anyway. But none of these things are the reason he has to keep her from accompanying him on his journey. It goes beyond love or money. It is survival.

The laser flashes again, this time to the right. He waits for the crash.

THE STATUE. It is not a pretty pose. She lies frosted in an ice cave, looking like one of Rodin's less comfortable figures, partly propped on her left side, right elbow raised above her head, hand hanging near her face, shoulders against the wall, left leg completely buried.

She has on a gray parka, the hood slipped back to reveal twisted strands of dark blond hair; and she wears blue trousers; there is a black boot on the one foot that is visible.

She is coated with ice, and within the much-refracted light of the cave what can be seen of her features is not unpleasant but not strikingly attractive either. She looks to be in her twenties.

There are a number of fracture lines within the cave's walls and floor. Overhead, countless icicles hang like stalactites, sparkling jewellike in the much-bounced light. The grotto has a stepped slope to it with the statue at its higher end, giving to the place a vaguely shrinelike appearance.

On those occasions when the cloud cover is broken at sundown a reddish light is cast about her figure.

She has actually moved in the course of a century—a few inches, from a general shifting of the ice. Tricks of the light makes her seem to move more frequently, however.

The entire tableau might give the impression that this is merely a pathetic woman who had been trapped and frozen to death here, rather than the statue of the living goddess in the place where it all began.

THE WOMAN. She sits in the bar beside the window. The patio outside is gray and angular and drifted with snow; the flowerbeds are filled with dead plants—stiff, flattened, and frozen. She does not mind the view. Far from it. Winter is a season of death and cold, and she likes being reminded of it. She enjoys the prospect of pitting herself against its frigid and very visible fangs. A faint flash of light passes over the patio, followed by a distant roaring sound. She sips her drink and licks her lips and listens to the soft music that fills the air.

She is alone. The bartender and all of the other help here are of the mechanical variety. If anyone other than Paul were to walk in, she would probably scream. They are the only people in the hotel during this long off-season. Except for the sleepers, they are the only people in all of Playpoint.

And Paul...He will be along soon to take her to the dining room. There they can summon holo-ghosts to people the other tables, if they wish. She does not wish. She likes being alone with Paul at a time like this, on the eve of a great adventure.

He will tell her his plans over coffee, and perhaps even this afternoon they might obtain the necessary equipment to begin the exploration for that which would put him on his feet again financially, return to him his self-respect. It will of course be dangerous and very rewarding. She finishes her drink, rises, and crosses to the bar for another.

And Paul...She had really caught a falling star, a swashbuckler on the way down, a man with a glamorous past just balanced on the brink of ruin. The teetering had already begun when they had met two years before, which had made it even more exciting. Of course, he needed a woman like her to lean upon at such a time. It wasn't just her money. She could never believe the things her late parents had said about him. No, he does care for her. He is strangely vulnerable and dependent.

She wants to turn him back into the man he once must have been, and then of course that man will need her, too. The things he had been—that is what she needs most of all—a man who can reach up and bat the moon away. He must have been like that long ago.

She tastes her second drink.

The son of a bitch had better hurry, though. She is getting hungry.

THE CITY. Playpoint is located on the world known as Balfrost, atop a high peninsula that slopes down to a now-frozen sea. Playpoint contains all of the facilities for an adult playground, and is one of the more popular resorts in this sector of the galaxy from late spring through early autumn—approximately fifty Earth years. Then winter comes on like a period of glaciation, and everybody goes away for half a century—or half a year, depending on how one regards such matters. During this time Playpoint is given into the care of its automated defense and maintenance routine. This is a self-repairing system, directed toward cleaning, plowing, thawing, melting, warming everything in need of such care, as well as directly combating the encroaching ice and snow. And all of these functions are done under the supervision of a well-protected central computer that also studies the weather and climate patterns, anticipating as well as reacting.

This system has worked successfully for many centuries, delivering Playpoint over to spring and pleasure in reasonably good condition at the end of each long winter.

There are mountains behind Playpoint, water (or ice, depending on the season) on three sides, weather and navigation satellites high above. In a bunker beneath the administration building is a pair of sleepers—generally a man and a woman—who awaken once every year or so to physically inspect the maintenance system's operations and to deal with any special situations that might have arisen. An alarm may arouse them for emergencies at any time. They are well paid, and over the years they have proven worth the investment. The central computer has at its disposal explosives and lasers as well as a great variety of robots. Usually it keeps a little ahead of the game, and it seldom falls behind for long.

At the moment, things are about even because the weather has been particularly nasty recently.

Zzzzt! Another block of ice has become a puddle.

Zzzzt! The puddle has been evaporated. The molecules climb toward a place where they can get together and return as snow.

The glaciers shuffle their feet, edge forward. *Zzzzt!* Their gain has become a loss.

Andrew Aldon knows exactly what he is doing.

CONVERSATIONS. The waiter, needing lubrication, rolls off after having served them, passing through a pair of swinging doors.

She giggles. "Wobbly," she says.

"Old World charm," he agrees, trying and failing to catch her eye as he smiles.

"You have everything worked out?" she asks after they have begun eating.

"Sort of," he says, smiling again.

"Is that a yes or a no?"

"Both. I need more information. I want to go and check things over first. Then I can figure the best course of action."

"I note your use of the singular pronoun," she says steadily, meeting his gaze at last.

His smile freezes and fades.

"I was referring to only a little preliminary scouting," he says softly.

"No," she says. "We. Even for a little preliminary scouting."

He sighs and sets down his fork.

"This will have very little to do with anything to come later," he begins. "Things have changed a lot. I'll have to locate a new route. This will just be dull work and no fun."

"I didn't come along for fun," she replies. "We were going to share

207

everything, remember? That includes boredom, danger, and everything else. That was the understanding when I agreed to pay our way."

"I'd a feeling it would come to that," he says, after a moment.

"Come to it? It's always been there. That was our agreement."

He raises his goblet and sips the wine.

"Of course. I'm not trying to rewrite history. It's just that things would go faster if I could do some of the initial looking around myself. I can move more quickly alone."

"What's the hurry?" she says. "A few days this way or that. I'm in pretty good shape. I won't slow you down all that much."

"I'd the impression you didn't particularly like it here. I just wanted to hurry things up so we could get the hell out."

"That's very considerate," she says, beginning to eat again. "But that's my problem, isn't it?" She looks up at him. "Unless there's some other reason you don't want me along?"

He drops his gaze quickly, picks up his fork. "Don't be silly."

She smiles. "Then that's settled. I'll go with you this afternoon to look for the trail."

The music stops, to be succeeded by a sound as of the clearing of a throat. Then, "Excuse me for what may seem like eavesdropping," comes a deep, masculine voice. "It is actually only a part of a simple monitoring function I keep in effect—"

"Aldon!" Paul exclaims.

"At your service, Mr. Plaige, more or less. I choose to make my presence known only because I did indeed overhear you, and the matter of your safety overrides the good manners that would otherwise dictate reticence. I've been receiving reports that indicate we could be hit by some extremely bad weather this afternoon. So if you were planning an extended sojourn outside I would recommend you postpone it."

"Oh," Dorothy says.

"Thanks," Paul says.

"I shall now absent myself. Enjoy your meal and your stay."

The music returns.

"Aldon?" Paul asks.

There is no reply.

"Looks as if we do it tomorrow or later."

"Yes," Paul agrees, and he is smiling his first relaxed smile of the day. And thinking fast.

THE WORLD. Life on Balfrost proceeds in peculiar cycles. There are

208

great migrations of animal life and quasi-animal life to the equatorial regions during the long winter. Life in the depths of the seas goes on. And the permafrost vibrates with its own style of life.

The permafrost. Throughout the winter and on through the spring the permafrost lives at its peak. It is laced with mycelia—twining, probing, touching, knotting themselves into ganglia, reaching out to infiltrate other systems. It girds the globe, vibrating like a collective unconscious throughout the winter. In the spring it sends up stalks that develop gray, flowerlike appendages for a few days. These blooms then collapse to reveal dark pods that subsequently burst with small, popping sounds, releasing clouds of sparkling spores that the winds bear just about everywhere. These are extremely hardy, like the mycelia they will one day become.

The heat of summer finally works its way down into the permafrost, and the strands doze their way into a long period of quiescence. When the cold returns they are roused, spores send forth new filaments that repair old damages, create new synapses. A current begins to flow. The life of summer is like a fading dream. For eons this had been the way of things upon Balfrost, within Balfrost. Then the goddess decreed otherwise. Winter's queen spread her hands, and there came a change.

THE SLEEPERS. Paul makes his way through swirling flakes to the administration building. It has been a simpler matter than he had anticipated, persuading Dorothy to use the sleep-induction unit to be well rested for the morrow. He had pretended to use the other unit himself, resisting its blandishments until he was certain she was asleep and he could slip off undetected.

He lets himself into the vaultlike building, takes all of the old familiar turns, makes his way down a low ramp. The room is unlocked and a bit chilly, but he begins to perspire when he enters. The two cold lockers are in operation. He checks their monitoring systems and sees that everything is in order.

All right, go! Borrow the equipment now. They won't be using it.

He hesitates.

He draws nearer and looks down through the view plates at the faces of the sleepers. No resemblance, thank God. He realizes then that he is trembling. He backs away, turns, and flees toward the storage area.

Later, in a yellow snowslider, carrying special equipment, he heads inland.

As he drives, the snow ceases falling and the winds die down. He smiles. The snows sparkle before him, and landmarks do not seem all that unfamiliar. Good omens, at last.

Then something crosses his path, turns, halts, and faces him.

209

ANDREW ALDON. Andrew Aldon, once a man of considerable integrity and resource, had on his deathbed opted for continued existence as a computer program, the enchanted loom of his mind shuttling and weaving thereafter as central processing's judgmental program in the great guardian computerplex at Playpoint. And there he functions as a program of considerable integrity and resource. He maintains the city, and fights the elements. He does not merely respond to pressures, but he anticipates structural and functional needs; he generally outguesses the weather. Like the professional soldier he once had been, he keeps himself in a state of constant alert—not really difficult considering the resources available to him. He is seldom wrong, always competent, and sometimes brilliant. Occasionally he resents his fleshless state. Occasionally he feels lonely.

This afternoon he is puzzled by the sudden veering off of the storm he had anticipated and by the spell of clement weather that has followed this meteorological quirk. His mathematics were elegant, but the weather was not. It seems peculiar that this should come at a time of so many other little irregularities, such as unusual ice adjustments, equipment glitches, and the peculiar behavior of machinery in the one occupied room of the hotel—a room troublesomely tenanted by a non grata ghost from the past.

So he watches for a time. He is ready to intervene when Paul enters the administration building and goes to the bunkers. But Paul does nothing that might bring harm to the sleepers. His curiosity is dominant when Paul draws equipment. He continues to watch. This is because in his judgment, Paul bears watching.

Aldon decides to act only when he detects a development that runs counter to anything in his experience. He sends one of his mobile units to intercept Paul as the man heads out of town. It catches up with him at a bending of the way and slides into his path with one appendage upraised.

"Stop!" Aldon calls through the speaker.

Paul brakes his vehicle and sits for a moment regarding the machine.

Then he smiles faintly. "I assume you have good reason for interfering with a guest's freedom of movement."

"Your safety takes precedence."

"I am perfectly safe."

"At the moment."

"What do you mean?"

"This weather pattern has suddenly become more than a little unusual. You seem to occupy a drifting island of calm while a storm rages about you."

"So I'll take advantage of it now and face the consequences later, if need

210

be."

"It is your choice. I wanted it to be an informed one, however."

"All right. You've informed me. Now get out of my way."

"In a moment. You departed under rather unusual circumstances the last time you were here—in breach of your contract."

"Check your legal bank if you've got one. That statute's run for prosecuting me on that."

"There are some things on which there is no statute of limitations."

"What do you mean by that? I turned in a report on what happened that day."

"One which—conveniently—could not be verified. You were arguing that day...."

"We always argued. That's just the way we were. If you have something to say about it, say it."

"No, I have nothing more to say about it. My only intention is to caution you—"

"Okay, I'm cautioned."

"To caution you in more ways than the obvious."

"I don't understand."

"I am not certain that things are the same here now as when you left last winter."

"Everything changes."

"Yes, but that is not what I mean. There is something peculiar about this place now. The past is no longer a good guide for the present. More and more anomalies keep cropping up. Sometimes it feels as if the world is testing me or playing games with me."

"You're getting paranoid, Aldon. You've been in that box too long. Maybe it's time to terminate."

"You son of a bitch, I'm trying to tell you something. I've run a lot of figures on this, and all this shit started shortly after you left. The human part of me still has hunches, and I've a feeling there's a connection. If you know all about this and can cope with it, fine. If you don't, I think you should watch out. Better yet, turn around and go home."

"I can't."

"Even if there is something out there, something that is making it easy for you—for the moment?"

"What are you trying to say?"

"I am reminded of the old Gaia hypothesis—Lovelock, twentieth century...."

"Planetary intelligence. I've heard of it. Never met one, though."

"Are you certain? I sometimes feel I'm confronting one."

"What if something is out there and it wants you—is leading you on like a will-o'-the-wisp?"

"It would be my problem, not yours."

"I can protect you against it. Go back to Playpoint."

"No thanks. I will survive."

"What of Dorothy?"

"What of her?"

"You would leave her alone when she might need you?"

"Let me worry about that."

"Your last woman didn't fare too well."

"Damn it! Get out of my way, or I'll run you down!"

The robot withdraws from the trail. Through its sensors Aldon watches Paul drive away.

Very well, he decides. *We know where we stand, Paul. And you haven't changed. That makes it easier.*

Aldon further focuses his divided attention. To Dorothy now. Clad in heated garments. Walking. Approaching the building from which she had seen Paul emerge on his vehicle. She had hailed and cursed him, but the winds had carried her words away. She, too, had only feigned sleep. After a suitable time, then, she sought to follow. Aldon watches her stumble once and wants to reach out to assist her, but there is no mobile unit handy. He routes one toward the area against further accidents.

"Damn him!" she mutters as she passes along the street, ribbons of snow rising and twisting away before her.

"Where are you going, Dorothy?" Aldon asks over a nearby PA speaker.

She halts and turns. "Who—?"

"Andrew Aldon," he replies. "I have been observing your progress."

"Why?" she asks.

"Your safety concerns me."

"That storm you mentioned earlier?"

"Partly."

"I'm a big girl. I can take care of myself. What do you mean *partly?*"

"You move in dangerous company."

"Paul? How so?"

"He once took a woman into that same wild area he is heading for now. She did not come back."

"He told me all about that. There was an accident."

"And no witnesses."

"What are you trying to say?"

"It is suspicious. That is all."

She begins moving again, toward the administrative building. Aldon switches to another speaker, within its entrance.

"I accuse him of nothing. If you choose to trust him, fine. But don't trust the weather. It would be best for you to return to the hotel."

"Thanks but no thanks," she says, entering the building.

He follows her as she explores, is aware of her quickening pulse when she halts beside the cold bunkers.

"These are the sleepers?"

"Yes. Paul held such a position once, as did the unfortunate woman."

"I know. Look, I'm going to follow him whether you approve or not. So why not just tell me where those sleds are kept?"

"Very well. I will do even more than that. I will guide you."

"What do you mean?"

"I request a favor—one that will actually benefit you."

"Name it."

"In the equipment locker behind you, you will find a remote-sensor bracelet. It is also a two-way communication link. Wear it. I can be with you then. To assist you. Perhaps even to protect you."

"You can help me to follow him?"

"Yes."

"All right. I can buy that."

She moves to the locker, opens it.

"Here's something that looks like a bracelet, with doodads."

"Yes. Depress the red stud."

She does. His voice now emerges clearly from the unit.

"Put it on, and I'll show you the way."

"Right."

SNOWSCAPE. Sheets and hills of white, tufts of evergreen shrubbery, protruding joints of rock, snowdevils twirled like tops beneath wind's lash...light and shade. Cracking sky. Tracks in sheltered areas, smoothness beyond.

She follows, masked and bundled.

"I've lost him," she mutters, hunched behind tghe curved windscreen of her yellow, bullet-shaped vehicle.

"Straight ahead, past those two rocks. Stay in the lee of the ridge. I'll tell you when to turn. I've a satellite overhead. If the clouds stay parted—strangely parted..."

"What do you mean?"

"He seems to be enjoying light from the only break in the cloud cover over the entire area."

"Coincidence."

"I wonder."

"What else could it be?"

"It is almost as if something had opened a door for him."

"Mysticism from a computer?"

"I am not a computer."

"I'm sorry, Mr. Aldon. I know that you were once a man...."

"I am still a man."

"Sorry."

"There are many things I would like to know. Your arrival here comes at an unusual time of year. Paul took some prospecting equipment with him...."

"Yes. It's not against the law. In fact, it is one of the vacation features here, isn't it?"

"Yes. There are many interesting minerals about, some of them precious."

"Well, Paul wants some more, and he didn't want a crowd around while he was looking."

"More?"

"Yes, he made a strike here years ago. Yndella crystals."

"I see. Interesting."

"What's in this for you, anyway?"

"Protecting visitors is a part of my job. In your case, I feel particularly protective."

"How so?"

"In my earlier life I was attracted to women of your—specifications. Physical, as well as what I can tell of the rest."

Two-beat pause, then, "You are blushing."

"Compliments do that to me," she says, "and that's a hell of a monitoring system you have. What's it like?"

"Oh, I can tell your body temperature, your pulse rate—"

"No, I mean, what's it like being—what you are?"

Three-beat pause. "Godlike in some ways. Very human in others— almost exaggeratedly so. I feel something of an amplification of everything I was earlier. Perhaps it's a compensation or a clinging to things past. You make me feel nostalgic—among other things. Don't fret. I'm enjoying it."

"I'd like to have met you then."

"Mutual."

"What were you like?"

"Imagine me as you would. I'll come off looking better that way."

She laughs. She adjusts her filters. She thinks about Paul.

"What was *he* like in his earlier days—Paul?" she asks.

"Probably pretty much the way he is now, only less polished."

"In other words, you don't care to say."

The trail turns upward more steeply, curves to the right. She hears winds but does not feel them. Cloud-shadow grayness lies all about, but her trail/*his* trail is lighted.

"I don't really know," Aldon says, after a time, "and I will not guess, in the case of someone you care about."

"Gallant," she observes.

"No, just fair," he replies. "I might be wrong."

They continue to the top of the rise, where Dorothy draws a sharp breath and further darkens her goggles agains the sudden blaze where a range of ice fractures rainbows and strews their shards like confetti in all directions.

"God!" she says.

"Or goddess," Aldon replies.

"A goddess, sleeping in a circle of flame?"

"Not sleeping."

"That would be a lady for you, Aldon—if she existed. God and goddess."

"I do not want a goddess."

"I can see his tracks, heading into that."

"Not swerving a bit, as if he knows where he's going."

She follows, tracing slopes like the curves of a pale torso. The world is stillness and light and whiteness. Aldon on her wrist hums softly now, an old tune, whether of love or martial matters she isn't certain. Distances are distorted, perspectives skewed. She finds herself humming softly along with him, heading for the place where Paul's tracks find their vanishing point and enter infinity.

THE LIMP WATCH HUNG UPON THE TREE LIMB. My lucky day. The weather...trail clean. Things changed but not so out of shape I can't tell where it is. The lights! God, yes! Iceshine, mounds of prisms.... If only the opening is still there.... Should have brought explosives. There has been shifting, maybe a collapse. Must get in. Return later with Dorothy! But first—clean up, get rid of...it. If she's still there.... Swallowed up maybe. That would be good, best. Things seldom are, though. I—When it happened. Wasn't as if. Wasn't what. Was.... Was shaking the ground. Cracking, splitting. Icicles ringing, rattling, banging about. Thought we'd go under. Both of us. She was going in. So was the bag of the stuff. Grabbed the stuff. Only because it was nearer. Would have helped her if—Couldn't. Could I? Ceiling was slipping. Get out. No sense both of us getting it. Got out. She'd've done the same. Wouldn't she? Her eyes....Glenda! Maybe...No! Couldn't have. Just couldn't. Could I? Silly. After all these years. There was a moment. Just a moment, though. A lull. If I'd known it was coming I might have. No. Ran. Your face at the window, on the screen, in a sometime dream, Glenda. It wasn't that I didn't. Blaze of hills. Fire and eyes. Ice. Ice. Fire and snow. Blazing hearthful. Ice. Ice. Straight through the ice the long road lies. The fire hangs high above. The screaming. The crash. And the silence. Get out. Yet. Different? No. It could never have. That was the way. Not my fault....Damn it. Everything I could. Glenda. Up ahead. Yes. Long curve. Then down. Winding back in there. The crystals will.... I'll never come back to this place.

THE LIMP TREE LIMB HUNG UPON THE WATCH. Gotcha! Think I can't see through the fog? Can't sneak up on me on little cat feet. Same for your partner across the way. I'll melt off a little more near your bases, too. A lot of housecleaning backed up here....Might as well take advantage of the break. Get those streets perfect....How long? Long....Long legs parting....Long time since. Is it not strange that desire should so many years outlive performance? Unnatural. This weather. A sort of spiritual spring....Extend those beams. Burn. Melt in my hot, red-fingered hands. Back off, I say. I rule here. Clear that courtyard. Unplug that drain. Come opportunity, let me clasp thee. Melt. Burn. I rule here, goddess. Draw back. I've a bomb for every tower of ice, a light for any darkness. Tread carefully here. I feel I begin to know thee. I see thy signature in cloud and fog bank, trace thy ice tresses upon the blowing wind. Thy form lies contoured all about me, white as shining death. We're due an encounter. Let the clouds spiral, ice ring. Earth heave. I rush to meet thee, death or maiden, in halls of crystal upon the heights. Not here. Long, slow fall, ice facade, crashing. Melt. Another....Gotcha!

FROZEN WATCH EMBEDDED IN PERMAFROST. Bristle and thrum. Coming now. Perchance. Perchance. Perchance. I say. Throstle. Crack. Sunder. Split. Open. Coming. Beyond the ice in worlds I have known. Returning. He. Throstle. The mind the mover. To open the way. Come now. Let not to the meeting impediments. Admit. Open. Cloud stand thou still, and wind be leashed. None dare oppose thy passage returning, my killer love. It was but yesterday. A handful of stones....Come singing fresh-armed from the warm places. I have looked upon thy unchanged countenance. I open the way. Come to me. Let not to the mating. I—Girding the globe, I have awakened in all of my places to receive thee. But here, here this special spot, I focus, mind the mover, in place where it all began, my bloody handed, Paul my love, calling, back, for the last good-bye, ice kiss, fire touch, heart stop, blood still, soul freeze, embrace of world and my hate with thy fugitive body, elusive the long year now. Come into the place it has waited. I move there again, up sciatic to spine, behind the frozen eyeballs, waiting and warming. To me. To me now. Throstle and click, bristle and thrum. And runners scratching the snow, my heart slashing parallel. Cut.

PILGRIMAGE. He swerves, turns, slows amid the ragged prominences—ice fallen, ice heaved—in the fields where mountain and glacier wrestle in slow motion, to the accompaniment of occasional cracking and pinging sounds, crashes, growls, and the rattle of blown ice crystals. Here the ground is fissured as well as greatly uneven, and Paul abandons his snowslider. He secures some tools to his belt and his pack, anchors the sled, and commences the trek.

At first, he moves slowly and carefully, but old reflexes return, and soon he is hurrying. Moving from dazzle to shade, he passes among ice forms like grotesque statues of glass. The slope is changed from the old one he remembers, but it feels right. And deep, below, to the right....

Yes. That darker place. The canyon or blocked pass, whichever it was. That seems right, too. He alters his course slightly. He is sweating now within his protective clothing, and his breath comes faster as he increases his pace. His vision blurs, and for a moment, somewhere between glare and shadow, he seems to see....

He halts, sways a moment, then shakes his head, snorts, and continues.

Another hundred meters and he is certain. Those rocky ribs to the northeast, snow rivulets diamond hard between them....He has been here before.

The stillness is almost oppressive. In the distance he sees spumes of windblown snow jetting off and eddying down from a high, white peak. If he stops and listens carefully he can even hear the far winds.

There is a hole in the middle of the clouds, directly overhead. It is as if he were looking downward upon a lake in a crater.

More than unusual. He is tempted to turn back. His trank has worn off, and his stomach feels unsettled. He half-wishes to discover that this is not the place. But he knows that feelings are not very important. He continues until he stands before the opening.

There has been some shifting, some narrowing of the way. He approaches slowly. He regards the passage for a full minute before he moves to enter.

He pushes back his goggles as he comes into the lessened light. He extends a gloved hand, places it upon the facing wall, pushes. Firm. He tests the one behind him. The same.

Three paces forward and the way narrows severely. He turns and sidles. The light grows dimmer, the surface beneath his feet, more slick. He slows. He slides a hand along either wall as he advances. He passes through a tiny spot of light beneath an open ice chimney. Overhead, the wind is howling a high note now, almost whistling it.

The passage begins to widen. As his right hand falls away from the more sharply angling wall his balance is tipped in that direction. He draws back to compensate, but his left foot slides backward and falls. He attempts to rise, slips, and falls again.

Cursing, he begins to crawl forward. This area had not been slick before....He chuckles. Before? A century ago. Things do change in a span like that. They—

The wind begins to howl beyond the cave mouth as he sees the rise of the floor, looks upward along the slope. She is there.

He makes a small noise at the back of his throat and stops, his right hand partly raised. She wears the shadows like veils, but they do not mask her identity. He stares. It's even worse than he had thought. Trapped, she must have lived some time after....

He shakes his head.

No use. She must be cut loose and buried now—disposed of.

He crawls forward. The icy slope does not grow level until he is quite near her. His gaze never leaves her form as he advances. The shadows slide over her. He can almost hear her again.

He thinks of the shadows. She couldn't have moved just then....He stops and studies her face. It is not frozen. It is puckered and sagging as if waterlogged. A caricature of the face he had so often touched. He grimaces and looks away. The leg must be freed. He reaches for his axe.

Before he can take hold of the tool he sees movement of the hand, slow and shaking. It is accompanied by a throaty sigh.

"No...," he whispers, drawing back.

"Yes," comes the reply.

"Glenda."

"I am here." Her head turns slowly. Reddened, watery eyes focus upon his own. "I have been waiting."

"This is insane."

The movement of the face is horrible. It takes him some time to realize that it is a smile.

"I knew that one day you would return."

"How?" he says. "How have you lasted?"

"The body is nothing," she replies. "I had all but forgotten it. I live within the permafrost of this world. My buried foot was in contact with its filaments. It was alive, but it possessed no consciousness until we met. I live everywhere now."

"I am—happy—that you—survived."

She laughs slowly, dryly.

"Really, Paul? How could that be when you left me to die?"

"I had no choice, Glenda. I couldn't save you."

"There was opportunity. You preferred the stones to my life."

"That's not true!"

"You didn't even try." The arms are moving again, less jerkily now. "You didn't even come back to recover my body."

"What would have been the use? You were dead—or I thought you were."

"Exactly. You didn't know, but you ran out anyway. I loved you, Paul. I would have done anything for you."

"I cared about you, too, Glenda. I would have helped you if I could have. If—"

"*If?* Don't give me *if*s. I know what you are."

"I loved you," Paul says. "I'm sorry."

"You loved me? You never said it."

"It's not the sort of thing I talk about easily. Or think about, even."

"Show me," she says. "Come here."

He looks away. "I can't."

She laughs. "You said you loved me."

"You-you don't know how you look. I'm sorry."

"You fool!" Her voice grows hard, imperious. "Had you done it I would have spared your life. It would have shown me that some tiny drop of affection might truly have existed. But you lied. You only used me. You didn't care."

"You're being unfair!"

"Am I? Am I really?" she says. There comes a sound like running water from somewhere nearby. "You would speak to me of fairness? I have hated you, Paul, for nearly a century. Whenever I took a moment from regulating the life of this planet to think about it, I would curse you. In the spring as I shifted my consciousness toward the poles and allowed a part of myself to dream, my nightmares were of you. They actually upset the ecology somewhat, here and there. I have waited, and now you are here. I see nothing to redeem you. I shall use you as you used me—to your destruction. Come to me!"

He feels a force enter into his body. His muscles twitch. He is drawn up to his knees. Held in that position for long moments, then he beholds her as she

219

also rises, drawing a soaking leg from out of the crevice where it had been held. He had heard the running water. She had somehow melted the ice....

She smiles and raises her pasty hands. Multitudes of dark filaments extend from her freed leg down into the crevice.

"Come!" she repeats.

"Please...," he says.

She shakes her head. "Once you were so ardent. I cannot understand you."

"If you're going to kill me then kill me, damn it! But don't—"

Her features begin to flow. Her hands darken and grow firm. In moments she stands before him looking as she did a century ago.

"Glenda!" He rises to his feet.

"Yes. Come now."

He takes a step forward. Another.

Shortly, he holds her in his arms, leans to kiss her smiling face.

"You forgive me...," he says.

Her face collapses as he kisses her. Corpselike, flaccid, and pale once more, it is pressed against his own.

"No!"

He attempts to draw back, but her embrace is inhumanly strong.

"Now is not the time to stop," she says.

"Bitch! Let me go! I hate you!"

"I know that, Paul. Hate is the only thing we have in common."

"...Always hated you," he continues, still struggling. "You always were a bitch!"

Then he feels the cold lines of control enter his body again.

"The greater my pleasure then," she replies, as his hands drift forward to open her parka.

ALL OF THE ABOVE. Dorothy struggles down the icy slope, her sled parked beside Paul's. The winds lash at her, driving crystals of ice like microbullets against her struggling form. Overhead, the clouds have closed again. A curtain of white is drifting slowly in her direction.

"It waited for him," comes Aldon's voice, above the screech of the wind.

"Yes. Is this going to be a bad one?"

"A lot depends on the winds. You should get to shelter soon, though."

"I see a cave. I wonder whether that's the one Paul was looking for?"

"If I had to guess I'd say yes. But right now it doesn't matter. Get there."

When she finally reaches the entrance she is trembling. Several paces within she leans her back against the icy wall, painting. Then the wind changes direction and reaches her. She retreats farther into the cave.

She hears a voice: "Please...don't."

"Paul?" she calls.

There is no reply. She hurries.

She puts out a hand and saves herself from falling as she comes into the chamber. There she beholds Paul in a necrophiliac embrace with his captor.

"Paul! What is it?" she cries.

"Get out!" he says. "Hurry!"

Glenda's lips form the words, "What devotion. Rather, let her stay, if you would live."

Paul feels her clasp loosen slightly.

"What do you mean?" he asks.

"You may have your life if you will take me away—in her body. Be with me as before."

It is Aldon's voice that answers "No!" in reply. "You can't have her, Gaia!"

"Call me Glenda. I know you, Andrew Aldon. Many times have I listened to your broadcasts. Occasionally have I struggled against you when our projects were at odds. What is this woman to you?"

"She is under my protection."

"That means nothing. I am stronger here. Do you love her?"

"Perhaps I do. Or could."

"Fascinating. My nemesis of all these years, with the analog of a human heart within your circuits. But the decision is Paul's. Give her to me if you would live."

The cold rushes into his limbs. His life seems to contract to the center of his being. His consciousness begins to fade.

"Take her," he whispers.

"I forbid it!" rings Aldon's voice.

"You have shown me again what kind of man you are," Glenda hisses, "my enemy. Scorn and undying hatred are all I will ever have for you. Yet you shall live."

"I will destroy you," Aldon calls out, "if you do this thing!"

"What a battle that would be!" Glenda replies. "But I've no quarrel with you here. Nor will I grant you one with me. Receive my judgment."

Paul begins to scream. Abruptly this ceases. Glenda releases him, and he turns to stare at Dorothy. He steps in her direction.

"Don't—don't do it, Paul. Please."

"I am—not Paul," he replies, his voice deeper, "and I would never hurt you...."

"Go now," says Glenda. "The weather will turn again, in your favor."

"I don't understand," Dorothy says, staring at the man before her.

"It is not necessary that you do," says Glenda. "Leave this planet quickly."

Paul's screaming commences once again. This time emerging from Dorothy's bracelet.

"I will trouble you for that bauble you wear, however. Something about it appeals to me."

FROZEN LEOPARD. He has tried on numerous occasions to relocate the cave, with his eyes in the sky and his robots and flyers, but the topography of the place was radically altered by a severe icequake, and he has met with no success. Periodcally he bombards the general area. He also sends thermite cubes melting their ways down through the ice and the permafrost, but this has had no discernible effect.

This is the worst winter in the history of Balfrost. The winds howl constantly and waves of snow come on like surf. The glaciers have a set speed records in their advance upon Playpoint. But he has held his own against them, with electricity, lasers, and chemicals. His supplies are virtually inexhaustible now, drawn from the planet itself, produced in his underground factories. He has also designed and is manufacturing more sophisticated weapons. Occasionally he hears her laughter over the missing communicator. "Bitch!" he broadcasts then. "Bastard!" comes the reply. He sends another missile into the mountains. A sheet of ice falls upon his city. It will be a long winter.

Andrew Aldon and Dorothy are gone. He has taken up painting, and she writes poetry now. They live in a warm place.

Sometimes Paul laughs over the broadcast band when he scores a victory. "Bastard!" comes the immediate response. "Bitch!" he answers, chuckling. He is never bored, however, or nervous. In fact, let it be.

When spring comes the goddess will dream of this conflict while Paul turns his attention to his more immediate duties. But he will be planning and remembering, also. His life has a purpose to it now. And if anything, he is more efficient than Aldon. But the pods will bloom and burst despite his herbicides and fungicides. They will mutate just sufficiently to render the poisons innocuous.

"Bastard!" she will mutter sleepily.

"Bitch!" he will answer softly.

The night may have a thousand eyes and the day but one. The heart, often, is better blind to its own workings, and I would sing of arms and the man and the wrath of the goddess, not the torment of love unsatisfied, or satisfied, in the frozen garden of our frozen world. And that, leopard, is all.